Justice on the Prairie

150 Years of the
Federal District
Court of Kansas

John Brown as depicted by Kansas artist John Steuart Curry in "Tragic Prelude," a mural painted in the Kansas statehouse between 1937 and 1942.

JUSTICE ON THE PRAIRIE

150 YEARS OF THE FEDERAL DISTRICT COURT OF KANSAS

BY MICHAEL H. HOEFLICH

ROCKHILL
B O O K S

Rockhill Books
Kansas City, Missouri

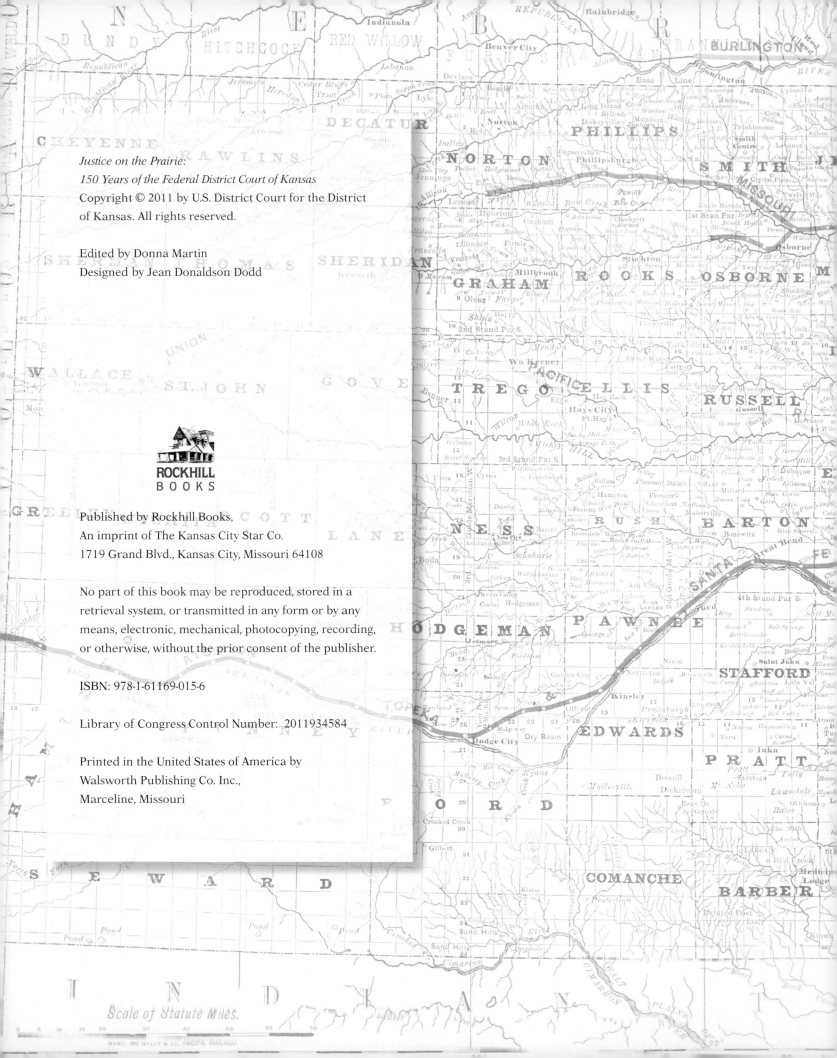

Published by Rockhill Books,
An imprint of The Kansas City Star Co.
1719 Grand Blvd., Kansas City, Missouri 64108

ISBN: 978-1-61169-015-6

Library of Congress Control Number: 2011934584

Printed in the United States of America by
Walsworth Publishing Co. Inc.,
Marceline, Missouri

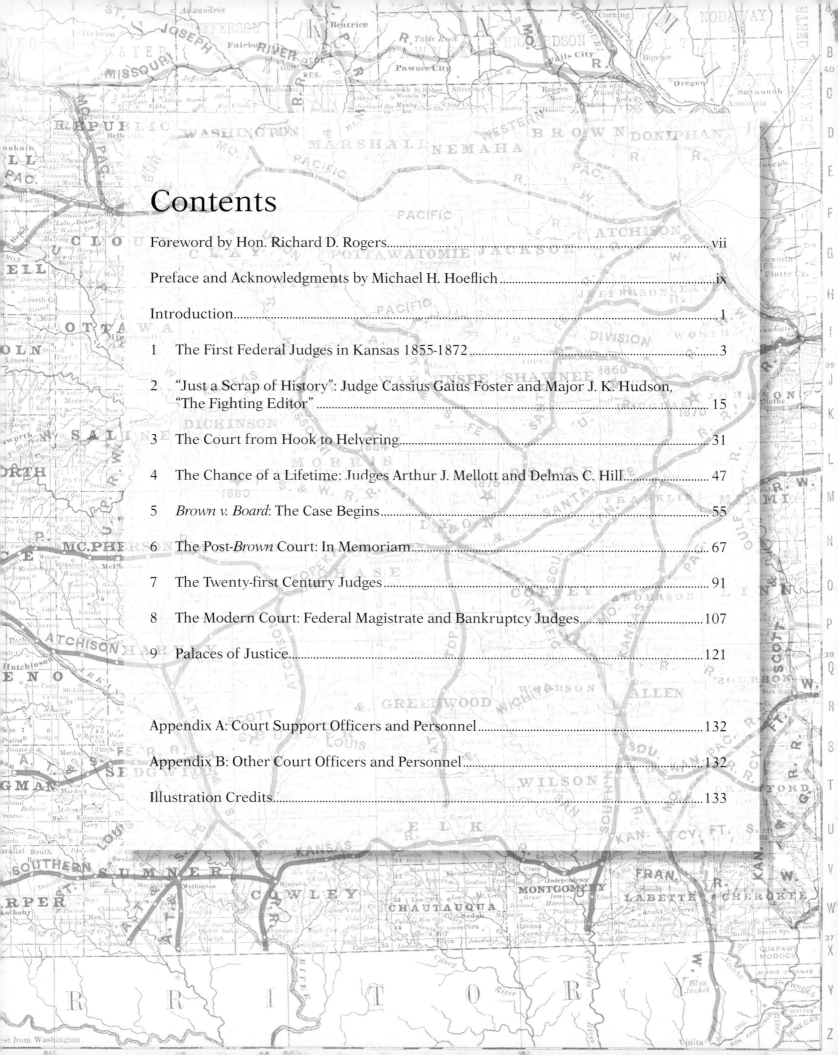

Contents

United States Courthouse and Post Office, Leavenworth, Kansas.

United States Courthouse and Post Office, Topeka, Kansas.

United States Post Office and Courthouse, Wichita, Kansas.

United States Post Office and Courthouse, Salina, Kansas.

United States Courthouse and Post Office, Fort Scott, Kansas.

United States Post Office, Kansas City, Kansas (artist's rendering).

United States Post Office and Courthouse, Fort Scott, Kansas.

United States Post Office and Courthouse, Wichita, Kansas.

United States Courthouse and Post Office, Topeka, Kansas.

Federal Building, Kansas City, Kansas.

Frank Carlson Federal Building and United States Courthouse, Topeka, Kansas.

Robert J. Dole United States Courthouse, Kansas City, Kansas.

Foreword

By Hon. Richard D. Rogers

Sir Winston Spencer Churchill, who wrote a great number of history books, once wrote: "History with its flickering lamp stumbles along the trail of the past, trying to reconstruct its themes, to revive its echoes and kindle with pale gleams the passion of former days."

The difficulty of reconstructing history is given in the following poem written at the death of Colonel Shalor W. Eldridge of Lawrence, a Civil War veteran:

> The muffled drum's sad call has beat
> the soldiers last tattoo,
> No more on life's parade shall meet these comrades
>   brave and true.
> On fame's eternal camping ground
> Their silent tents are spread,
> And glory guards with solemn sound
> The bivouac of the dead.

The 150-year history of the federal judiciary in Kansas has been well covered in the nine chapters written by former Dean Michael Hoeflich of the University of Kansas Law School. These chapters were meticulously researched and masterfully written and bring the court's history from the territorial judges down to the present occupants of the court.

It is interesting to find that the state and federal judges have maintained a connection with the Kansas State Historical Society throughout the past years, starting with Samuel A. Kingman, Kansas Supreme Court justice in 1876, followed by four federal judges, Judge George Templar in 1971, Judge Arthur Stanley Jr. in 1975, Judge Richard D. Rogers in 1994, and 10th Circuit Judge James K. Logan in 2008. Indeed, many presidents of the Kansas State Historical Society became governors, United States senators, or United States congressmen at some point in their careers.

Kansas was admitted to the Union as the thirty-fourth state on January 29, 1861. On April 4 of the same year, James S. Lane and S. C. Pomeroy were chosen by the state legislature to be United States senators. On April 12, 1861, Fort Sumter was attacked and two days later surrendered to the troops of the secessionists. On April 15, President Lincoln made his first call for seventy thousand volunteers. The Civil War had begun.

The period of time covered by the 150 years of history of the Federal Court of Kansas constituted one of the most precarious, consequential, and dangerous times in the history of the nation. As the period opened, the Civil War was pending. Lincoln had just been elected. America was as unprepared for war then as we were later in history at the time of Pearl Harbor, when our army was smaller than Portugal's. The United States Army had suffered a great loss by the resignation of high officers, including General Joseph E. Johnson, Quartermaster Samuel Cooper, and Colonel Robert E. Lee, and many other capable officers. Lincoln's main protection before his inauguration was his former partner at law, Ward Hill Lamon, who was a giant at six feet, four inches and weighing 260 pounds, armed with every weapon imaginable.

Edgar Langsdorf, a well-known historian with the Kansas State Historical Society, wrote an article on Senator Jim Lane and the Kansas Frontier Guard, sixty men strong, who went to Washington, lived in the White House, and protected the president. A new article on this subject has the title "The Kansas Lawyer Who Saved Lincoln's Life" by James P. Muehlberger, a Kansas lawyer with the Shook, Hardy & Bacon firm. Senator James H. Lane organized the Kansas Frontier Guard and they went immediately to Washington, D.C., to protect the president until the Sixth Massachusetts Regiment fought its way through Baltimore, Maryland, a city with many Southern sympathizers, and arrived in Washington. Many prominent Kansans who later became officers in Kansas government were in the Frontier Guard organization.

The view of history during the 150 years also caught my eye in the law practice of Leavenworth County lawyers and partners William C. Sherman, Thomas Ewing Jr., Hugh Ewing, and Daniel M. Cook. From this law firm we find one lieutenant general, William C. Sherman, and three brigadier generals in the other three partners.

Thomas Ewing Jr. was the first chief justice of the Kansas Supreme Court. He resigned to become a colonel of the 11th Kansas Regiment. His military history was excellent. His fifteen hundred men fought fifteen thousand of General Price's army at Pilot's Knob, Missouri, as Price invaded Kansas in 1864. Price was eventually defeated at the Battle of Westport, Missouri, by the Kansas militia force and other federal troops. This was followed by a second defeat for General Price at the Battle of Mine Creek in Kansas, which ended the battles in the West. Price's army fled to Arkansas after losing two Confederate generals at Mine Creek.

General Thomas Ewing Jr. is hated in Missouri because after the Quantrill massacre at Lawrence, he issued Order No. 11, which moved forcibly the populations from four counties in Missouri facing Kansas to other locations in Missouri where they could not raid Kansas.

The interesting accounts of the earlier judges in Kansas bring about some observations. First, the early days of the territorial judges in Kansas brought out the proslavery stance of the presidents who appointed them. We originally had a proslavery legislature. Then, as the population of Kansas changed to an antislavery population and the state moved to new legislatures and the Wyandotte constitution, the battle was won. Kansas became an antislavery state. The later judges appointed were antislavery judges agreeable to the Civil War amendments. The voters from Missouri were totally rejected.

According to the early history, federal judges spent far more time on personal issues than the judges of today. They also had views on state issues, such as prohibition, and announced their views and at times took an active part in controversial state issues. The later appointed judges restricted their activities to the cases actually filed in their courts where they had jurisdiction. The addition of magistrate judges and bankruptcy judges over the years brought greater efficiency to the federal courts and added a new era of expertise to the court system.

The fascinating history of Kansas, coupled with the 150 years of the court's history, brings to mind an old poem written during the early days of the Kansas struggles:

Of all the states, but three will remain in story;
Massachusetts with its Plymouth Rock,
Virginia with its native stock,
And sunny Kansas with its woes and glory.

This poem refers to the fact that most states were founded for commercial reasons, but the three states mentioned were Massachusetts, which was founded for political liberty; Virginia, which was founded for religious liberty; and Kansas, which was founded to halt the spread of slavery. All of these efforts were great and necessary objectives.

We can be proud of our Kansas history and the 150-year history of the federal judiciary.

Preface and Acknowledgments

This book has been a collaborative effort among a number of people. It is not a scholarly history of the court nor is intended to break new historical ground. Instead, it is a celebratory account of the first one hundred and fifty years of the Federal District Court for the District of Kansas aimed at the general public. It is an attempt to bring this history to a wider audience than has hitherto been done in specialist publications. As a result the text of the book is very dependent upon the research and publications of several generations of lawyers, judges, and historians.

In particular, the entire book draws closely upon the classic history of the District Court in Kansas: George Templar et al., "Kansas: The Territorial and District Courts," available online at: http://www.10thcircuithistory.org/pdfs/1992_historical_book/4Chapter2.pdf

The chapter on *Brown v. Board of Education* closely follows the account of the case given by Richard Kluger: *Simple Justice: The History of Brown v. Board of Education and Black America's Struggle for Equality* (New York: Knopf, 1975).

Individual judges' biographies rely upon not only Templar's article but also the series of biographies written by Robert Richmond and published privately by the Mennonite Press.

Alleen VanBebber, Esq., substantially rewrote the biographical section on Judge VanBebber based upon the biography found on the Tenth Circuit Historical Society website listed above.

For the sake of reading ease, I have not attempted to provide notes for every instance in which the text depends upon these and other sources. Notes are included for major points and to help with further reading.

In addition to the sources listed above and cited in the notes I have used several sources for this history. For basic biographical facts, I have used the biographies provided online by the Federal Judicial Center at: http://www.fjc.gov/public/home.nsf/hisj.

I have also made frequent use of the website Judgepedia: http://judgepedia.org/index.php/Main_Page. Once again, I have not attempted to cite to these sources in the text unless there is a special reason to do so.

Among the other primary sources for this history are articles published by various newspapers and magazines as well as interviews of living judges conducted either by the District Court staff or by Jessica Micklowski and Ryan Schwarzenberger during 2010.

As noted above, a number of individuals have made major contributions to this book. Jess Micklowski and Ryan Schwarzenberger researched, wrote, and edited portions of every chapter. Jeff Kincaid did valuable research on *Brown v. Board*. Jennifer Brake and Skyler O'Hara contributed substantially to the chapter on federal magistrate and bankruptcy judges. Ken Lyon, of Fort Scott, Kansas, did much of the research used in the section on Fort Scott's federal buildings. A version of Chapter 2 appeared in the *University of Kansas Law Review*.

Tim O'Brien and Neely Fedde of the Kansas Federal District Court should be listed as co-authors of this book. They did research, writing, and editing for nearly every page of the volume. This book would not exist but for their labors.

Jean Svadlenak, museum consultant and consultant to the Kansas Federal District Court, played an enormous role in producing this book as well. She was, in many respects, the true author of Chapter 9 and the vast majority of the images used in the book come from her research. The staff of the Kansas State Historical Society and the National Archives Kansas City Region provided invaluable assistance in this search, especially Nancy Sherbert, curator of photographs at KSHS and Jake Ersland at NARA.

Federal District Judges Tom Marten and Eric Melgren, members of the court committee charged with supervising the production of this book, were of great help, both for their insightful comments and their unflagging support of the project. Chief District Judge Kathryn Vratil conceptualized and championed the book as part of the court's 150th anniversary celebration.

Since this is a commissioned history of the Kansas Federal District Court, I have attempted to be as objective and nonpolitical in the account as possible. Any remarks that may have political overtones reflect only the author's opinions and not the opinions of either the judges or the District Court.

MICHAEL H. HOEFLICH

Drawing of courtroom during 1857 treason trial of Charles Robinson, governor of Kansas Territory, before the federal Territorial Supreme Court.

Introduction

There is something about Kansas that inspires men and women to excel. Perhaps it is the tough climate or the struggle the soil demands before it will yield crops. Perhaps it is the open skies, purple and pink at dawn and dusk. Perhaps it is the very idea of Kansas, a state whose birth started the process by which all Americans would find equality under the law. But whatever it is, there is something special about this state and its people. It is something special which pervades everything in the state.

The Federal District Court for the District of Kansas came into existence in 1861 when the United States Congress accepted the Kansas Constitution and admitted Kansas as a state. Born from the territorial judges who maintained the federal legal presence in the Territory of Kansas during the tumultuous first years of its existence, the Federal District Court of Kansas began slowly, with a single judge, a borrowed courthouse, and a few cases. Indeed, for most of the first century of its existence, the Federal District Court in Kansas consisted of only a single judge, whose caseload grew from just a few cases to nearly one thousand. But even during these years the distinct character of Kansas federal jurisprudence began to make itself apparent. The judges of the United States District Court have consistently demonstrated their independence of mind, their integrity in the face of often substantial external pressures, and their commitment to justice under law. These three characteristics–independence, integrity, commitment to justice–are manifest throughout the existence of the Federal District Court of Kansas and throughout the pages of the history of that court which follow.

Independence

Since the very beginning of the history of the Federal District Court of Kansas, its judges have cherished their independence and have not surrendered to either bureaucratic pressure or judicial fad. Kansas judges have always understood that as Article III judges, the life tenure they enjoy is not for their individual benefit but for the purpose of enabling them to follow the law to its appointed ends, regardless of politics or favor. Thus it was that Cassius Gaius Foster battled the prohibitionist fervor which captured Kansas during his time on the bench. So it was that Judges Walter A. Huxman, Delmas C. Hill, and Arthur J. Mellott laid the groundwork that enabled the United States Supreme Court in *Brown v. Board of Education* to finally do away with decades of Jim Crow laws in public schooling. So it is that Judge Thomas Marten has created an innovative voir dire procedure in his court in the cause of greater efficiency and lower costs. Independence is not always an easy characteristic to manifest. When Judge Patrick Kelly stood up to the Operation Rescue protesters in Wichita who refused to follow his rulings, he was met not by praise from his superiors in Washington, but by an unprecedented intervention by the Justice Department in favor of the protesters. Did Justice Kelly cave in? Not at all, and because of his courage and independence the violence which might have enveloped Wichita for weeks or months ended in days.

Integrity

A federal judge is the living manifestation of the law of the United States. It is the federal judge who presides over the vast responsibility of ensuring that the laws of the United States are applied, and applied correctly and in timely fashion. The federal district courts are the first line, the entry points into the federal system, and the federal magistrate judges and the federal district judges are the face of the federal system at these entry points. Integrity in office is an absolute necessity.

In the earliest days of the Federal District Court of Kansas it may be that some of the federal judges were a bit too fond of spirituous liquors. But never was there any suggestion during the entire century and one-half existence of the court that district judges had ever sacrificed the law which they dispensed for their own personal gain. While New York had to suffer the humiliation of having a leading federal judge, Martin Manton, impeached and sent to prison, such ignominy never touched–and hopefully never will touch–the Federal District Court of Kansas.

Commitment

One of the things which characterize the Kansas District is a continuous tradition of judges who serve the district in various capacities and who continue to work long after they need not. Over the years the judges of the Federal District Court of Kansas have often served the court in various capacities before they became district judges. Many judges in recent years began as law clerks for their predecessors. Others served as United States attorneys. Others served as federal magistrate judges or bankruptcy judges. The fact is that many of the judges have dedicated much of their lives to serving the legal system and the federal courts in particular.

Length of service is another striking aspect of the Federal District Court of Kansas. No other federal court–nor state court so far as is known–can boast of having a centenarian judge who has sat on the bench as long as Judge Wesley Brown. Judge Richard Rogers turns ninety this year and Judge Sam Crow turned eighty-five. Yet all three stay active on the bench, hearing cases and dispensing judgments. At a time when they could be retired and enjoying the well-deserved fruits of their labors these men continue to show a remarkable commitment to service and justice.

Anyone who gets to know the judges, the staff, and the history of the Federal District Court of Kansas must come away with a sense of awe, a sense of tradition, a sense of integrity and commitment, a sense that the citizens of Kansas have been and continue to be well served by the Federal District Court. If this volume can help others to understand the profound service to the state and to justice performed every day for 150 years by the Federal District Court here in Kansas, then it will have achieved its purpose.

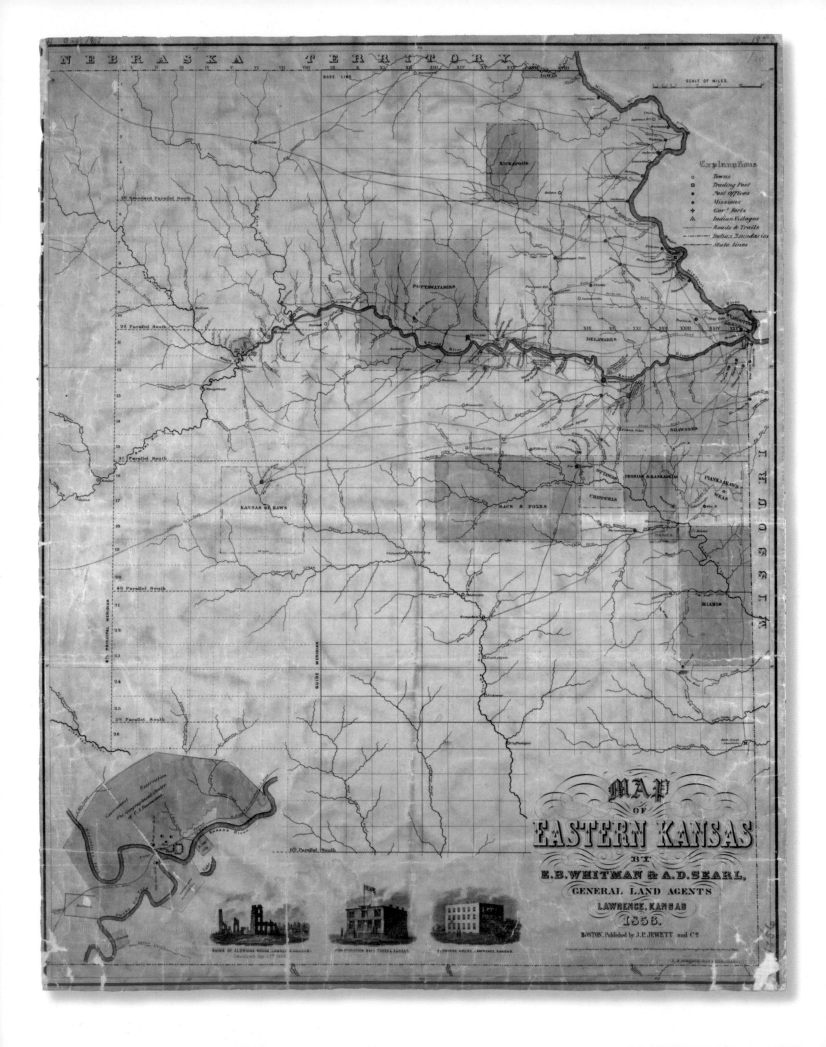

MAP
OF
EASTERN KANSAS
BY
E. B. WHITMAN & A. D. SEARL,
GENERAL LAND AGENTS
LAWRENCE, KANSAS
1856.

BOSTON, Published by J. P. JEWETT and C.º

I

THE FIRST FEDERAL JUDGES IN KANSAS: 1855-1872

The Territorial Judges

The first quarter-century of the federal judiciary in Kansas began in controversy and ended in controversy. That this was so is not in the least surprising because the history of the first decades of Kansas' existence as a territory and as a state was marked by intense political and legal disputes over slavery.

The Kansas-Nebraska Act was signed into law by President Franklin Pierce on May 30, 1854.[1] The act provided for the creation of a Territorial Supreme Court in Kansas, which would consist of a chief justice and two associate justices. Less than a month later the president appointed Madison Brown as chief justice and Rush Elmore and Sanders Johnson as associate justices.[2] All three supported the admission of Kansas to the Union as a slave state. Although appointed to the chief justiceship, Brown refused the job, and in October 1854, the president appointed Samuel D. Lecompte to replace him. Lecompte, like Brown, Elmore, and Johnson, was

Samuel D. Lecompte.

proslavery.

Although appointed in October, Lecompte did not arrive in Kansas Territory until December.[3] In the meantime, Justices Elmore and Johnson, along with Governor Andrew H. Reeder, made an expedition to the western portion of the territory to obtain property, a trip that would result in negative consequences for them in the future. In April 1855, the Territorial Supreme Court was established at Leavenworth, and the three justices settled down to business. And they had quite a bit of business. Only a month before, after a controversial election in which many Missourians had crossed the border to vote, the first Kansas Legislature (now often referred to as the "Bogus Legislature") was elected, met, and passed state laws that embraced the legality of slavery and ensured the rights of slave owners. Governor Reeder, convinced that the legislature had been constituted illegally, had vetoed its legislative productions. Thus, one of the first tasks facing the new Territorial Supreme Court was to determine whether the vetoed laws were, in fact, valid. Lecompte and Elmore issued an opinion upholding the proslavery legislative package, establishing a precedent that, on political questions, the Territorial Supreme Court would support the proslavery forces.[4]

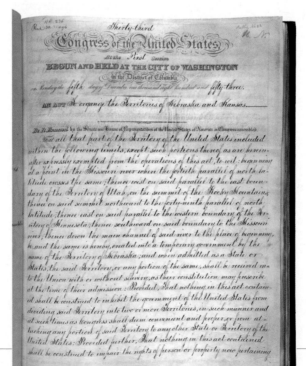

Left: Map of eastern Kansas Territory in 1856 by E.B. Whitman and A.D. Searl. Right: The Kansas-Nebraska Act of 1854 created the territories of Kansas and Nebraska. Initially intended to facilitate development of a transcontinental railroad, the act also included a provision that allowed people within those territories to decide whether or not to allow slavery within their borders. Settlers — both pro- and antislavery — then raced to Kansas to try to control territorial elections. Conflict erupted in Kansas and eventually engulfed the United States in civil war.

Within a few months of its first sitting, the Territorial Supreme Court lost two of its justices: Elmore and Johnson. Their trip to the West and acquisition of land from the Indians resident there led to complaints that reached President Pierce. At his order, both were removed from the bench. Governor Reeder, too, lost his job. Reeder was replaced by John W. Geary, and Elmore and Johnson were replaced by Sterling Cato and Jeremiah Burrell. Once again, both associate justice appointees were ardent proslavery adherents. Almost immediately, Cato became involved in the political controversies of the day, issuing writs for the arrest of several Free-State politicians. Burrell, on the other hand, fell ill virtually upon his arrival and returned home to Pennsylvania, where he quickly died. Burrell was replaced by another Pennsylvanian, Thomas Cunningham, but as soon as he arrived in Kansas and learned of the conditions there, he turned around and went back east.[5] Finally, in 1857, President James Buchanan filled the third Kansas justiceship with Joseph Williams. Williams was a veteran western judge, having served on the Territorial Supreme Court of Iowa and, once Iowa achieved statehood, as chief justice of its Supreme Court.

Mordecai Oliver, William Blair Lord, William A. Howard, John Upton, and John Sherman, members of the congressional committee appointed to investigate the claims of voting fraud in Kansas, in 1856. Oliver, a Missouri native, supported the proslavery movement.

Charles Robinson, c. 1861.

Wilson Shannon, c. 1884.

From 1855 to 1857, when effectively there were only two territorial justices, Lecompte and Cato, the Territorial Supreme Court served as one of the strongest allies of the proslavery partisans in Kansas. This political partisanship is not surprising since both judges were appointed by presidents whose sentiments lay with the proslavery forces.[6] Nevertheless, both Cato and Lecompte were far more involved in territorial politics than any modern judge would consider appropriate. Indeed, Lecompte was instrumental in the events that led to the infamous "Sack of Lawrence" in 1856 and the escalation of violence in the Kansas Territory that followed.[7] By early 1856 the political

situation in Kansas was deteriorating rapidly. Two legislatures had been elected, one proslavery and the other Free State. Two governors claimed the office: Charles Robinson for the Free-State Party and Wilson Shannon by presidential appointment. As a result of this situation, Congress appointed an investigating committee to travel to Kansas to report back on the governmental and political chaos. Almost simultaneously, Sheriff Jones, a proslavery partisan and ally of Governor Shannon, along with some federal troops, came to Lawrence to arrest several Free-State leaders. On the night of April 23, after taking his prisoners into custody, Jones was shot in the back by a sniper. By early May, the shooting of Jones had led Justice Lecompte to convene a grand jury that issued indictments for treason against James Lane, Charles Robinson, and Andrew Reeder, three of the most important Free-State leaders. Robinson was arrested; Lane fled the territory; and Reeder, a member of the Congressional Investigating Committee, was in peril.[8] Lecompte issued a warrant for the arrest of the three Free-Staters, and a U.S. marshal armed with the arrest warrant approached Lawrence.[9] At the same time, proslavery partisans from Missouri approached the Free-State citadel, which was preparing for a battle. This came on May 21. The "Sack of Lawrence" became a national sensation and a

Left: In April 1865, Missourians captured a Free-State supporter and set him adrift down the Missouri River on a raft that flew this flag.

Below: "Wanted" poster for runaway slaves, June 7, 1860.

Above: Abolitionist John Brown, who left North Elba, New York, and joined his adult sons in Kansas Territory to oppose proslavery supporters in 1855.

Right: Poster calling for election of district delegates to represent the Free-State Party at its convention in Big Springs, Kansas Territory, in September of 1855.

The Sacking of Lawrence on May 21, 1856, helped ratchet up the guerrilla war in Kansas Territory that became known as Bleeding Kansas.

rallying cry for abolitionist and Free-State supporters around the nation. Among those roused to action was John Brown, whose subsequent violent acts in Kansas and elsewhere eventually led to his arrest, trial, execution, and martyrdom. While one cannot say with certainty that none of this would have occurred but for Justice Lecompte's actions, certainly Lecompte's use of his position on the territorial bench to assist the proslavery forces was a major factor in fomenting the violence that led the territory during this period to be called "Bleeding Kansas."[10]

In 1857 Lecompte was finally removed from judicial office by the president and replaced by John Pettit, a former congressman and senator from Indiana.[11] Although Pettit might have been a more learned jurist than Lecompte, he was certainly no less a proslavery partisan.[12] Throughout his term in office his decisions in political cases, with one major exception, favored the proslavery forces.[13] The one exception was the case of *United States v. Weld* decided by Pettit in 1860,

in which Weld and other Free-Staters had been charged with obstructing the enforcement of the Fugitive Slave Act of 1850.[14] This act, of course, in the minds of abolitionists and Free-State supporters, was one of the greatest outrages perpetrated by Congress, since it permitted the capture and return of runaway slaves who had reached nonslavery states and the enforcement by federal judges of such recapture and return.[15] Weld's acts were highly popular with the Free-State supporters and anathema to proslavery partisans. Thus, Pettit's decision not to penalize Weld and his confederates is somewhat puzzling. One commentator on the case, James C. Durham, has speculated that Pettit's decision was a "triumph of his conscience over the literal demands of the law."[16] Judge George Templar has suggested a more pragmatic cause: the presence of Free-State supporters in Leavenworth and threats against Pettit's life were he to find against Weld.[17] There is also a third possible reason for Pettit's decision: by 1860 the Free-State forces in Kansas were clearly the victors in the struggle over whether Kansas would be a free or slave state.[18] A decision against Weld, therefore, would have found very little support in Kansas and would have potentially led to strong popular protest.

Although the political partisanship of Lecompte and Cato has come to dominate historical discussions of the territorial bench, both justices heard cases which were not political in nature. The types of cases that came before the Territorial Supreme Court were those which one would expect to arise in a frontier community. From 1855 to 1861 Kansas Territory's population of white settlers increased substantially.[19] Although much of this immigration was motivated by politics, the immigrants nonetheless needed places to live and work.[20] This led to an intense period of town formation and of land claims by immigrants and their companies. The frequency of land claims inevitably led to controversies of rights to property, controversies which often ended in litigation before the Territorial Supreme Court.[21]

These cases make for good reading and give an intimate portrait of life on the Kansas frontier. Land claims were disputed, cattle were rustled, contracts were broken, and eastern bonds were dishonored. We also get a particularly poignant view of what it was like to be a judge on a frontier court. For the most part, the justices of the Territorial Court were men from the East, used to practicing law and serving as judges where courts were held in courthouses, where law books were easily available, and where the bar itself was well organized and usually quite convivial. What they found when they arrived in Kansas to take up their offices was that there were no courthouses but, rather, they were forced to hold court wherever adequate space could be maintained.[22] There were few law books available and fewer law booksellers.[23] Either they brought their law books with them or they sent for them back east by mail order. As to a convivial bar, the political struggles that enveloped the state made for little peaceful social life. Indeed, as one justice discovered, not even official court papers were safe from theft and destruction.[24]

The justices of the Territorial Supreme Court were well aware of the conditions under which they were required to do their work and, on occasion, they expressed their frustration in their opinions. Perhaps the most moving of these declarations is to be found in the 1860 case of *Bliss v. Burnes*.[25] This case involved a disputed promissory note but, on appeal to Justice Pettit, the crucial issues were those of civil procedure and jurisdiction under the common law and under the newly enacted Kansas Code of 1858. The central question was whether the enactment of the 1858 code had changed the common law and, if so, what effect it would have on the case. It was not an easy question because it should have required substantial common-law research on the point, research that was impossible to do under the circumstances in which Justice Pettit worked. Thus, in the second to last paragraph of his opinion, Justice Pettit wrote:

> This decision was made by me in the hurry and turmoil incident to a district court in this territory, without argument and without presentation of authorities or even the reading of the petition; but I am fully convinced that I committed an error in overruling the demurrer. It gives me sincere pleasure to give my view in its correction.

Partisan Pettit may have been, but he still took great pride in his skills as a jurist and felt an obligation to state the law as he best could. In many ways, the non-political cases decided by the justices of the Territorial Supreme Court are the result of the heroic efforts of serious jurists placed in highly difficult circumstances.

The First Federal District Judge:
Archibald Williams

On February 9, 1861, Kansas was admitted to the Union as a state.[26] With the extinction of the territory also came the end of the Territorial Supreme Court. Lecompte was in private

Judge Archibald Williams, United States District Court of Kansas.

practice in Leavenworth and was, ultimately, to become a Republican. Pettit left Kansas and returned to his home state of Indiana. Cato left Kansas and, presumably, returned to his home in Alabama.[27] And Rush Elmore, who replaced Cato until statehood, then left the bench.[28] By an Act of January 29, 1861, Congress voted that Kansas should be a single federal judicial district court.[29] Initially, the Federal District of Kansas was not part of any federal circuit and functioned, for the most part, as both a district and circuit court. On July 15, 1862, Kansas was assigned to the Ninth United States Circuit and remained thus until assigned to the Eighth Circuit in 1866. When the Eighth Circuit was split into the Ninth and Tenth Circuits in 1929, Kansas joined the Tenth Circuit.

Although the number of federal judges in Kansas declined from three to one with the admission of Kansas as a state and the organization of the Federal District Court, the caseload of the new District Court was reduced significantly since the newly organized Kansas state courts assumed jurisdiction in many cases which would have gone before the Territorial Court. The first person to be appointed to the new District Court, who was appointed by President Abraham Lincoln, was Archibald Williams, a well-known lawyer and politician in Illinois.[30] Like Lincoln, Williams was born in Kentucky and moved to Illinois. He practiced law in Quincy, Illinois, and served in both the Illinois House and Senate and, from 1849 until 1853, as the U.S. attorney for the District of Illinois.[31] Williams, like Lincoln, was a volunteer soldier in the Black Hawk War.[32] When appointed as the first judge of the Federal District of Kansas, he was sixty years old.[33]

There can be no question that Judge Williams was qualified for his appointment. According to Judge George Templar, the first great historian of the federal court of Kansas, Williams and Lincoln were friends as well as business associates, and Lincoln recommended Williams for appointment as U.S. attorney in Illinois in 1849.[34] Lincoln also visited Quincy in 1854 to campaign for Williams in his race for Congress. It is not clear, however, that Williams's long-

Justice David Davis, United States Supreme Court, c. 1870.

standing relationship with Lincoln was solely responsible for his appointment to the federal bench in 1861. That honor may well belong to Judge David Davis, Lincoln's long-time political ally and his campaign manager in the 1860 presidential election.

Judge David Davis was one of the most influential political and legal figures on the Illinois scene during Lincoln's time in Illinois. From 1848 until 1862, Davis was the presiding judge of the Eighth Judicial Circuit in Illinois, the circuit in which Lincoln practiced.[35] In 1860 Davis was the Republican delegate from Illinois to the convention,[36] and it was his influence that played a major role in Lincoln's nomination for president. But Davis's actions were not altruistic. Davis was a classic Illinois politician and he expected those he had assisted politically to return the favor. Apparently, Davis did not hesitate to ask the new president for patronage positions. (In fact, Davis, himself, was appointed by Lincoln to a seat on the United States Supreme Court in 1862.)[37] According to a statement made by Henry C. Whitney to William H. Herndon, Lincoln did not appoint Williams out of friendship alone and was, in fact, hectored by Davis to make the appointment. Lincoln told Whitney:

> I am much annoyed about something that just happened: Davis, with that way of making a man do a thing whether he wants to or not made me appoint [Archibald] Williams Judge in Kansas … and I've got a hat full of dispatches already from Kansas chiefly protesting against it, and asking if I was going to fill up all the offices from Illinois.[38]

Although Judge Williams's appointment may have been made by the president under pressure from Judge Davis and against the wishes of many Kansans, he took up his office in 1861 and discharged his judicial duties for two years until he returned to Quincy to die.[39] During his roughly two years in office, Judge Williams decided a number of significant cases, but these were limited to a narrow field of cases involving Indian tribes, the jurisdiction of which was vested in the Federal District Court, as well as cases involving violation of federal statutes. The most important cases, those involving the aftermath of the Civil War in Kansas, were to be left to his successor on the court: Mark Delahay.

The Delahay Court

On October 6, 1863, President Lincoln appointed an old colleague and supporter, Mark Delahay, to replace Archibald Williams as the federal district judge for Kansas.[40] At the time of his appointment, Delahay was thirty-five years old and a well-known figure in Kansas territorial politics. His

Lincoln in Kansas

In late fall 1859, at the urging of a young ambitious Mark Delahay, Republican presidential nominee Abraham Lincoln took the long, cold train journey from Illinois to Kansas. He arrived in Leavenworth on December 3. In the audience that day was a young Leavenworth lawyer, Daniel M. Valentine, who was later to be a long-serving justice of the Kansas Supreme Court. Before the speech there was a reception held for Lincoln at the Mansion House. After the reception Lincoln and the crowd moved on to Stockton Hall, where the candidate spoke for two hours, not uncommon for speeches of the period. In his diary for December 3, Valentine noted that the crowd was large, perhaps as many as five hundred. Valentine described the candidate's performance:

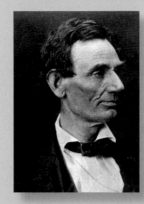

...the old man spoke 2 hours. It was a sound deep & logical speech, he is not eloquent like Burlinghame, —his language is not so beautiful, his periods not so nicely turned his questions not so graceful, his hands were placed one on the other & both at his belly at the commencement, towards the conclusion he kept them on his groins or upper part of his thighs one on each thigh the most of the time, he occasionally made gestures with his hands, he is not Poetical, he states everything fairly. His forte is (after stating his opponents a views and arguments fairly & justly) to reduce those views & arguments to a palpable absurdity & to Show them in a ridiculous & Ludicrous light, The Points he touched on were as ably handled as I have ever heard or seen them handled. I think it as able a speech as I ever heard he had a few notes to look at, the first part of his speech was historical to show that the Fathers of the Republic thought Slavery very wrong, The most of his speech was in opposition to popular sovereignty & those that think Slavery a matter of in- difference.

In 1860, Abraham Lincoln presented this banner (which he had received two years earlier from students at Lombard College) to Judge Mark Delahay.

In this letter to Judge Delahay, Abraham Lincoln declines an invitation to attend the convention to formally organize the Republican Party in Kansas on May 18, 1859. Lincoln would visit Kansas later that year.

Two days later Lincoln made a second speech and Valentine recorded his impressions of Lincoln once more:

Went to Hear Hon. Abe Lincoln make another speech – he has the actions of a Kentuckian he aims to say something funny but he does not try to use beautiful Language, he got off several good hits, his Language is his own & Original – Do all Kentucky orators try to say something funny?

Lincoln's Leavenworth appearance had greater significance than an ordinary campaign stop. The first speech he gave at Leavenworth became the basis for his far more famous speech at Cooper Union, a speech that many historians believe to have had a substantial positive impact on his campaign. And, of course, one may certainly speculate that the role of the young Mark Delahay in arranging this campaign trip may well have led Lincoln and Stanton to appoint Delahay as the federal district judge for Kansas when, after Lincoln's election, the seat fell vacant.

relationship with Lincoln went back at least to 1853, when Delahay had practiced law in Illinois on the Eighth Judicial Circuit with the future president. Before this, Delahay had been a newspaper editor in Virginia, Illinois,[41] and may well have known Lincoln in that capacity. In 1853 Delahay left Illinois for Alabama but remained there only two years when he decided to move to the newly created Kansas Territory. He settled in Leavenworth and became the publisher of the *Territorial Register*. At this time Delahay was apparently a Democrat but personally opposed to slavery.[42] In 1856 Delahay became a member of the Free-State Party and was instrumental in the drafting of the Topeka Constitution of 1856.[43] At the elections held thereafter, when Charles Robinson was elected governor, Delahay was elected to be the Free-State Party's delegate to the U.S. Congress. During the ensuing months of violence, Delahay seems to have been absent from Kansas, instead traveling around Illinois campaigning for Fremont.[44] Delahay was back in Kansas in 1857 and again immersed himself in territorial politics.[45] At the same time, he became convinced that his old colleague Lincoln could be a successful presidential candidate. By 1859 Delahay had become an open supporter of Lincoln in Kansas and twice invited Lincoln to come to Kansas to campaign.[46] His first invitation was rejected, but Lincoln accepted the second and spoke several times in Northeast Kansas in December 1859, accompanied by Delahay.[47]

Judge Mark W. Delahay.

Although Delahay was unable to deliver the Kansas Republican Convention to Lincoln (the Kansans supported Seward at the 1860 Convention), Lincoln continued to value his loyal friend.[48] This continued reliance on Delahay's loyalty was not misplaced for, after the election and the bombardment of Fort Sumter—a time in which the threat of presidential assassination was all too real—Delahay traveled with James Lane to Washington, D.C., and joined the "Frontier Guard," the group of

Mark W. Delahay certificate of appointment as "Judge of the District Court of the United States for the District of Kansas" dated October 6, 1863.

volunteers who came together to protect the president from attack.[49] Soon thereafter, a grateful president appointed Delahay as the surveyor-general of the new State of Kansas, a rich political patronage plum.[50]

Two years later, when Archibald Williams was forced

Above: Justice Samuel Freeman Miller, United States Supreme Court, was assigned to "ride the circuit" in Kansas, c. 1870. Below: Judge John Forrest Dillon, United States Court of Appeals for the Eighth Circuit.

to resign his judgeship because of illness, the president appointed Delahay to the position. Once again, Lincoln's appointment of a former Illinoisan met with protest from Kansans, but neither the president nor the Senate was moved by these complaints and Delahay was duly confirmed.[51] He spent almost the next decade in this judicial position, although it has been suggested that Delahay had hoped to obtain a better position after a few years, a hope that was dashed by Lincoln's assassination in 1865.[52]

Delahay's period on the federal bench was one of great importance, especially in the years after the defeat of the Confederacy and the restoration of the Union. The war had disrupted business and social intercourse between the Union and Confederacy, and this interruption had inevitably led to difficult legal issues. Unfortunately, as reported by both his contemporaries and later historians of the period, Delahay was not highly qualified as either a lawyer or a judge.[53] He had spent much of the decades preceding his judicial appointment as a newspaper editor and politician.[54] It is doubtful that Delahay was competent enough as a lawyer

Above: Summons for "Wild Bill" Hickok and Jack Harvey to appear before a grand jury in the Federal District Court of Kansas on April 11, 1867.

Left: Notice of land condemnation action against a Confederate soldier filed in the Federal District Court of Kansas in 1863.

Below: Complaint filed by J.B. "Wild Bill" Hickok in the Federal District Court of Kansas in 1869.

Circuit Courts for the District of Kansas

The Judiciary Act of 1789 established the federal court system for the new nation. Originally there were thirteen federal districts, three federal circuits, and the United States Supreme Court. Both the district courts and the circuit courts had original jurisdiction over specific matters (i.e., were trial courts of the first instance), and the circuit courts also had limited appellate jurisdiction. The Supreme Court had final appellate jurisdiction. The 1789 act required that Supreme Court justices sit on the circuit courts with district judges, but this was changed by the Judiciary Act of 1801, which created sixteen circuit judgeships and relieved the Supreme Court justices of their obligation to "ride the circuits." In 1802 Congress repealed the 1801 act, expanded the number of circuits to six, and provided that each circuit court have one Supreme Court justice and one District Court judge sit twice annually to hear cases. Between 1855 and 1869 three additional circuits were added, including the Federal Circuit of Kansas which was established by Act of Congress on July 15, 1862, to make a total of nine circuits. Nine circuit judges were appointed, one to each circuit, and the circuit-riding obligation of Supreme Court justices was reduced to a required sitting once in every two years.

The legislation that reorganized and expanded the federal circuit courts in 1869 left the circuit courts with only very limited appellate jurisdiction. Most appeals from district court cases continued to go directly to the U.S. Supreme Court. By 1890 it was generally believed that the 1869 legislation was in need of radical reform. As a result Congress created a series of intermediate appellate courts and thus began the system of Federal Circuit Courts of Appeal still in place today. The old system of federal circuit courts, including that for the District of Kansas, was allowed to wither away, and these courts were finally abolished on January 1, 1912, by the Judicial Code of 1911. The Circuit Court for the Federal District of Kansas never played a significant role in the Kansas legal order. Altogether eleven judges served on this court from 1862 until 1911. They held court in five Kansas cities during this period: Topeka, Leavenworth, Fort Scott, Wichita, and Kansas City, Kansas. Today this court and its judges are a little-remembered part of the state's judicial heritage.

to decide the often highly complex cases that came before his court. Fortunately, Delahay, although the sole district judge for Kansas, did have help on the bench: U.S. Supreme Court Justice Samuel Freeman Miller, appointed by President Lincoln to the United States Supreme Court in 1862, and Judge John Forrest Dillon, appointed to the United States Eighth Circuit Court of Appeals by President Ulysses S. Grant in 1869. Both men were far superior to Delahay as jurists and one or the other wrote many of the most difficult opinions decided by the District of Kansas while Delahay was the incumbent.

Of the cases that came before the Kansas District Court during this period, by far the most interesting from both a legal and political perspective was *Brown v. Hiatt*, decided in 1870.[55] In this case the judges were presented with a set of difficult questions arising from a property transaction in Kansas completed before the outbreak of hostilities. The case turned specifically on whether the Kansas statute of limitations had been tolled by the Civil War and disruption of communications between the Confederacy and the Union and, as a result thereof, whether a former Confederate citizen could argue that the war had stopped the statute's operation so that he could still assert his claims after the period of limitations had otherwise run.[56] Politically, a decision in favor of the former Confederate would have been unpalatable. From the legal standpoint, however, this was a case with no exact precedent controlling it. Thus the District Court of Kansas was forced to decide a case with potentially national ramifications.

The decision, written by Justice Miller, was brilliantly researched and argued. Justice Miller cited not only federal and Supreme Court cases, but also learned treatises by Emmerich de Vattel and Justice Joseph Story.[57] Perhaps the most interesting part of the opinion is the section where Justice Miller discusses a point made by Justice Joseph Story, and rejects it. The importance of the decision, since it could potentially affect all contracts made between Union and Confederate citizens before the outbreak of the Civil War, led to its appeal to the United States Supreme Court where it was reversed in part and affirmed in part.[58] On the main question as to whether the Confederate citizen's rights to sue were preserved because the war had tolled the statute of limitations, Justice Stephen Field found in favor of the Confederate and allowed him to collect his debt. Because of its potential broad applicability, it was also one of the first Kansas opinions to be discussed in national legal periodicals, including the *American Law Register* and the *Chicago Legal News*.

Although Judge Delahay had served faithfully for nearly a decade, by 1872 a personal failing, an affection for alcoholic beverages, had become so evident that talk of impeachment was becoming serious.[59] In order to avoid the embarrassment of such a proceeding, Judge Delahay resigned from the bench in 1872. He died five years later.[60]

Notes to Chapter 1

1. Kansas-Nebraska Act, 10 Stat. 277 (1854).

2. George Templar et al., *Kansas: The Territorial and District Courts, in* THE FEDERAL COURTS OF THE TENTH CIRCUIT: A HISTORY 15, 16 (James K. Logan ed.,1992) [hereinafter *Kansas: Territorial and District Courts*].

3. *Id.* at 17.

4. *Id.* at 18.

5. *Id.* at 19.

6. Paul E. Wilson, *How the Law Came to Kansas*, KANSAS HISTORY15, 30. (Spring 1992) [hereinafter *How the Law Came to Kansas*].

7. *See e.g.*, James K. Logan, *The Federal Courts and Their Judges—The Impact on Kansas History, in* THE LAW AND LAWYERS IN KANSAS HISTORY 57, 59–62 (Virgil W. Dean ed., 1993).

8. George Templar, *The Federal Judiciary of Kansas, in* REQUISITE LEARNING AND GOOD MORAL CHARACTER: A HISTORY OF THE KANSAS BAR 59, 61 (Robert W. Richmond, ed. 1982) [hereinafter *The Federal Judiciary of Kansas*]; Logan, *supra* note 7, at 61.

9. *Kansas: Territorial and District Courts*, at 19.

10. Logan, *supra* note 7, at 57.

11. *Id.* at 61.

12. *Id.* at 62.

13. *See Kansas: Territorial and District Courts*, at 21.

14. 1 Kan. Rep. 591 (D. Kan. 1860); *Kansas: Territorial and District Courts*, at 21.

15. *See* Logan, *supra* note 7, at 62.

16. Durham, *U.S. v. Lewis L. Weld: Judicial Creativity or Judicial Subversion?* 56 J. Kan. B.A. 5, 8 (1987).

17. *Kansas: Territorial and District Courts*, at 21.

18. *See How the Law Came to Kansas*, at 32–33.

19. *See* Paul E. Wilson, *The Early Years: The Bench and Bar Before 1882, in* REQUISITE LEARNING AND GOOD MORAL CHARACTER: A HISTORY OF THE KANSAS BAR, 27, 35–37, 40–41 (Robert W. Richmond, ed., 1982) [hereinafter *The Early Years*].

20. *Id.* at 30.

21. *How the Law Came to Kansas*, at 25–26.

22. *Kansas: Territorial and District Courts*, at 18–19.

23. *The Early Years*, at 35.

24. *Kansas: Territorial and District Courts*, at 20.

25. *Bliss v. Burnes*, McCahon (Kan.) 91. *See also The Early Years*, at 35.

26. *Kansas: Territorial and District Courts*, at 21.

27. *Id.* at 18.

28. *Id.* at 21.

29. *History of the Federal Judiciary–U.S. District Court for the District of Kansas: Legislative History*, FED. JUD. CTR., http://www.fjc.gov/history/home.nsf/page/courts_district ks.html (last visited Jan. 01, 2011).

30. *Kansas: Territorial and District Courts*, at 22.

31. *Id.; History of the Federal Judiciary: Williams, Archibald*, FED. JUD. CTR., http://www.fjc.gov/servlet/nGetInfo?jid=2592 (last visited Feb. 3, 2011) [hereinafter *FJC: Williams*].

32. Jim Barry, *Archibald Williams*, LINCOLN'S LEGACY, http://www.lincolndouglasquincydebate.com/html/Williams.html (last visited Oct. 7, 2009).

33. *See FJC: Williams*.

34. *Kansas: Territorial and District Courts*, at 22.

35. *History of the Federal Judiciary: Davis, David*, FED. JUD. CTR., http://www.fjc.gov/servlet/nGetInfo?jid=573 (last visited Feb. 16, 2011) [hereinafter *FJC: Davis*].

36. HORACE GREELEY, PROCEEDINGS OF THE FIRST THREE REPUBLICAN NATIONAL CONVENTIONS OF 1856, 1860 AND 1864: INCLUDING PROCEEDINGS OF THE ANTECEDENT NATIONAL CONVENTION HELD AT PITTSBURGH, IN FEBRUARY, 1856 AS REPORTED BY HORACE GREELEY 173 (C. W. Johnson 1893).

37. *See* Letter from Henry C. Whitney to William H. Herndon (ca. 1887), *in* HERNDON'S INFORMANTS at 648–50 (Douglas L. Wilson & Rodney O. Davis, eds., 1998), *available at* http://lincoln.lib.niu.edu/file.php?file=herndon647b.html

38. *See id.* at 649.

39. *See Kansas: Territorial and District Courts*, at 22.

40. *History of the Federal Judiciary: Delahay, Mark W.*, FED. JUD. CTR., http://www.fjc.gov/servlet/nGetInfo?jid=598 (last visited Jan. 01, 2011) [hereinafter *FJC: Delahay*]; *See* John G. Clark, *Mark W. Delahay: Peripatetic Politician*, KAN. HIST. Q., Autumn 1959, at 301.

41. *FJC: Delahay*.

42. *Kansas Historical Society: Delahay Portraits*, http://www.kshs.org/c0012/delahay.htm (last visited Jan. 01, 2011) [hereinafter *Delahay Portraits*].

43. *See* Clark, *supra* note 40, at 302.

44. *Id.* at 303.

45. *See id.* at 304.

46. *Id.* at 307–08.

47. *Id.* at 308–09.

48. *Id.* at 309.

49. *Id.* at 311.

50. *See FJC: Delahay*.

51. *See* Letter from Henry C. Whitney to William H. Herndon, *supra* note 37.

52. Clark, *supra* note 40, at 311–12.

53. *See e.g., Kansas: Territorial and District Courts*, at 23; Clark, *supra* note 40.

54. Clark, *supra* note 40.

55. 4 F. Cas. 384 (C.C.D. Kan. 1870).

56. *Id.* at 386.

57. *Id.* at 387–88.

58. *Brown v. Hiatt*, 82 U.S. 177 (1872).

59. *Kansas: Territorial and District Courts*, at 23.

60. *See FJC: Delahay*.

2

"JUST A SCRAP OF HISTORY": JUDGE CASSIUS GAIUS FOSTER AND MAJOR J. K. HUDSON, "THE FIGHTING EDITOR"

In a shady spot in the Topeka Cemetery is the last resting place of Cassius Gaius Foster. The grave is marked by a small, tasteful gray stone monument which gives little hint of the tumultuous life lived by the man buried beneath.[1] Few remember Judge Foster today, but during the last quarter of the nineteenth century he was the sole representative of federal justice in Kansas.[2] He was also one of the most controversial figures of his era, the scourge of temperance advocates across the state and a litigant in one of the nastiest and most bizarre law cases in Kansas in the nineteenth century.

Cassius Gaius Foster was born in upstate New York in 1837. He went to school there and in 1859 he entered the law office of a local attorney in Rochester to read law with the hope of joining the bar and becoming a practicing attorney. But Foster soon realized, as did so many young lawyers and law students of his era, that the bar in the northeastern states was crowded and that it would be difficult to make a living. And, thus, he took Horace Greeley's famous advice, "Go West, young man," to heart and traveled to Atchison, Kansas, to live and work.

In 1859, when Foster settled in Atchison, it was a frontier town. The era of "Bleeding Kansas" was coming to an end, but the clouds of war hung ominously over the whole nation.[3] The city had been founded in July 1854 by a group led by Senator David R. Atchison of Missouri.[4] The city at this time, and for three years following, was a proslavery stronghold. Indeed, in 1855, the citizens took

Judge Cassius Gaius Foster.

out their anger against the abolitionist cause by expelling the Reverend Pardee Butler, an outspoken opponent of slavery, by tying him to a log raft and setting him adrift on the Missouri River.[5] In the same year, a band of Atchison men took part in a raid on Lawrence, the Free-State capital.[6] But within the next two years, the Free-State forces in Kansas were politically victorious and the citizens of Atchison decided to give up their proslavery politics and concentrate on building the city's economy. Quite quickly, the business community grew and prospered. By 1859, the year of Foster's arrival in Atchison, the biggest political issue was not slavery, but road improvements.[7]

Foster seems to have settled quickly and successfully into the Atchison community. He practiced law full time from 1859 until 1863, when he was elected to serve as a state senator. He returned to private practice in 1864 and was elected mayor of Atchison in 1867. Once again, in 1868 he returned to his law practice and remained in that position until 1874, when he was nominated by President Grant to serve as federal district judge for the District of Kansas. He was then forty-seven years old.[8]

Foster had two predecessors on the federal bench in Kansas: Archibald Williams, who served from only 1861 to 1863,[9] and Mark Delahay, who served from 1863 to 1873.[10] Williams's tenure ended by illness and death. Delahay resigned

Facing page: Upper left: Tombstone of Cassius Gaius Foster, Topeka Cemetery. Upper right: Judge Cassius Gaius Foster. Bottom: Atchison, Kansas, Territory, c. 1860.

Left: Front Street in Dodge City, Kansas, c. 1880-85. Above: Cattle round-up near Ashland, Kansas, 1897.

under threat of impeachment and removal as a result of his drunkenness on and off the bench. Interestingly, Foster was also quite ill during much of his quarter-century on the bench and did not produce a large number of decisions.[11] However, while his judicial productivity was low, he was extremely active in the fight against prohibition in Kansas. Indeed, during much of his time as a judge he was, in fact, most deeply involved as a vociferous opponent of prohibition. This opposition led him to become one of two parties in a series of widely publicized cases in the Kansas state courts, participation which made him one of the most infamous Kansans of his era.

The Kansas Prohibition Movement

Robert Smith Bader, author of the standard work on the history of the prohibitionist movement in Kansas, has pointed out that many of the immigrants to Kansas during the territorial period came with twin political goals.[12] The first, of course, was to ensure that Kansas would be a free state without slavery. The second was that Kansas be a dry state. Once the battle over slavery was won, the battle over prohibition began.

To a large extent, the political controversy over prohibition in Kansas grew out of several factors. First, as a frontier state, and one with too many cowboys and too few lawmen, Kansas was a rough place in which drinking, gambling, and whoring were prevalent. Second, as the state became more civilized, more families moved into Kansas, and while the men might well have been willing to tolerate a "Wild West" society, the women settlers wanted a more civilized and tranquil environment in which to live and raise their children.

Indeed, even during the territorial period, the prohibition movement gained strength and supporters in the northeastern part of the state. As early as 1856, a group of Topeka women petitioned the Territorial Legislature to ban the sale or importation of liquor and other alcoholic beverages. In the summer of that year, a group of women, armed with hatchets, attacked a saloon in Lawrence, a communal activity which soon became common.[13]

There were, however, certain impediments to the burgeoning temperance and prohibitionist movement. The first—and greatest— impediment was that Kansas women had no general right to vote in elections, other than for school boards. Although the subject of women's suffrage was raised at the Wyandotte Convention in 1859, in spite of vigorous arguments on behalf of women's rights the convention chose to give only very limited suffrage to female Kansans.[14] However, while women could not themselves vote in favor of prohibitionist legislation, they could do everything in their power to force their husbands and male relatives to support their cause. And

Carry Nation, c. 1865-75. Nation, a member of the Women's Christian Temperance Union and prohibition crusader, gained fame for her practice of violently attacking saloons with rocks and hatchets.

this they did. Over the next three decades, women would lead the charge—eventually successful—for prohibition.[15]

The second impediment to passing prohibitionist legislation in Kansas was a combination of geography and demography. During the first decades of statehood, western Kansas remained very much a frontier whose primary industry was cattle. Saloons and drinking were an integral part of the "cowboy way." Even in northeastern Kansas there was a split. In Lawrence, Topeka, and Emporia, where the population was dominated by immigrants from the northeastern states, prohibitionist feeling was strong. But in Leavenworth and Atchison counties, whose population was dominated by immigrants from Germany, the situation was quite different. To put it bluntly, the German immigrants were not willing to give up their beer and their beer halls.[16]

As a result of these factors, much of Kansas politics in the 1860s and 1870s was focused on the prohibition question. The tide turned in favor of statewide prohibition only when John Pierce St. John was elected governor on the Temperance and Republican tickets.[17] St. John had come to Kansas in 1869 and settled in Olathe to practice law. Very quickly, St. John also became known for his good looks (which no doubt helped gain him votes), his oratory, and his strong temperance

Prohibition meeting at Bismark Grove, Kansas, 1878.

Above: Political cartoon published in the Freethought Ideal, *an Ottowa, Kansas. newspaper, on March 1, 1901. The cartoon depicts Carry Nation leading a mob against a saloonkeeper. Left: The cover of pamphlet written by J.R. Detwiler and published by the Temperance Banner Print in Osage Mission, Kansas, 1880. The pamphlet lists various objections to prohibition from the temperance perspective.*

views. He did not, however, campaign on the prohibitionist issue.

Once John St. John assumed the governorship, the stage was set for a serious political push for prohibition. A young member of the Kansas Christian Temperance Union (KCTU) from Fort Scott, John Detwiler, convinced his fellow KCTU members that the best strategy to follow in their fight was to push for a constitutional amendment rather than legislation. Petitions were circulated and presented to the legislature in January 1879.[18] The legislature voted to support a state referendum on the issue in a particularly close vote in which many members switched from one side to the other. The "dry" and "wet" forces lined up against each other and a massive political campaign on the amendment ensued. Western Kansas and the Kansas German population stood against; the vast majority of other Kansans favored the amendment. Certainly, there were some respected political leaders who opposed the amendment.[19] The most notable was Charles Robinson, former governor and hero of the Free-State

struggle. A second notable opponent was Judge Cassius Gaius Foster, federal district judge for the District of Kansas.[20]

The vote on the prohibition amendment took place in 1880. It passed by a small margin,[21] as one would expect, with little support in western Kansas and in the German-dominated counties of Leavenworth, Atchison, Doniphan, Barton, and Wyandotte. In 1881 the legislature passed enabling legislation, and on May 1, 1881, Kansas became a "dry" state. Although the prohibitionists had won their amendment, the issue was far from dead. For the next ten years debate and conflict over the "dry" status of Kansas continued. There were even minor riots against prohibition. Most importantly, in those counties and cities which had opposed the amendment, enforcement was difficult, if not impossible. The antiprohibitionist forces continued to find ways of avoiding the provision, and the temperance forces continued to pressure the governor, the legislature, and city and county officials to increase enforcement. Although prohibition was in force, a thirsty man could still get a drink in most parts of Kansas.

The ongoing battles over enforcement of prohibition consumed Kansas politics during the 1870s. The antiprohibitionists soon came to be the "resubmissionists": those who favored a revote on the constitutional amendment. The resubmissionist movement gained increasing strength, and during the 1880s and 1890s, debates—political and social—raged. Just as Judge Foster had been a champion of the antiprohibitionist forces in the 1870s, he became one of the leaders of the resubmissionist movement of the 1880s and 1890s.

There is no evidence that Judge Foster himself was a frequenter of saloons, nor is there any indication in the record that he overindulged in alcohol. Instead, it would seem that Judge Foster's position on prohibition had both philosophical and historical roots. Foster had spent his early years in Kansas at Atchison, where his political career began. Atchison, as a German community, was among the leaders against prohibition. Second, by his own words, Judge Foster was troubled by the philosophical and political implications of government intervention in the private lives of its citizens. To Judge Foster the moral arguments against easy availability of alcoholic beverages were far outweighed by his sense of personal liberty and opposition to government regulation of private activities. There is absolutely no reason to doubt Foster's motives.[22]

Beginning with the earliest territorial years, newspapers in Kansas were the most powerful political voices in the state's public discourse.[23] During the 1870s and the run-up to the 1881 prohibition law, almost two hundred newspapers allied themselves with the temperance and prohibitionist movement.[24] Among these, the *Topeka Daily Capital* was in the forefront. Its editor was Major J. K. Hudson.

Above: Topeka Daily Capital *founder, owner and editor J.K. Hudson, superimposed over the front page of the April 21, 1888, edition.*
Left: The Hudson Building in Topeka, Kansas, c. 1880-85. The Hudson Building was named after J.K. Hudson and housed the Topeka Daily Capital *from 1886 to 1908.*

J. K. Hudson was born and raised in Ohio.[25] His father was the editor of an antislavery newspaper. In 1861 Hudson traveled to Kansas, where he joined the Third Regiment of the Kansas Volunteers, known as "Lane's Brigade" after James K. Lane. He was mustered out in 1865 and moved to Wyandotte County. In 1871 he was elected to the Kansas Legislature and in 1873 made an unsuccessful run for the United States Congress. Later that year he published a newspaper, the *Kansas Farmer,* and resettled in Topeka. In 1879 he started the *Topeka Daily Capital,* which he edited for the next several decades. Hudson was a crusading newspaperman and one of his many causes was the temperance and prohibition movement. According to one biographer, Hudson was known "for the vigorous style of his work" and by another as "the fighting editor." This was, as will become clear, a remarkable understatement. In 1890 Major Hudson and Judge Foster entered into a public battle in which both displayed the "vigor" of their voices. The beginning of the battle between Hudson and Foster began innocently enough in 1889. Judge Foster was called upon to speak at a resubmissionist rally. This was reported by Hudson in the *Daily Capital*:

RESUBMISSION RALLY AT THE GRAND OPERA HOUSE.

On December 28, 1889, after a season of much advertising, a great state rally of the resubmissionists was held at the Grand opera house, in Topeka. Invitations had been sent to all the cities of the state, and special railroad rates secured. A dozen speakers were announced from Leavenworth, Wichita, Topeka, and elsewhere. In point of numbers and ability the meeting was a great failure. Judge Foster, it had been announced, would preside and make a speech. From the Daily Capital, of December 29, we take the following account of Judge Foster's speech:

Judge Foster, when introduced, said that his election as chairman of this convention was entirely unexpected. He was glad to see so many visitors from abroad, and said, "I desire to say on the part of at least one-half of the people of this city, who are not cranks and intolerants, that you are welcome; yes, thrice welcome. We have been inflicted with disquisitions and speeches from various gentlemen, from the governor down to the young attorney who, having nothing else to do, sits down and interviews himself, and has the interview published in the newspapers." The Judge then became rather humorous, and thought that a law prohibiting the sale of feather beds, because some people were lazy and were not early risers, would be as reasonable as the law prohibiting the sale of liquor. The feather-bed story was concluded at 8:40 o'clock. "They tell us," said Judge Foster, "that money spent for liquor is thrown away; but don't we spend money foolishly in many other ways? Whoever thought of passing a law declaring how men shall or shall not spend their money?" The Judge said that he believed that four times as many men are killed every year by the use of tobacco as by the use of liquor, and yet, said he, you will see these rabid prohibitionists going around with a quid of tobacco in their mouth as big as a goose egg. "I don't wish at all to be understood that I am in love with the saloon. Liquor men

are inclined to be aggressive; they are inclined to overstep the bounds of propriety, but the traffic may be regulated."[26]

While it would appear that Judge Foster's speech may not have been an oratorical masterpiece, Major Hudson's response to the speech was really a bit harsh and insulting:

(Editorial Comments *Daily Capital* on Judge Foster's Speech.)

Those who are training the Judge for senator are greatly chagrined by his failure at his first appearance on the platform and in type. They say that he wasn't "at himself." So it seems to the people.

The people have a right to be indignant when a judge, instead of using argument, scolds them in bad English. Judge, if you must abuse your neighbor, leave out slang, and give us good grammar.[27]

Hudson's printed attack on Foster drove the judge into a frenzy and, unfortunately, Judge Foster, at that point, decided to elevate the dispute from a war of words into a legal battle. The path he took was unwise in the extreme, and the legal basis for his charges was shaky. Hudson's newspaper had been used for years to print legal notices of matters in the District Court. Suddenly, Judge Foster discovered that the litigants had been overcharged for the notices and that too few notices had been run. Thus, he decided to do two things: take the legal notice business away from the *Daily Capital* and, also, to require Hudson to repay the so-called overcharges:

A few days ago my attention was called to the alarming fact that you have for years past been systematically disregarding the act of congress and the orders of this court in publishing these notices. Instead of publishing them six times, as the law and the order itself required, you have stopped on five publications, and hurried in your bill for a fee at least three times the amount allowed you by law. Titles to a vast amount of real estate have been based on these defective notices, and are absolutely worthless. How can you, Major Hudson, say you are not guilty of gross carelessness and culpable negligence in this matter? Every day this court is now called upon to set aside decrees and titles by reason of your blunders. Ask your attorney if you are liable for damages to the injured party. It is not for me to decide.

David Josiah Brewer

David Brewer was born to missionary parents in Smyrna in Asia Minor in 1837. He returned with his family to the United States and was educated at Yale College and Albany Law School. He also spent a year "reading law" with his uncle, David Dudley Field, the great New York lawyer and jurist. Well-prepared for the practice of law, he left the settled East and moved to Leavenworth, Kansas, in 1858. Brewer quickly gained a reputation as a good lawyer. In 1861 he was appointed a commissioner for the Federal Circuit Court for the Circuit of Kansas. The next year he was elected a judge of the probate and criminal courts of Leavenworth and in 1862 took a seat as a judge of the Kansas First Judicial Circuit of Kansas. In 1869 he became the city attorney of Leavenworth and, in 1870, he became the youngest justice of the Kansas Supreme Court at thirty-three. He served in this capacity until 1884, when President Chester A. Arthur appointed him to the United States Court of Appeals for the Eighth Circuit.

As a member of the Eighth Circuit, the circuit to which Kansas then belonged, Judge Brewer heard numerous cases on appeal from the Kansas Federal District Court and assumed a major role in the shaping of federal law in Kansas. While his time on the Eighth Circuit was of great significance for the development

Above: Fifth Street in Leavenworth, Kansas, 1867. Left: Justice David J. Brewer, United States Supreme Court, 1887.

of federal jurisprudence in Kansas, his stay on the Circuit Court was brief. In 1889 President William Henry Harrison nominated Judge Brewer to the Supreme Court of the United States to succeed Justice Stanley Matthews. Justice Brewer remained on the U.S. Supreme Court until his death in 1910. He was the first Kansan to take a seat on the Supreme Court. During his two decades on the Supreme Court Judge Brewer wrote numerous opinions and was a major voice on the court. He was also a popular speaker throughout the country and an ardent advocate for peace. He is still remembered as one of Kansas' greatest lawyers and judges.

* * *

You will be given a chance to explain these charges in court, for an order will be made retaxing the printer's fees in every case for the past two years, there being over 40 cases. Any balances ascertained to have been wrongfully drawn from the registry of the court by you will be ordered returned within a stated time.

Perhaps it might be well for you to understand beforehand that your zeal in the cause of prohibition will not be received as any reason why you shall not comply with the law; nor need you fear that your unfair treatment of the circuit and district judges of this court, for many years past,

will in the least influence the court in dealing out to you evenhanded justice.[28]

Most politicians and judges have learned that it is very unwise to attack the press unless one's charges are absolutely iron-clad. Not only is the press protected by the First Amendment, but an attack on one newspaper tends to be a clarion call to all newspapers to come to the defense of the one attacked. Knowing this, Major Hudson was unwilling to bow down to Judge Foster. Instead, like a toreador waving his red cape in front of a crazed bull, Major Hudson raised the heat of his rhetoric against Judge Foster:

My dear Judge, your condescension is

something to be grateful for; it marks a red-letter day in my history, and it gives the people an opportunity to take a look at the practical working of your judicial brain, for which all will be duly thankful. There are dogs and dogs, my dear Judge, and we have known large ones that looked fierce but only barked. I appreciate the honor you have conferred on me by breaking your extraordinary record, and hope to convince you that it would have been much wiser had you maintained that judicial silence which has so long passed for wisdom. When you condescend to a newspaper discussion, you are necessarily compelled to say something, and there are wicked people, my dear Judge, who will rend you ermine, so to speak, if you fail to talk sense and to make a good case—a danger that does not menace you on the bench, where you may be a tyrant or a fool, and none dare to question your right to be either, for you are there for life. The generous missionary spirit which prompts you to make this very, very bad break in your beautiful record for my benefit, displays at once an exalted and noble quality of mind and heart which will surprise your most intimate friends.

* * *

These are the fees that have been charged for notices in Judge Foster's court for over 15 years, and their legality has never been questioned. These are the facts out of which Judge Foster makes his case.

And now as to the responsibility: Is it possible, Judge Foster, that with your presumed knowledge of the law, you have permitted these illegal fees to be charged in your court for over 15 years, invalidating titles and involving untold expense and litigation? Has the judge no responsibility? If you are ignorant of the law, why did you not come out like a man and say so, and not hide behind a weak and cowardly insinuation that I will be held responsible for the excess of legal fees, and given a stated time in which to return them? Is the clerk of your court not informed as to the legality of fees charged and paid by him? The notices in this paper for your court have been published and charged for as your clerk directed. Is he not responsible also? What are the attorneys who practice in your court doing for their clients that they permit illegal fees to be charged against their clients? Are the attorneys who have witnessed these fees charged for 15 years free from responsibility? My dear Judge, don't you see how dangerous it is to rush into print after 15 years'

silence? Don't you wish your missionary zeal had not run away with your stupid discretion?

But this is not all. If this irregularity has been going on in your court for over 15 years because you were not informed as to the provisions of the law, does it not raise a fair presumption that your lack of information may not stop with this one blunder? You arraign a publisher for charging what your own clerk directs him to charge, and threaten him with litigation, all of which poorly covers the bad case you make for yourself and the lack of legal information you yourself have had on the subject. Every publisher, every lawyer and every man of common sense knows that legal publications are printed just as often as they are ordered by the lawyers or the clerk or whoever orders them. No publisher would do otherwise. The bills are not rushed into the court, as Judge Foster states, as they are never settled until the cases are completed, a fact that our condescending and humorous Judge is probably not familiar with.

Proceed with the prosecution for illegal fees, my dear Judge. My defense I am willing to give to you now. It will be something like this: "Your honor, I knew no more about the legal printers' fees than you did, which was less than nothing; no more, your honor, than your clerk, and no more than all the lawyers who practice at your bar. And while I know that ignorance of the law is no plea to make in an ordinary court, there seems to be so d—d much of it in your court that I shall offer it, and throw myself upon your missionary sympathy."

Your working out of a problem of printers' fees in detail will not take attention from the fact that your new love for mathematics does not clear you of the responsibility of this irregularity. You ought to have reached this little sum in multiplication about 15 years ago.[29]

* * *

(Editorial from the *Daily Capital*, Sunday, January 12, 1890.)

TO JUDGE CASSIUS GAIUS FOSTER
It has not been my intention to further expose your lack of legal information and your political pettifogging mind to the people of Kansas, because, in common with all citizens, I have a high respect for the judiciary. The courts form the great bulwark of American liberty, and are the safeguards of justice to the citizen. The people will tolerate with patience for a long time a man upon the bench

who fails in the measure of his duty as a just judge rather than utter a harsh criticism upon him or his methods. What the people expect of the judge is that he honor the position that honors him.

You, as United States circuit judge, saw proper in your letter addressed to me on January 8 to charge me with having collected illegal fees for printing notices sent from your court for publication in the Capital, and to threaten me with a prosecution which must be tried in your court. You have the very distinguished honor of being, in all human probability, the first United States circuit judge in this part of the country to threaten a private citizen with litigation as a revenge for political differences of opinion, when the trial must be heard by himself. It is a spectacle that has made the people in this community, without regard to party or political opinion, discuss the importance of an impeachment trial at which you would appear as the defendant.

I did not intend to again address you upon the subject, believing your better judgment would prevent you from carrying out the threat contained in your letter of January 8. In this I was mistaken. I received at the hands of the bailiff of your court the following document:

In the circuit court of the United States, for the district of Kansas
Topeka, Kas., January 9, 1890.
Whereas, it has been made to appear to this court that there has been illegal and extortionate printing fees, charged in the following cases, it is therefore ordered that the clerk of this court, on Tuesday, the 14th day of January, 1890, proceed to retax the printer's fees in said cases, according to the rates allowed by law, and that notice of this order be served on J. K. Hudson at least three days before the said retaxation: Cases Nos. 5495, 5328, 5930, 5892, 6008, 5340, 5976, 5355, 6030, 5507, 5686, 5641, 5792, 6206, 6192, 6160, 6161, 6152, 6186, 6141, 6142, 6007, 5945, 6001, 5758, 6365, 6188, 6189, 6261, 6274, 6303, 6338, and 6359. It is further ordered that the clerk proceed to ascertain and report to this court all cases in which the service of publication on nonresident defendants is illegal for want of proper publication.
United States of America, district of Kansas, ss.:
I, George F. Sharitt, clerk of the circuit court of the United States of America for the district of Kansas, do hereby certify the foregoing to be a true,

full and correct copy of an order of said court, from the record thereof.

In testimony whereof, I hereunto set my hand and affix the seal of said court, at my office in Topeka, in said district of Kansas, this 9th day of January A. D. 1890.
GEO. F. SHARITT, Clerk.
(Seal.)[30]

By the time Foster had actually had his clerk, George Sharitt, produce a court order to retax the legal notice fees and require Hudson to appear in the District Court, all semblance of propriety and dignity had disappeared from the dispute. Kansas newspapers now treated Foster as a fool, a drunkard, and the devil himself. Hudson delighted in publishing the negative comments of his brother editors:

(From the *Daily Capital* of January 19, 1890.)

JUDGE FOSTER.

The Overwhelming Testimony Against Him from the Republican Press of Kansas.

Here's Your Verdict, Judge.

His Condemnation as a Politician, as a Lawyer, and as a Judge.

A Resub.—Submitted.—Lost.

A Reply to His Prostitution of Judicial Power Such as no Man Ever Received.

Burn the Next Letter.

Condemnation of His Conduct Crystallizes in a General Demand that He Resign.

"I will Skin that Editor."

The Republican Press of Kansas Represents the Sentiments of the People.

The Skinner Skunned.

The Proof that no Man is Beyond the Reach of Public Sentiment.

Dinna Ye Hear the Slogan?

The Testimony of an Indignant People Against a Judge Dragging the Judicial Ermine Through the Slums of Saloon Politics

Nineteenth-Century Newspapers in Kansas

From earliest territorial days Kansas has always been awash in newsprint. In the nineteenth century, newspapers did not simply report the news; instead, newspapers were often openly partisan, supporting various political parties, religious groups, or even social clubs. Editors were frequently owners and used their newspapers to further their personal views, help them to obtain governmental office or contracts, and assist their other businesses such as law. J.K. Hudson's crusade on behalf of the prohibitionist movement in Kansas was much in keeping with this tradition, as was his attempt to obtain the lucrative contract to be state printer.

Today we live in a world where many cities have only one newspaper, if they have a newspaper at all. Kansas in the nineteenth century was far different. In 1875, for instance, Topeka was home to myriad newspapers including the *Topeka Commonwealth* and the *Blade* (both subsequently merged into Hudson's *Topeka Daily Capital*), the *American Young Folks* newspaper, the *Leader*, and the *North Topeka Times*. In neighboring Douglas County, Lawrence residents had available the *Kansas Collegiate*, the *Kansas Daily Tribune*, the *Kansas Weekly Tribune*, the *Republican Daily Journal*, the *Spirit of Kansas*, the *Western Home Journal*, the *Kansas Pacific Homestead*, the *Standard of Reform,* and the *State Sentinel*.

In an era without electronic media, out-of–state newspapers were expensive and difficult to obtain. Local newspapers such as these, which provided the citizenry with news, advertisements, political manifestoes, poetry, the weather, and other information, were a crucial part of everyday life.

Western Kansas World, *the "official paper of Trego County, Kansas," was first published on March 21, 1885, and remains in circulation today. Below: Sol Miller established the* White Cloud Kansas Chief *in 1857. In 1872, he moved the paper to Troy, Kansas, and changed its name to the* Weekly Kansas Chief, *where it was published until 1918.*

* * *

(From the *Daily Capital* of January 26, 1890.)

THE VERDICT

Of the People of Kansas, as Shown in the Capital, January 19, and To-day, is

Against Cassius Gaius Foster.

As a Judge, as a Lawyer, and as a Politician.—The Sentiment is Overwhelming,

And the Demand is, Resign.

Never Before in the History of Kansas has any Public Officer Received Such General Condemnation.

The Verdict is In, and We Rest Our Case.

Nobody is Fooled on the Legal Fees.—All See the Real Issue in this Contest.—Judge

Foster for the Saloon; the Capital Against It.[31]

Hudson gleefully let the proceedings go forward and reported everything that happened in detail:

On January 7, 1890, Judge C. G. Foster, of the United States district court, made an order requiring all legal publications to be printed in the new resubmission daily, the Topeka Republican, which was at that date exactly seven days old. In giving this order, Judge Foster stated that the reason he made it was that the publisher of the Capital had been charging illegal fees. On January 8 the Capital commented on this singular order, editorially. On January 9, Judge Foster replied to the editorial in an open letter to the Capital in which he defended his action, and threatened the editor with prosecution in his court. To this there was an appropriate editorial reply. On January 11 there was served on the editor of the Capital an order of the court giving him three days' notice to appear at the retaxing of printers' fees in 33 cases, which was printed and received editorial attention in the Capital, January 12. On January 14 an order was received by J. K. Hudson from Judge Foster's court stating that the illegal fees charged in the cases retaxed amounted to $159, and he was given five days (from

January 14) to appear and return said money. To this order there was an editorial reply denying the indebtedness, and denouncing the illegal proceedings on the part of the judge. No further attention was paid to the order. No appearance by attorney or in person was offered in court at any time during the discussion or since. After publishing the overwhelming verdict of the press of Kansas against the course of Judge Foster, the case rested without comment or reference to it by the Capital until the organization of the grand jury for the United States district court, April 14, when Judge Foster made good his threat of presenting the editor of the Capital for indictment, and thus we reach the second trial of this case.

After Hudson lost his case in the District Court he took his appeal to Circuit Court. In that court, Foster and the U.S. Attorney attempted to justify their position, but Judge Henry C. Caldwell found the reasoning insufficient and found for Hudson. Once, again, Hudson reported the courtroom drama with glee:

JUDGE CALDWELL'S DECISION.

The following is the decision of Judge Caldwell:

In the circuit court of the United States of the district of Kansas.

The United States of America, plaintiff, vs. Joseph K. Hudson, defendant.

There is nothing in this case that is unusual. The indictment found by the grand jury is presented, and the question has arisen as to whether it charges, with sufficient particularity and distinctness, an offense under the laws of the United States. The only question is whether this paper which I hold in my hand charges, in apt and sufficient terms, an offense.

In connection with this transaction, there may have been one or more offenses committed. The question is whether it appears sufficiently on the face of this indictment that any offense was committed by this defendant. To determine that, we must see whether the indictment is sufficiently specific to advise the defendant of the offense with which he is charged; because it is undoubtedly a fundamental rule in criminal proceedings, recognized by all courts—and by none with more distinctness than the federal courts and the supreme court of the

United States—that a criminal charge in the shape of an indictment must advise the defendant distinctly and particularly of the offense of which he is accused, and of the particular act or acts alleged to constitute, that offense.

To understand the legal value of this indictment, it is essential to understand the law regulating and governing the deposit of moneys in the courts of the United States, and their withdrawal from those courts. In 1871, the Congress of the United States passed an act on this subject. The first section of that act is as follows:

"That all moneys in the registry of any court of the United States, or in the hands or under the control of any officer of such court, which were received in any case pending or adjudicated in such court, shall, within 30 days after the passage of this act, be deposited with the treasurer, an assistant treasurer or a designated depository of the United States, in the name of and to the credit of such court."

That applied to all moneys then in the hands of the clerk, or, in the language of the act, "in the registry of the court," and made it obligatory upon the officers, within 30 days, to deposit the same with the treasurer, an assistant treasurer or a designated depository of the United States, in the name of and to the credit of the court. A designated depository of the United States is a national bank, designated by the treasurer of the United States as a bank authorized to receive and pay out the public funds of the United States. All banks have not that authority. The authority to receive the public funds of the United States must come from the treasurer of the United States, in pursuance of an appointment made by that officer. No court, and no officer of a court, can deposit, and no court can authorize its officers to deposit, any fund belonging to the registry of a court, in any national bank except such as may have been designated by the treasurer of the United States as banks that may receive and pay out the funds of the United States. Having made proper provision for getting all such moneys into a safe place, into the custody of the treasurer, an assistant treasurer or a designated national depository of the United States, Congress then proceeds to legislate for the future. There had been abuses; it had transpired that officers of courts receiving funds had retained them and used them for their private purposes, and when they were wanted they were not forthcoming. This act was passed to correct that abuse. It proceeded,

The First Clerk of Court

By the time John T. Morton was appointed in 1861 as the first clerk of the Federal District Court of Kansas, the position had become much larger in scope than was specified in the Judiciary Act of 1789. The clerk not only summoned jurors and "record[ed] the decrees, judgments and determinations…" of the court, he also performed a vast array of administrative tasks and recorded naturalization petitions and copyright claims. The clerk was compensated by the fees collected from litigants. Eventually, limitations were placed upon how much a clerk could keep and the remainder was required to be turned over to the Treasury Department. In 1853, Congress enacted a fee schedule for courts nationwide and thus eliminated the substantial cost differences between districts. Only in 1919 did the clerks of the district court finally become salaried.

John T. Morton, first clerk of court for the Federal District Court of Kansas, c. 1861-63.

Today's clerk functions as the chief operating officer of the court with mainly administrative duties. Each court has its own staff of information technology, finance, and human relations personnel. Of course, the clerk's office still maintains the records (albeit electronically) and provides customer service to the litigants and attorneys with questions or issues. The clerk also provides guidance and leadership in administrative matters to the court and works closely with the Administrative Office of the Courts to provide service to the judges.

in the first place, to get in, gather together into a safe place, all moneys and funds in the hands of the court, and then it legislates for the future in these terms: "And all such moneys which are hereafter paid into such courts, or received by the officers thereof, shall be forthwith deposited in like manner." That is, with the treasurer, an assistant treasurer or a designated national depository of the United States. "That no money, deposited as aforesaid shall be withdrawn, except by order of the judge or judges of said courts respectively, in term or in vacation, to be signed by such judge or judges, and to be entered and certified of record by the clerk." The clerk has no authority to draw a check. His name as drawer of the check on the treasurer, an assistant treasurer or a designated national depository of the United States, is of no more legal effect or force or validity than the name of the crier of the court would be. It is to be got out by the order of the court or judge, to be signed by such judge or judges, and entered and certified of record by the clerk: "and every such order shall state the cause in or on account of which it is drawn."

I have read the original act because it throws some light on the revision.

In making the revision, there was only a very slight change made in the language of the original act. Of course the first provision had served its purpose; the 30 days had elapsed, and the first clause of the first section is omitted, but the balance of the act is retained. Section 995 of the Revised Statutes says: "All moneys paid into any court of the United States, or received by the officers thereof, in any cause pending or adjudicated in such court shall be forthwith deposited with the treasurer, an assistant treasurer or a designated depository of the United States, in the name of and to the credit of such court. No money deposited as aforesaid shall be withdrawn except by order of the judge or judges of said courts respectively in term or in vacation, to be signed by such judge or judges, and to be entered and certified of record by the clerk," who does all the recording for the court: "and every such order shall state the cause in or on account of which it is drawn."

Now, I may state here, my practice has been, conforming to that act, to have a printed record, a volume of blank printed orders, leaving the title of the case, the name of the payee of the check, and the amount, blank; also leaving space for my name or the name of any other judge that happens to be holding court. Then I have a copy of that which is a record. Having two of these, the original is signed by me and given to the party entitled to the fund; the other is kept, an exact copy, and is entered of record. The clerk attests the record by his signature, and also attests the check, but the check is drawn as required by law, and signed by the judge.

That is the only way that a fund can be got out of the registry of the court when it once goes there—

using the term "registry" in the sense in which the learned counsel for the government uses it in this indictment.

The penal provisions of the Revised Statutes are the same in substance that they are in the original act. It first relates to the clerk and other officers of the court: "Every clerk or other officer of a court of the United States who fails forthwith to deposit any money belonging in the registry of the court, or hereafter paid into court, or received by the officers thereof, with the treasurer, assistant

> "Whether there was an act committed which, if properly set out, would constitute an offense under this section, I do not decide. That is not the point; the court must not speculate upon that. It is a homely phrase, but a good one for the court to follow, not to cross a bridge until you come to it."

treasurer or a designated depository of the United States, in the name of and to the credit of such court, or who retains or converts to his own use, or to the use of another, any such money, is guilty of embezzlement," etc.; and "every person who knowingly received from a clerk or other officer of a court of the United States any money belonging in the registry of such court as a deposit, loan or otherwise, is guilty of embezzlement."

Now, this defendant is indicted under that last section of the act. Before I proceed to test the sufficiency of this indictment, it is necessary to show what may occur. The court may have its funds in a dozen, or, for that matter, a hundred different places; as, for instance, the court over which I have had the honor to preside in Arkansas for 25 years, has moneys now deposited in a national depository at Little Rock—that is, a national bank, designated by the secretary of the treasury to receive a deposit of national funds. It has funds with the assistant treasurer of the United States at St. Louis, and with the assistant treasurer of the United States in New York City, and with the assistant treasurer of the United States in the city of Boston, which are all lawful depositories under the act; three of them assistant treasurers, and one a designated national depository. Now, suppose a man is indicted in the district of Arkansas for unlawfully obtaining money out of the registry of the court. What registry? From the national depository at Little Rock, or from the assistant treasurer in Boston? I don't know how many depositories the circuit court for this district may have; it may have a great many more, for aught I know, or it may have less; but I do know that this indictment doesn't tell this defendant what depository he is accused of taking this money out of, or what registry; that is very clear. It nowhere appears with sufficient distinctness what depository of this court is meant.

There are very many questions that might be raised as to the sufficiency and particularity of this indictment. The act itself is not charged with sufficient particularity.

Now, "on pretense of false and illegal claim for services for publishing illegal notices." Why, that is nothing; you might have said on pretense of being a handsome man; it would be legally worth as much as that. How does the court know what the pleader thinks is a "pretense of a false or illegal claim?" What does the court understand a pleader to mean by "false pretense," or "on pretense," without stating what the pretense was? One man may think a thing is a false pretense, and another that it is a meritorious and just one. What was the pretense? It is not for the pleader to say it was on false pretense; that is a mere conclusion of law. You must show what he did, in language to this effect: "and that he did make a false pretense in this, to-wit: That, whereas, he had performed a service for which he was entitled to be paid a certain sum of money, to-wit, so many dollars; that he, thereafter, knowingly, fraudulently and willfully made out an account of those services for so many dollars, and presented it, and by a false oath or by some other pretense, induced the court to make an illegal order in his favor, by which he obtained that money from the registry of the court," naming the registry. Or, if the money was not obtained in this mode, then the manner in which it was obtained

must be particularly set out. There are other points that might be alluded to, but it is not necessary. It is sufficient to say that this indictment, as it stands, does not sufficiently specify the act done by the defendant. Whether there was an act committed which, if properly set out, would constitute an offense under this section, I do not decide. That is not the point; the court must not speculate upon that. It is a homely phrase, but a good one for the court to follow, not to cross a bridge until you come to it. The only thing the court is called upon to decide is that this indictment is uncertain and insufficient, and that it fails to charge, with sufficient distinctness, an offense under that section.

For that reason the motion to quash will be granted.[32]

The battle between Major Hudson and Judge Foster seemed to be at an end in 1890 when Judge Caldwell quashed the indictment against Hudson. For the next five years the two men seem to have avoided each other. Hudson continued to edit his newspaper, and Foster continued to sit on the federal bench, disturbed only by intermittent bouts of illness. But the peace between them did not last forever. The battle was rejoined in 1895; this time, Foster made the first move. Hudson had attempted to be appointed state printer. Judge Foster, no doubt still angry about his loss five years before, immediately took steps to block Hudson from his goal. Once again, the two men became public adversaries:

(Editorial from the *Daily Capital* of Sunday, June 2, 1895.)

THE LEAN AND LANK CASSIUS ONCE MORE.

We see that Judge Cassius Gaius Foster is very unnecessarily sticking his nose into the state-printer contest. He was not too sick last winter to go to the statehouse to lobby against the election of Major Hudson, although not able to do the work of United States district judge, for which he was drawing full pay. We understand that it is upon Judge Foster's advise that the populist Snow makes a contest for an office he was not elected to fill. This is not the first time the narrow personal prejudices of Judge Foster have run away with what discretion and sense he may have. Once before, when Major Hudson was concerned, he forgot the dignity of his position, and exposed his lack of knowledge of law and justice, in a newspaper controversy over a trial taking place in his own court. To a packed grand jury, this travesty upon a just judge gave such instructions as to insure a verdict against the collection of fees he himself had indorsed as correct in the particular cases under trial, and in similar ones for 15 years before. When the case came to be reviewed by Judge Caldwell, a man of real legal learning and high judicial honor, the petty personal spitework of Judge Cassius Gaius Foster was swept aside, and the legal tyrant's large ears exposed to the ridicule of the people. Since that time he has been engaged in drawing the salary, for which he has not rendered the services it should pay for, and holding on to an office which he has never been large enough to fill, trying through friends to bulldoze the government into retiring him upon full pay. A part of the mission of this judicial cadaver is to follow, with the malice born of small souls, a man who neither feared his power nor respected his ignorance of law. We copy Judge Foster's facetious opinion upon the right of a man to an office whose claim rests, not upon being the choice of a majority of the representatives of the people, nor upon the fact that he was elected at all, but upon the supposition of a technical violation of the statutory law in Major Hudson's election. When it is known that the populist majority of the senate, in a caucus the night preceding, agreed to try to prevent the election of a state printer by remaining out of the joint convention, the whole basis of Snow's dishonest claim, advocated by Judge Foster and the anarchist Clemens, fails, because conspiracy to defeat a constitutional duty is neither good public policy nor good law. The following is the profound legal opinion of Cassius Gaius Foster upon a question which involves principles of constitutional rights, of justice to the people's representatives, and the question of the supremacy of the majority, all of which do not seem to be within the view of the judge who is pleading the case of an unprincipled political pirate. The letter is as follows:

Topeka, May 27, 1895.

E. H. Snow: Dear Sir—In answer to your note, asking me to read the letters of Senator Baker and Judge Thacher on the state-printer matter, and if I could express my views on the subject, I need only say, I have read the letters, and summarize their arguments thus:

1. Because the constitution says there shall be a joint convention of the legislature on the third Tuesday of January, to elect a state printer, therefore there was a joint convention.

2. As the law of 1879 requires a majority of the members elected to each house to concur in the election of a printer, it might prevent the dominant political party electing its candidate, therefore the law is unconstitutional.

For several reasons, which suggest themselves to the average legal mind, to say nothing of the decided cases, there is, in my opinion, nothing in either proposition. How would it do to try your side of the case in the courts?

Very truly,

C. G. FOSTER.[33]

This time Hudson had overreached. One simply doesn't refer to a federal judge as an "unprincipled political pirate." But Hudson probably did not expect what came next. Rather than carry on the battle in newspapers, Judge Foster turned to the Kansas courts and brought a criminal libel action against Hudson.[34] The spectacle of a federal judge suing a newspaper editor for libel in a state court was one not seen before in Kansas. But odd as the suit may have been, Foster had the law on his side this time. The suit was brought in the Kansas District Court in Atchison, Foster's hometown. Once again, Major Hudson used his newspaper to defend himself and to attack Foster. But neither Foster nor Hudson really seemed to have had much taste for another major battle like the one they had fought five years before. The case against Hudson opened on September 28, and Hudson's lawyer immediately made a motion to quash.[35] The two sides argued the motion but the judge, rather than deciding at that point, took the motion under advisement until the next day. At that time the district judge, Judge Z. T. Hazen, overruled the motion and set the stage for the trial to begin; however, it did not do so. Instead, the prosecutor asked for a delay in the proceedings on the ground that Judge Foster was ill and could not appear as a witness. On October 5, the prosecutor, at the request of Judge Foster, withdrew the charges. According to Hudson, the judge in the case "complimented the contestants on their good sense." Hudson had apologized to Foster and that ended the matter.

Withdrawal of the libel action in 1895 marked the end of the epic battles between Foster and Hudson. Foster petitioned Congress just a few years later to be allowed to retire with a pension from the Federal District Court, and as soon as this was granted, he did so.[36] He soon died. Hudson, on the other hand, continued his journalistic career, although, perhaps, never did he again so deserve the title of "Fighting Joe Hudson" as he did during his struggle with Judge Cassius Gaius Foster.

Notes to Chapter 2

1. http://www.findagrave.com/cgi-bin/fg.cgi?page=gr&GSln=Foster&GSiman=1&GScty=49465&GRid=6635642&

2. *History of the Federal Judiciary: Foster, Cassius Gaius,* FEDERAL JUDICIAL CENTER, http://www.fjc.gov/servlet/nGetInfo?jid=784 [hereinafter *FJC: Foster*].

3. Nicole Etcheson, *Bleeding Kansas: Contested Liberty in the Civil War Era* (Lawrence: University Press of Kansas, 2006).

4. William G. Cutler, *History of the State of Kansas* (Chicago: A. T. Andreas, 1883), 369–71. Online at http://www.kancoll.org/books/cutler/atchison/atchison-co-p2.html#FIRST_SETTLERS.

5. *Id.* at 371–72. Online at http://www.kancoll.org/books/cutler/atchison/atchison-co-p3.html#BORDER_RUFFIAN WARFARE.

6. *Id.,* at 371–72.

7. *Id.,* at 372.

8. *FJC: Foster.*

9. *History of the Federal Judiciary: Williams, Archibald* at http://www.fjc.gov/public/home.nsf/hisj.

10. *History of the Federal Judiciary: Delahay, Mark* at http://www.fjc.gov/public/home.nsf/hisj.

11. His most important decision also involved alcoholic beverages in Indian territory; see William E. Unruh, "United States v. Downing, Judge Cassius Foster and the Sale of Spiritous Liquors to the Indians in Indian Country," in The Law and Lawyers in Kansas History: A Collection of Papers Presented at the 116th Annual Meeting of the Kansas State Historical Society October 4–5, 1991, at 1 and 10–12 (1992).

12. Robert Smith Bader, *Prohibition in Kansas* (Lawrence: University Press of Kansas, 1986), at 107–108 [hereinafter *Bader*].

13. *Id.* at 15.

14. *Id.* at 20–21, 99.

15. *Id.* at 31.

16. *Id.* at 16–18.

17. *Id.* at 23.

18. *Id.* at 19–20.

19. *Id.* at 21–22.

20. *Id.* at 22.

21. *Id* at 37–39.

22. See J.K. Hudson, *The Legal and Political History of the Suits Brought by Hon. Cassius Gaius Foster, Judge of the U.S. District Court of Kansas, Against Maj. J. K. Hudson, Editor Daily Capital, of Topeka, Kansas: Giving the Origin, Facts, Letters, Charges, Indictments, Editorials, and Decisions of the Cases of 1890 and 1895* (Topeka, 1915) (1895) [hereinafter *Legal History*]. See also Cecil Howes, "Pistol Packin' Pencil Pushers," *Kansas Historical Quarterly* (1944), v.13, pp. 116–38.

23. William E. Connelley, *A History of Kansas Newspapers, 1854–1916* (Topeka: Kansas State Printing Plant, 1916).

24. *Bader* at 57.

25. Biographical details about J. K. Hudson are from *The National Magazine: A Monthly Journal of American History* (1894), pp.50–51; see also *Legal History*.

26. *Legal History* at 7.

27. *Id.* at 7.

28. *Id.* at 9–10.

29. *Id.* at 11.

30. *Id.* at 18.

31. *Id.* at 29.

32. *Id.* at 61–62.

33. *Id.* at 69–70.

34. *Id.* at 70.

35. For an account of the proceedings and the settlement, see *id.* at 70–74.

36. Fifty-fifth Congress, H.R. Report No. 1716 (January 4, 1899).

"Abilene in Its Glory," an illustration by Henry Worrall, 1874.

Atchison, Topeka & Santa Fe Railway workers, c. 1890–1900.

3

THE COURT FROM HOOK TO HELVERING

With the retirement of Judge Cassius Gaius Foster, the Kansas District Court left what may be called its formative period. The advent of the new century brought with it a series of new social and legal challenges to confront the court. Except for a short period from 1928 to 1929 there continued to be only a single federal district judge for the Kansas District.[1] Three judges served relatively short terms on the court. William Cather Hook's and George Thomas McDermott's tenures as district judges were both ended by their appointments to the U.S. Court of Appeals for the Sixth and Eighth Circuits.[2] Guy Tresillian Helvering, appointed to the district judgeship at age sixty-five after a distinguished legal career including a decade as commissioner of internal revenue, died only three years after his appointment.[3] Two judges, however, had long tenures on the court: John Calvin Pollock served for thirty-four years[4] and Richard Joseph Hopkins served for fourteen years.[5]

Judge William Cather Hook

William Cather Hook was appointed to be judge of the Federal District Court of Kansas in 1899 to replace Judge Cassius Gaius Foster, who had retired as a result of illness.[6] Hook was born in Pennsylvania on September 24, 1857.[7] His parents immigrated to Nebraska in 1863 and then to Leavenworth, Kansas, in 1867.[8] He entered as an apprentice in the Leavenworth offices of Clough & Wheat as a teenager and then attended Washington University in St. Louis, at the time one of the leading law schools in the United States. He graduated with an LLB[9] in 1878 and returned to Leavenworth to practice law. He remained in private practice and served as city attorney until his appointment to the District Court in 1899.

Although Judge Hook spent only four years as a federal district judge, he wrote one of the most important and influential decisions of the era. On November 27, 1899, less than a year after his appointment, Judge Hook published his

Judge William Cather Hook.

decision in the case of *Western Union Telegraph Company v. Myatt.*[10] It was a masterpiece of judicial craftsmanship.

In 1898 the Kansas Legislature passed a series of new laws designed to give the state greater control of railroads and telegraph companies operating in Kansas.[11] Until the new legislation, regulation of railroads and telegraph companies rested with a Board of Railroad Commissioners, whose regulatory powers were relatively weak.[12] At this time, railroads, telegraph companies, and other corporations that operated under licenses from the state and were thereby "clothed with the public interest" were an essential part of the Kansas economy.[13] They were also immensely powerful

Above: Membership card issued to R.F. Andrews by the Order of Railroad Telegraphers, a labor union established to promote the interests of telegraph operators who worked for the railroads.
Right: Telegram from F.E. Shaw, sheriff of Atchison County, Kansas, to Governor John Martin on March 26, 1886, regarding a strike by railroad workers

corporations that had few competitors and whose control of prices for transportation, freight, and communications was virtually unchallenged. By the time the Kansas Legislature passed the 1898 legislation soon to be tested in Judge Hook's court, many Kansans believed that this was an unacceptable situation. Thus, in a special session called in 1898, the legislature passed a series of laws to abolish the Board of Railroad Commissioners, create a new "Court of Visitation," and expanded the regulatory powers of the state vested in this new court.[14] Indeed, the legislation gave the new court the power not only to set rates charged by these public service corporations it controlled, but also to adjudicate the reasonableness of these rates and to determine whether such rates were permissible under Kansas law.[15]

Soon after the 1898 legislation was signed into law the Court of Visitation set rates for the transmission of telegraph messages. Unfortunately for Western Union, the primary telegraph company serving Kansas, the rates set by the Court of Visitation were below the company's actual costs.[16] A Mr. Maxwell attempted to send some telegraphic messages but refused to pay the company's charges and would only pay the rates set by the Court.[17] Western Union refused to send his messages. He then filed a complaint with the attorney general of Kansas, Aretas Allen Godard, who began state court proceedings to force Western Union to charge no more than the court-established rates. Western Union thereupon brought an action in the Federal District Court of Kansas before Judge Hook seeking an injunction to stop the state proceedings.

The decision by Judge Hook in this case is quite remarkable for both its learning and its analysis. Judge Hook

not only granted the injunction but also invalidated the legislation which set up the Court of Visitation.[18] At the heart of the opinion was his analysis of the question whether the Court of Visitation's mix of judicial and legislative functions violated the separation of powers inherent in the Kansas Constitution as well as the due process requirements of the United States Constitution.[19] In this analysis, Judge Hook made a bold venture into the respective powers of state and federal courts as well as established new doctrines in constitutional jurisprudence. In so doing he also demonstrated the depth of his legal learning.

In his discussion of the doctrine of the separation of powers, Judge Hook provided a learned discourse on the origins of the doctrine going back to the Founding Fathers.[20] He cited passages from Blackstone, Montesquieu, and Kent.[21] He then went on to show a remarkable knowledge of Kansas state constitutional law, using state cases to demonstrate that Kansas had adopted the doctrine, although its own constitution did not say so explicitly.[22]

The end result of Judge Hook's opinion was to define more clearly than had been done before the distinction between judicial and legislative powers and to prove that the doctrine had been incorporated into the state constitution although not expressed directly. Once Judge Hook had built this jurisprudential edifice, it became simple for him then to ask whether the Court of Visitation's setting of telegraphic rates below the actual cost to the company was a violation of due process under the United States Constitution. The answer was a resounding "yes."[23] Within his first year on the federal bench, Judge Hook invalidated one of the most important populist laws passed by the Kansas Legislature, enjoined the Kansas court system from hearing a case, and extended American jurisprudence on both separation of powers and due process. Quite a first year, indeed!

Judge Hook's decision had national importance and attracted the attention of lawyers and politicians throughout the United States.[24] As a result, when Judge Henry Clay Caldwell retired from the U.S. Court of Appeals for the Eighth Circuit in 1903, President Theodore Roosevelt nominated Judge Hook to replace him.[25] Judge Hook remained on the Circuit Court from then until his death in 1921. Although Judge Hook's career subsequent to his time on the Federal District of Kansas is beyond the scope of this book, it merits a few paragraphs, at least.

The learning and judicial abilities which Judge Hook demonstrated in the Western Union opinion helped to make him one of the best and most respected federal circuit judges of his era. His decisions in the newly developing field of antitrust law were perhaps the most important.[26] It was Judge Hook's definition of monopoly and restraint of trade in the Standard Oil case which became the basis for the understanding of these terms in later cases and legislation.[27]

> "Magnitude of business does not, alone, constitute a monopoly, nor effort at magnitude an attempt to monopolize. To offend the act the monopoly must have been secured by methods contrary to the public policy as expressed in the statutes or in the common law."
>
> -- *Judge William Cather Hook*

In 1910, Justice David Brewer's death left an opening on the United States Supreme Court. Soon thereafter, Chief Justice Melville Fuller died, and several months later Justice John Marshall Harlan died as well. This meant that within the space of little more than a year, Judge Hook had three chances for nomination to the Supreme Court by President William Howard Taft. Each time he was considered the favorite, but each time the nomination failed to come about.[28] He seemed almost a sure thing to replace Justice Brewer, but instead, his colleague Willis Devanter got the nod.[29] The later chances evaporated when Judge Hook's concurrence in an Oklahoma

"Jim Crow" case came to light. The great Booker T. Washington himself lobbied against Hook's opinion in strong words:

> I do not see how any colored man after reading this decision could advocate the cause of Judge Hook. It is a deliberate insult to a whole race of people. He goes further in trying to humiliate us than any Southern judge has ever done.[30]

With such strong feelings against Hook, the president chose another. Judge Hook remained on the U.S. Circuit Court of Appeals for the Eighth Circuit for the remainder of his life.[31]

John Calvin Pollock

Early photograph of Judge John Calvin Pollock.

Federal District Judge John Calvin Pollock was born on October 5, 1857, in Belmont, Ohio.[32] After his education in Belmont,[33] Pollock attended Franklin College, from which he obtained an AB in 1882.[34] Immediately upon college graduation, Pollock entered the law offices of a well-known local attorney of his home county as an apprentice.[35] In 1884 he concluded his office study and immigrated to Newton, Iowa, where he was admitted as an attorney.[36] In February 1885, he left Newton and moved to Wright County, Missouri. He remained in practice there for three years. In 1887, he again moved; this time to Winfield, Kansas. He built a

Winfield, Kansas, 1900, where Judge Pollock practiced law before his appointment to the Kansas Supreme Court, and birthplace of Judge McDermott.

Judge John Calvin Pollock.

successful practice during the next four years. In 1901 a seat opened on the Kansas Supreme Court due to the death of one of the justices. Judge Pollock was appointed by the governor to fill the vacancy.[37] In 1902, at the end of the term he had been appointed to fill, Judge Pollock successfully ran for the seat in his own right. Throughout his period in private practice and on the state bench, Judge Pollock was active in Republican Party politics,[38] a fact which, no doubt, assisted him in his early rise to judicial office.

In 1903, with the elevation of Judge Hook to the Eighth Circuit, President Theodore Roosevelt was given the opportunity to find his replacement as federal district judge for the District of Kansas. There were several candidates for the position, each supported by members of the Kansas congressional delegation.[39] Judge Pollock was supported by Senator Chester Long and Representatives Victor Murdock and Philip Campbell.[40] Chief Justice Johnson of the Kansas Supreme Court was supported by Representatives William Calderhead and Charles Scott. Senator Joseph Burton supported Topeka attorney Charles Blood Smith. Representatives Jason Miller and Charles Curtis favored

Judge J. G. Slonecker of Topeka, and Representatives Justin Bowersock and William Reeder backed N. H. Loomis.

This chaotic situation was worsened when a whisper campaign was begun against Judge Pollock. Rumors stated that Judge Pollock had been drinking whiskey and "playing poker" with members of the bar and "winning at it." President Roosevelt asked the attorney general of the United States to investigate these charges. At the same time, the president ordered the Kansas delegation to go back to Congress and vote until they had a single candidate to recommend. However, when the president learned from the attorney general that there was no substance to the charges, he decided to appoint Judge Pollock to the vacancy despite the fact that the Kansas delegation had still not settled on their choice. Judge Pollock's nomination was confirmed by the Senate on December 1, 1903, and he received his commission on the same day.[41] For the next thirty-four years he served as the federal district judge for the District of Kansas.

When Judge Pollock took the federal bench in 1903, his court was changing. President Roosevelt was a progressive activist who believed that the federal government had broad authority to legislate and to adjudicate. This meant more business for Congress and more business for the federal courts. After President Roosevelt's departure from office, the United States faced the even more radical transformation caused by its entry into the First World War, the war which made the United States a global power. The war also brought with it fears of spies, treason, and the spread of Bolshevism. All of these newly increased problems led to more federal legislation and more business for the federal courts. During Judge Pollock's three decades on the federal bench, he decided numerous cases. Some of these were of great importance to the litigants but of little national or historical significance. Nevertheless, they demonstrate what kind of man and judge he was. In 1908 Judge Pollock heard the case of a young bank clerk who was being prosecuted for the theft of a five-dollar remittance from the bank.[42] Upon questioning by Judge Pollock, the young man confessed to the crime and explained that he had taken the money to send to his sick brother and produced a money order receipt to prove his statement. When Judge Pollock saw the receipt, he sentenced the young man to time served and freed him. On the other hand, in another criminal case, a man was being prosecuted for stealing $2.50 from a post office. When the thief showed no remorse, Judge Pollock sent him to Leavenworth Prison for eighteen months.

During his long tenure on the bench, Judge Pollock decided one case of great national and historical importance. The International Workers of the World (IWW or "Wobblies") was established by a group of radical labor activists at the beginning of the twentieth century.[43] By 1917—and the entry of the United States into World War I—it was considered to

The "Wobblies"

The International Workers of the World, popularly known as "Wobblies," was founded as a universal labor union in 1905. Almost from its founding convention the IWW locked horns with both the federal and various state governments. In the year following its founding, members of the IWW engaged in numerous strikes and other industrial action and its leaders were accused of attempted murder and assassination. To government officials, the IWW was seen as a militant socialist organization with a subversive agenda. To its members, the IWW was the best hope for workers' rights and the reform of industry in the United States. There was, perhaps, an element of truth in both perspectives. By 1910 the Wobblies were split between those members who favored "direct action" and those who sought to achieve their goals through the traditional political process. It was in this year that IWW publications began to speak openly of sabotage as a strategic tool. Such radicalization served only to further convince government that the IWW was a dangerous organization, ensuring that government actions to repress it would be further reinforced.

Between 1910 and 1915 IWW direct actions led to multiple strikes at corporate sites across the United States. In 1915 agents of the copper mining companies killed Wobbly leader Joe Hill. The IWW now had its first martyr and his death became a rallying point for IWW members across the nation. The entry of the United States into the First World War, however, shifted the political climate in the U.S. Industrial actions such as strikes now became, in the

Political cartoon that uses a Kansas wheat field to depict the Wobblies invasion, July 24, 1920.

public mind, acts of treason designed to derail the war effort. In 1920 the attorney general of the United States, Mitchell Palmer, authorized the arrest and deportation of thousands of alien workers, the so-called Palmer raids, in the name of national security. Although the IWW continues in existence to this day, by the middle of the 1920s its significance on the national stage had been permanently diminished.

be one of the most dangerous groups in the United States by government officials, law enforcement, the press, and the general public. Although the most notorious of the prosecutions brought against the IWW took place in Chicago, Judge Pollock presided over a second prosecution in Kansas City.

The Kansas action against the IWW began with the then United States attorney for the District of Kansas, Fred Robertson. In 1917 Robertson became convinced that members of the IWW planned to sabotage railroads, industrial facilities, and farms in Kansas.[44] In November 1917 Robertson arrested more than forty members of the group.[45] In March 1918, a grand jury sitting in Wichita indicted the men for espionage and plotting to sabotage food production.[46] Robertson, however, had been quite negligent in preparing his case and when the indictment came before Judge Pollock,

it was quashed.[47] A second indictment, with evidence little better than the first, came before Judge Pollock. The judge once again felt constrained to quash it.[48] It would appear, however, that in spite of the poor job done by the prosecution, Judge Pollock wanted to see the IWW members in his court as defendants.[49]

In order to accomplish his goal, Judge Pollock met with Robertson and outlined for him prosecution strategy which the judge felt he could accept.[50] In June 1919, a special grand jury again indicted the Wobblies, but this time the counts were those which Judge Pollock had instructed the prosecution to bring. Not surprisingly, this time the indictment held and Judge Pollock found himself presiding over the case.[51] The case attracted national attention and public sentiment was against the IWW. The prosecution spent a week presenting its case.[52] In a surprise move, when it was the time for the

United States Penitentiary in Leavenworth, Kansas, c. 1895-1910.

defense to present its case, it chose not to do so but to simply allow the case to go to the jury.[53] Judge Pollock's charge to that jury was anything but neutral: "the IWW organization, during the period of this war, was, in and of itself, a disloyal organization, the members conspiring with each other to violate these several laws."[54] The defendants were found guilty and soon were on their way to Leavenworth and prison.

This was far from Judge Pollock's first contact with Leavenworth. As the federal penitentiary in Kansas and one of the best maximum security prisons in the United States, the prison at Leavenworth was often the destination of those found guilty in federal court. On occasion, Leavenworth was also the source of criminal cases. One case which arose from Leavenworth Penitentiary put one of America's most famous criminals in Judge Pollock's courtroom.

Mug shot of Robert Stroud, the "Birdman of Alcatraz," c. 1942, from the Alcatraz Warden's Notebook.

Robert Stroud is now popularly known as the "birdman of Alcatraz."[55] But, in fact, much of his early life behind bars was spent as an inmate at Leavenworth. In 1908, then an eighteen-year-old worker in Alaska, Robert Stroud brutally murdered F. K. "Charlie" Von Dahmer in revenge for Von Dahmer's beating of Stroud's girlfriend. In early 1909,

Stroud was convicted of murder, sentenced to twelve years imprisonment, and sent to McNeil Island Penitentiary. At McNeil, Stroud was involved in a fight with another inmate and, after stabbing the other inmate, had his twelve-year sentence extended by six months.[56] In 1912 Stroud was transferred to Leavenworth's maximum security compound.[57] He was viewed by prison authorities as a dangerous inmate, prone to violence. In 1915, Stroud developed Bright's disease and was transferred to the prison infirmary. While there he came into contact with a prison guard named Andrew Turner. The two disliked each other intensely.[58] On March 26, 1916, Stroud and Turner began to fight in the prison dining hall. Stroud pulled a knife out of his clothing and stabbed Turner in the chest repeatedly until Turner was dead.

Immediately after Stroud killed Turner, the U.S. attorney for the Federal District of Kansas, Fred Robertson, decided to prosecute Stroud and attempt to have him condemned to death. In May 1916, Stroud was tried in Federal District Court before a jury with Judge Pollock presiding. On May 27, Judge Pollock sentenced Stroud to be hanged.

After sentence was passed, Stroud's family and friends began a campaign to reverse the sentence. They appealed the sentence to the U.S. Circuit Court and that court reversed and remanded the case for a second hearing before Judge Pollock. Stroud's mother, Elizabeth, intensified her campaign to spare her son from hanging and turned the case into a popular cause focused not on Stroud's guilt, but on the inhumanity of the death penalty. Many women's groups and other activists began a media campaign to influence the new trial. Judge Pollock, apparently, was infuriated by this outside interference in a case which he believed was absolutely clear-cut. His anger rose to the point where he was judged no longer sufficiently objective to try the case and was disqualified. On May 22, 1917, Judge J. W. Woodrough, federal district judge for the Eastern District of Oklahoma, took over the case. Once, again, Stroud was found guilty by the jury, but this time his life was spared.

In 1931 the lawyers and judges of Kansas and Missouri put on a testimonial dinner in honor of Judge Pollock's service on both the Kansas and federal bench.[59] The dinner was attended by virtually all of the legal luminaries of the two states as well as by the guest of honor, Judge Pollock.[60] In a night filled with speeches, Judge Pollock's legal learning, patriotism, and dedication to the law were repeated over and over again. Many of the speakers also told anecdotes about Judge Pollock. Perhaps the most fascinating and revealing of these was the story told by Judge Charles B. Faris of St. Louis. Judge Faris, like Judge Pollock, had left a seat on his state Supreme Court to become a federal district judge.[61] He related to his audience that this was not an easy decision and that he made it with some trepidation. His concerns, however, so he told, were allayed completely after a meeting with Judge Pollock. Judge Pollock calmed his colleague by a simple, short statement of his view of a federal judgeship:

> There are just two things about your job that
> you ought always to remember and be comforted:
> One is that you are here for life, and the other is,
> that you can do pretty near what you damn please.[62]

George Thomas McDermott

In 1928 Congress passed legislation to create a second federal district judgeship for the District of Kansas.[63] President Calvin Coolidge appointed George Thomas McDermott to fill that seat, which he held for just sixteen months, when he was elevated to the U.S. Court of Appeals for the Tenth Circuit.[64]

Early photograph of Judge George Thomas McDermott.

McDermott was born in 1886 in Winfield, Kansas. He attended Southwestern University for his undergraduate education[65] and received his law degree from the University of Chicago in 1909.[66] During law school McDermott showed his talent for law and served as a research assistant for Professor Floyd Mechem and assisted him in preparing the second edition of Mechem's treatise on agency.[67] He returned to Topeka and entered into private practice

Judge George Thomas McDermott..

with a leading lawyer of the day: Robert Stone.[68] The firm of Stone and McDermott prospered, and McDermott remained a member of the firm until he was appointed to the federal bench.

McDermott, during his years of private practice in Topeka, was actively involved both in politics and in bar activities. He was a long-time member of the Topeka Chamber of Commerce, including serving a term as president.[69] He was also member of the Kansas Board of Law Examiners, as well as of the Topeka Board of Education. For two years, from 1917 to 1919, he was a member of the United States Army and attained the rank of lieutenant.[70] Although he did not serve in the trenches, he was shipped to France in August 1918 to study French artillery techniques.[71] He returned to the United States in January 1919 and resumed his practice.

Back in practice, McDermott was appointed by the Kansas Supreme Court to assist in liquidating the Kansas bank guarantee fund and to serve as a commissioner of the court to hear a telephone rate case.[72]

Judge McDermott spent only a short time on the District

Membership composite of the Topeka, Kansas, Bar Association in 1931. Members include Judge McDermott, Judge Hopkins, and Elisha Scott, who would later represent the plaintiffs in Brown v. Board.

Court, and his influence there was not great. He was appointed to a seat on the newly created United States Court of Appeals for the Tenth Circuit in 1929 and served on this court until his death in 1937.[73] While on the Circuit Court, he was more active. He authored the majority opinion in 240 cases and wrote dissenting opinions in 22.[74] During this time he also taught constitutional law at Washburn Law School.[75] He was also elected to the council of the new American Law Institute in 1934, one of the most prestigious positions an American lawyer can hold.[76]

Throughout his time in practice and on the bench, Judge McDermott acquired a reputation as a brilliant and

hardworking jurist. He also was considered to be, as one colleague put it, "an unusual personality." From his earliest days in the legal profession, Judge McDermott stood out as a "human dynamo" and as an extremely aggressive advocate. When his nomination to the Federal Court was announced, some members of the bar were concerned that he did not possess a "judicial temperament." Apparently, these fears were realized in his earliest days as a judge but eventually he overcame them:

His unusual ability as an advocate led many of his friends to doubt whether his temperament would permit him to become a good judge. At first, it seemed difficult for him to restrain the spirit of advocacy and wait with judicial calm until each side had presented its case, but he shortly mastered that difficulty and became a great trial judge, forcing the lawyers to cut through the rubbish and present for decision the exact issue of facts as well as law.

And:

> As a trial judge, he was quick to find the nub of the case and to limit the trial to the exact controversy.... Woe betide the lawyer who went before Judge McDermott with a poorly prepared or with an ill-founded case! A few terse and pointed questions from the bench... and there wasn't much left of the lawsuit. Judge McDermott could discern and put his finger on the weak spots with discomforting skill.[77]

Judge McDermott was unafraid to make his opinions known not only in his courtroom, but also at every level of government and the judiciary. When President Herbert Hoover nominated Justice Chase T. Rogers to the Supreme Court of the United States in 1930, Judge McDermott wrote to the president to tell him that he approved of the nomination.[78] Judge McDermott also told the president his own thoughts on the importance of the federal judiciary:

> I doubt if any of your heavy responsibilities is greater than that of judicial appointments. Our government of constitutional limitations is still in the experimental stage; upon the judiciary rests the ultimate responsibility of holding the government within those limitations which the people themselves have established; if the judgment of the judges is to be deflected by considerations other than the law, the confidence of the people in the judiciary will be gone; and if that goes, I do not know where we will end.[79]

In 1929, when Judge McDermott left the District of Kansas for the Tenth Circuit, his seat on the District Court was filled by Richard Joseph Hopkins.[80]

Richard Joseph Hopkins

J udge Richard Joseph Hopkins was born in 1873[81] in Jefferson City, Missouri, and raised in Garden City, Kansas.[82] His father was a successful lawyer in Garden City. Hopkins attended the University of Kansas for two years and then transferred to Northwestern University, where he received his law degree in 1901. He became a member of the

Judge Richard Joseph Hopkins.

Illinois bar and was in private practice in Chicago until 1906. He then returned to Garden City and entered into partnership with his father. For the next thirteen years he remained in private practice and also was deeply involved in state politics. In 1908 he was elected to the Kansas House of Representatives and in 1909 became Speaker pro tempore of the House. During this period he was instrumental in the passage of the Kansas bank guarantee law. In 1910 he was elected as lieutenant governor and remained in this office through 1912. In his position as lieutenant governor he presided over the tumultuous Senate session of 1911. In 1913 Hopkins became the city attorney for Garden City and stayed in this position until 1918.[83] He was then elected attorney general of the State of Kansas and served

Garden City, Kansas, 1887; childhood hometown of Judge Hopkins.

Session of Haskell County District Court in Santa Fe, Kansas, 1912. Judge Hopkins is pictured fifth from right.

in this capacity from 1919 to 1923. In 1923 he was appointed as an associate justice of the Supreme Court of Kansas and served until 1929, when he was nominated to replace Judge McDermott as a federal district judge for the District of Kansas. He served as federal district judge until his death on August 28, 1943.

During his political career before his appointment first to the Kansas Supreme Court and ultimately to the Federal District Court, Judge Hopkins acquired a reputation as a fierce political advocate. Not only was he a state legislator during tense and difficult times, he was also a crusading attorney general. He was, perhaps, best known for his pursuit and prosecution of those who violated prohibition, but he also, perhaps unwisely, found himself caught in a conflict with the great editor of the *Emporia Gazette,* William Allen White. The dispute took place over the then newly created Court of Industrial Relations.

In the late nineteenth century, American workers began to become radicalized. This was the period of the formation of the International Workers of the World, or the Wobblies, of the Haymarket Riot, and of frequent strikes by labor unions in their battle for better wages and working conditions. Striking workers caused great disruption to many key American industries. Kansas, in particular, was plagued by more than seven hundred strikes to railroad and mining operations in the period from 1914 to 1919.[84] In November of 1919, the United Mine Workers' Union called a national strike in the coal mines.[85] In response, President Woodrow Wilson declared the strike illegal. Throughout the nation — except in Kansas — mine workers returned to the mines to ensure that there

would be adequate coal for the coming winter. In Kansas, however, the miners' leader, Alexander Howat, refused to comply with the presidential order. As a result, Kansas miners stayed away from work and coal mining in the state ceased. In an extraordinary move, Governor Henry J. Allen called for volunteers to go down into the mines to keep the supply of coal coming. More than ten thousand men volunteered, Kansas coal mines were reopened, and the Kansas union quickly settled the strike and returned to work.

Governor Allen was changed by the strike. He realized that another method of resolving labor grievances had to be found. His solution, about which he published a book, was to urge the Kansas Legislature to create a new "Court of

National Guard soldiers who replaced striking coal miners in November and December of 1919.

Miners and children in front of shaft mine 6 of the Crowe Coal Company in northeastern Crawford County, Kansas, 1904.

Industrial Relations" with broad powers to regulate certain key industries and to prevent strikes.[86] The legislature followed his lead and passed the necessary enabling laws.[87] The new three-man court, presided over by Judge William L. Huggins, was soon active.[88]

In 1922 another strike was called in Southeastern Kansas by railroad workers. The union sought to gain support and sympathy for their cause. One tactic they employed was to ask merchants to display yellow placards in their windows stating that the merchants were "100%" behind the striking workers.[89] The union approached William Allen White at the newspaper office and asked White if he would display such a placard.[90] White, in his inimitable way, told them that he could see both sides of the dispute so he would mount a yellow placard stating that he supported the union "50%."[91] And he did so. In the meantime, Governor Allen, under the Court of Industrial Relations legislation, issued an executive order banning posters supporting the strike.[92] He asked his close friend William Allen White to remove the placard from the *Gazette*'s front window. White refused and instead demanded that the

attorney general, Richard Hopkins, arrest him and bring him to trial. Neither Governor Allen nor Attorney General Hopkins relished the idea and both refused to act.[93] Not satisfied by the official response, White produced a scathing editorial which was soon published across America.[94] Both Allen and Hopkins were ridiculed and the Court of Industrial Relations was doomed.

Not everyone supported White. Indeed, rumors circulated in Kansas that White's actions were nothing but a

Above: In August of 1921, coal miners again went on strike in Franklin County, Kansas. Mine owners hired strike breakers or "scabs" and by December the striking miners were running out of money. So, their wives, sisters, mothers, and daughters organized themselves and marched on the mines, blocking the railways to prevent scabs from getting to the mines to work. Dubbed "the Army of Amazons," between two thousand and six thousand women marched on and effectively shut down sixty-three mines over a three-day period beginning December 12, 1921. Left: Atchison, Topeka & Santa Fe Railway shop workers posing immediately after the 1922 railroad strike.

Emporia Gazette owner and editor William Allen White, 1924. White became a leader of the Kansas Progressive movement and unsuccessfully ran for governor in 1924. He won two Pulitzer Prizes, one for a 1922 editorial about free speech inspired by the striking railroad workers, and another awarded posthumously for his autobiography.

publicity stunt.[95] White was sufficiently bothered by these rumors that he wrote a letter of explanation to Hopkins in November 1922.[96] By this time, the political damage White had done to Hopkins was moot, since Hopkins had been appointed to the Kansas Supreme Court (and Governor Allen had not been re-elected). Indeed, seven years later White championed Hopkins's appointment as federal district judge for the District of Kansas.[97]

In 1929 when Judge McDermott was appointed to the Tenth Circuit, Judge Hopkins was the leading choice for the then vacant district judgeship.[98] But Hopkins was seen as an ardent prohibitionist and his past political career was raised in opposition to the appointment.[99] Senators Arthur Capper and Henry Allen from Kansas, as well as many of the leading politicians and judges from Kansas, urged President Herbert Hoover to nominate Hopkins. Although President Hoover dithered for a time, he did eventually forward the nomination to the Senate for confirmation. It was not an easy confirmation, and the Senate split along party lines.[100] An attempt to kill Hopkins's nomination by a recommit vote on December 19, 1929, was defeated 48–25 and Hopkins's confirmation went forward.

During his fourteen years as federal district judge Hopkins heard a wide variety of cases. Some of the most interesting – and difficult – were the criminal cases. One such case was the prosecution of two bank robbers, Robert Suhay and Glenn Applegate, for the murder of an FBI agent, Wimberly Baker, in Topeka.[101] Judge Hopkins presided over the trial, which found the two guilty and sentenced them to be hanged at Leavenworth.

Judge Hopkins clearly stated his philosophy of law in his "Charge to the Grand Jury" convened in Kansas City, Kansas, on June 5, 1939. It is a long and scholarly disquisition both on American history and jurisprudence. Among its most important passages is this statement:

If we have wholesale disrespect for law,
Who shall maintain order in society?

Judge Hopkins was not content simply to write judicial opinions. He also was an author. He collaborated with the Girard, Kansas, publisher Emmanuel Haldeman-Julius, in producing two of Haldeman-Julius' "Little Blue Books." [102] These two volumes not only demonstrate Judge Hopkins's literary abilities and legal and historical thinking, they also show the reverence in which Judge Hopkins held President Abraham Lincoln. Judge Hopkins's essay "Abraham Lincoln" extols Lincoln's virtues as a man, as a lawyer, and as a national leader. [102] It leaves little doubt that Judge Hopkins, who had devoted his career to law, politics, and the judiciary, had thought of Lincoln as a role model for himself and all who aspired to law and political office.

Judge Hopkins died on August 28, 1943, having served his state and nation for more than thirty years.[103]

Guy Tresillian Helvering

Judge Guy T. Helvering was born in Ohio on January 10, 1878.[104] In 1887 his family moved to Beattie, Kansas, where he spent his youth.[105] In May 1898, at the outbreak of the Spanish-American War, Helvering enlisted in the Twenty-Second Regiment of the Kansas Infantry and served until November of that year. Upon his mustering out of the army, Helvering attended the University of Kansas and then transferred to the University of Michigan, from which he received the LLB in 1906. He returned to Kansas and settled in Marysville, joined the bar, and began his career as a lawyer. He was appointed as Marshall County prosecutor in 1907 and served in that position until 1911.[106] In 1910 he ran unsuccessfully as a Democrat for Congress, but his second attempt in 1913 was successful and he served three terms in Congress.[107] Upon his return to private life in 1919, Helvering moved to Salina.[108]

In Salina, Helvering continued to be active politically as well as to become a banker and businessman. He served as mayor of Salina from 1926 until 1930 and was the chairman of the Kansas Democratic Party from 1930 until 1934. He also served as the campaign manager for Harry Woodring's successful gubernatorial campaign in

Judge Guy Tresillian Helvering.

1930.[109] Governor Woodring rewarded Helvering by appointing him as the Kansas highway commissioner.[110] At this time, the Highway Commission was a primary source for gubernatorial patronage appointments and this led to passage of a bill in the Kansas Legislature to convene and investigation of the Highway Commission. Governor Woodring vetoed the bill and the investigation never took place. Upon Governor Woodring's defeat in his attempt at re-election, Woodring went to Washington, D.C., as the assistant secretary of war in the administration of President Franklin D. Roosevelt. President Roosevelt also nominated Helvering to serve as the commissioner of internal revenue.[111]

Judge Helvering's nomination was not without controversy. Congressional Republicans were opposed. Senator James Couzens of Michigan characterized Helvering "as a man of shifty eyes and shifty methods."[112] Senator Arthur Capper of Kansas, however, though a staunch Republican,

supported Helvering's nomination, and Helvering was confirmed as commissioner in June 1933. He served in that capacity until October 1943 thus becoming the longest serving commissioner in the history of the IRS.[113] It was a very difficult period for the IRS because of the need to raise revenue first to implement President Roosevelt's New Deal legislation and then to finance the United States' efforts in World War II.

Badge worn by Treasury Department investigators during Helvering's tenure as IRS commissioner.

As commissioner of internal revenue Helvering gained a reputation both for competence and for toughness. *Time* magazine, in a 1935 article, declared that Helvering had "distinguished himself chiefly by his firm stand against tax compromises."[114] In 1935 Helvering was also instrumental in persuading Congress to repeal one of the most disliked provisions of the Revenue Act of 1934. This provision required all taxpayers to file a "pink slip" with their annual returns. The pink slip contained data from the returns which were then to be made public. Apparently, Helvering's objection to the pink slips was not a concern for taxpayer privacy but rather that the implementation of the pink slips would have cost the IRS $500,000 per year which Helvering believed to be wasteful.

After ten years of service as IRS Commissioner, Helvering asked President Roosevelt to nominate him for the federal district judgeship for the District of Kansas, which had become vacant upon the death of Judge Hopkins.[115] The president agreed to the nomination and Judge Helvering received his

Judge Guy Tresillian Helvering.

commission as federal district judge in October 1943.[116]

As Judge George Templar observed in his classic article on the history of the judges of the Federal District Court in Kansas, Judge Helvering went on the bench at a particularly difficult time in United States history.[117] The New Deal had greatly expanded federal law and was the beginning of the modern administrative state. This, in turn, vastly increased the number of cases coming before the federal courts. The entry of the United States into World War II further increased the volume of cases before the courts because of the large number of wartime regulations which had to be enforced. Although there had been periodic pressure to add a second permanent judgeship to the District of Kansas, these efforts had failed. Thus, Judge Helvering, appointed to his judgeship at the relatively advanced age of sixty-five, found himself faced with an extraordinarily heavy caseload. This took its toll on Judge Helvering, and he died, while on a trip to Washington, D.C., on July 4, 1946.[118]

Notes to Chapter 3

1. George Templar et al., *Kansas: The Territorial and District Courts, in* FEDERAL COURTS OF THE TENTH CIRCUIT: A HISTORY 15, 27 (James K. Logan ed., 1992) [hereinafter *Kansas: Territorial and District Courts*].

2. *History of the Federal Judiciary: Hook, William Cather,* FED. JUD. CTR., http://www.fjc.gov/servlet/nGetInfo?jid=1089 (last visited Feb. 3, 2011) [hereinafter *FJC: Hook*]; *History of the Federal Judiciary: McDermott, George Thomas,* FED. JUD. CTR., http://www.fjc.gov/servlet/nGetInfo?jid=1541 (last visited Feb. 3, 2011) [hereinafter *FJC: McDermott*].

3. *See History of the Federal Judiciary: Helvering, Guy Tresillian,* FED. JUD. CTR., http://www.fjc.gov/servlet/nGetInfo?jid=1019 (last visited Feb. 3, 2011) [hereinafter *FJC: Helvering*].

4. *See History of the Federal Judiciary: Pollock, John Calvin,* FED. JUD. CTR., http://www.fjc.gov/servlet/nGetInfo?jid=1906 (last visited Feb. 3, 2011) [hereinafter *FJC: Pollock*].

5. *See History of the Federal Judiciary: Hopkins, Richard Joseph,* FED. JUD. CTR., http://www.fjc.gov/servlet/nGetInfo?jid=1092 (last visited Feb. 3, 2011) [hereinafter *FJC: Hopkins*].

6. *See FJC: Hook;* George Templar, *The Federal Judiciary of Kansas,* 37 KAN. HIST. Q. 1, 5–6 (Spring 1971) [hereinafter *The Federal Judiciary*].

7. *The Federal Judiciary.*

8. Thomas Amory Lee, *William C. Hook: Judge of the Eighth Circuit Court of Appeals of the United States,* 3:1 KAN. HIST. Q. 68, 70 (1934).

9. *FJC: Hook.*

10. 98 F. 335 (D. Kan. 1899).

11. *Id.* at 337–38. *See* H.B. No. 1, 1898, SPEC. SESS., 1898 KAN. SPEC. SESS. LAWS 76; H.B. No. 66, 1898 SEC. SESS., 1898 SPEC. SESS. LAWS 91; SUBSTITUTE FOR S.B. NO. 8, 1898, SPEC. SESS., 1898 SPEC. SESS. LAWS 117.

12. *Western Union,* 98 F. at 359.

13. *See e.g., id.* at 340–41.

14. *See* H.B. No. 1, 1898, SPEC. SESS., 1898 KAN. SPEC. SESS. LAWS 76; H.B. No. 66, 1898 SEC. SESS., 1898 SPEC. SESS. LAWS 91; SUBSTITUTE FOR S.B. NO. 8, 1898, SPEC. SESS., 1898 SPEC. SESS. LAWS 117. *See also Western Union,* 98 F. at 359.

15. *Western Union,* 98 F. at 337–40.

16. *Id.* at 340.

17. *Western Union,* 98 F. at 340.

18. *Id.* at 359–60.

19. *Id.* at 346–47.

20. *Id.* at 348.

21. *Id.* at 348–50.

22. *Id.* at 350–53.

23. *Id.* at 354–55.

24. Lee, *supra* note 8, at 72–73.

25. *Id. See also FJC: Hook.*

26. *See US v. Standard Oil Co. of New Jersey,* 173 F. 177 (C.C. Mo. 1909) (concurring opinion) and *US v. Union Pac. R. Co.,* 188 F. 102 (C.C. Utah 1911) (dissenting opinion); *US v. International Harvester Co.,* 214 F. 987 (1914).

27. *See* John H. Atwood, *William Cather Hook,* 7 A.B.A. J. 552, 553 (1921); Lee, *supra* note 8, at 73.

28. *See id.* at 76–80.

29. *Id.* at 76.

30. Letter from Booker T. Washington to Blanche Kelso Bruce (Feb. 17, 1912) *in* 11 THE BOOKER T. WASHINGTON PAPERS, 1911–1912, at 466 (Louis R. Harlan & Raymond W. Smock eds., Univ. of Illinois Press 1981), *available at* www.historycooperative.org/btw/V01.11/html/466.html.

31. *FJC: Hook.*

32. *FJC: Pollock.*

33. PERL W.MORGAN, ed., HISTORY OF WYANDOTTE COUNTY KANSAS AND ITS PEOPLE 517 (Chicago: The Lewis Publishing Co., 1911).

34. *FJC: Pollock.*

35. MORGAN, *supra* note 33, at 518–19.

36. *See* THE BENCH AND BAR, A TRIBUTE TO JUDGE JOHN CALVIN POLLOCK (Kansas City, Mo..: Brown-White Printing, 1931).

37. MORGAN, *supra* note 33, at 518–19.

38. *See id.* at 519.

39. *Judge Plays No Poker,* N.Y. TIMES, Nov. 26, 1903, at 1. *See also Kansas: Territorial and District Courts* at 25.

40. *Judge Plays No Poker.*

41. *FJC: Pollock.*

42. *Clerk Stole Money For Sick Brother,* KAN. CITY J., Apr. 29, 1908.

43. *See generally,* Clayton R. Koppes, *The Kansas Trial of the IWW, 1917–1919,* 16 LAB. HIST. 338 (2001).

44. *See id.* at 339.

45. *Id.* at 339–40.

46. *Id.* at 341.

47. *See id.* at 342.

48. *Id.* at 342.

49. *See id.* at 342–43.

50. *Id.* at 343.

51. *Id.* at 347.

52. *Id.* at 353.

53. *See id.* at 353.

54. *Id.* at 354.

55. Richard J. Hopkins, U.S. Dist. Judge, The Stroud Case, Address Before the Fortnightly Club (April 15, 1941), *in* 9 J. B. ASS'N ST. KAN. 373, 374 (May 1941).

56. *Id.* at 374.

57. *Id.* at 374.

58. *Id.* at 375–76.

59. *See* THE BENCH AND BAR, *supra* note 36.

60. *See id.* at 11, 79–86.

61. *Id.* at 30.

62. After Judge Pollock's death his seat on the court was not filled.

63. *See* 40 Stat. 1156.

64. *FJC: McDermott.*

65. *In Memoriam,* 88 F. 2d xiii, xxi.

66. *FJC: McDermott.*

67. *In Memoriam,* at xiv.

68. *Id.* at xxi.

69. *Id.* at xiv.

70. *FJC: McDermott.*

71. *In Memoriam,* at xxii–xxiii.

72. *Id.* at xvi.

73. *FJC: McDermott.*

74. *In Memoriam* at xix.

75. *Id.* at xx.

76. *Id.* at xxi.

77. *Id.* at xxi–xxii.

78. Letter from Circuit Judge George T. McDermott to President Herbert Hoover, Presidential Timeline of the Twentieth Century (May 2, 1930), www.presidentialtimeline. org/html/record.php?id=1361.

79. *Id.*

80. *See FJC: Hopkins.*

81. *Id.*

82. William E. Connelley, A Standard History of Kansas and Kansans 2330–32 (Chicago: Lewis Publishing Co., 1919).

83. *FJC: Hopkins.*

84. Richard J. Hopkins, Duties of Peace Officers: Kansas vs. Howat and Other Legal Matters 12 (1873).

85. *Coal Strike and the Court of Industrial Relations,* Kan. Hist. Soc., http://www.kshs.org/portraits/coal strike.htm (last visited Feb. 12, 2011).

86. *See* Henry J. Allen, The Party of the Third Part 283 (Harper, NY 1921). *See also* William A. White, The Autobiography of William Allen White 611 (1946).

87. *See* S.B. 1, 1920, Spec. Sess. (Kan. 1920).

88. *Coal Strike and the Court of Industrial Relations, supra* note 84; Herbert Feis, *The Kansas Court of Industrial Relations, Its Spokesmen, Its Record,* 37 Q. J. Econ. 705, 706 (Aug. 1923).

89. *See* White, *supra* note 86 at 612.

90. *See id.* at 611.

91. *Id.* at 612, 614; *Allen Peace Offer Spurned by White,* N.Y. Times, July 22, 1922.

92. *See id.* at 612.

93. *See William Allen White Case Dropped,* N.Y. Times, Dec. 8, 1922.

94. *See* White, *supra* note 86 at 613–14. (White's editorial "To an Anxious Friend" won a Pulitzer Prize for best editorial of the year.)

95. White, *supra* note 86 at 614.

96. *See* Letter from William Allen White to Richard J. Hopkins, Attorney General (Nov. 7, 1922), *in* Selected Letters of William Allen White 1899–1943, at 228–29 (Walter Johnson, ed., 1947).

97. *The Federal Judiciary* at 28.

98. *See id.* at 28.

99. *Id.* at 28–29.

100. *Senate Vote #120: To Recommit to the Committee on the Judiciary the Nomination of Richard J. Hopkins District Judge for the District of Kansas,* GovTrack (Dec 19, 1929), http://www. govtrack.us/congress/vote.xpd?vote=s71 2-120.

101. *See Suhay v. US,* 95 F.2d 890 (10th Cir. 1938) (affirming D. Crt. decision). *See also, To Die Aug. 12, Killers Happy It's Not 13th,* Dallas Morning News, Jun. 11, 1938, § 1 at 1, *available at* http://genealogytrails.com/kan/legalhangings1.html.

102. *See* Richard J. Hopkins, Abraham Lincoln–Lawyer, (E. Haldeman-Julius ed).

103. *FJC: Hopkins.*

104. *FJC: Helvering.*

105. *Helvering, Guy Tresillian, (1878–1946),* Biographical Directory U.S. Cong., http://bioguide.congress.gov/scripts/ biodisplay.pl?index=H000466 (last visited Feb. 12, 2011) [hereinafter *BDC: Helvering*].

106. *FJC: Helvering.*

107. *BDC: Helvering.*

108. *See FJC: Helvering.*

109. *Kansas: Territorial and District Courts* at 29.

110. *Records of the Kansas Governor's Office: Harry H. Woodring Administration Jan. 12, 1931–Jan. 9, 1933,* Kan. St. Hist. Soc., http://www.kshs.org/research/collections/documents/ govtrecords/governors/woodring.htm (last visited Feb 12, 2011).

111. *BDC: Helvering.*

112. *The Congress: Work Done, Jun. 12, 1933,* Time (Jun. 12, 1933), *available at* http://www.time.com/time/magazine/ article/0,9171,745666,00.html.

113. *Longest- and Shortest-Serving Commissioners of Internal Revenue,* IRS.gov, http://www.irs.gov/irs/ article/0,,id=111763,00.html (last visited Feb. 12, 2011).

114. *Taxation: Pink Slips,* Time, Mar. 25 1935, *available at* http://www.time.com/time/magazine/article/0,9171,748586,00. html.

115. *See Kansas: Territorial and District Courts* at 29.

116. *FJC: Helvering.*

117. *Kansas: Territorial and District Courts* at 29.

118. *FJC: Helvering.*

Judges Arthur J. Mellott, Delmas C. Hill, and Walter A. Huxman, 1951.

4

THE CHANCE OF A LIFETIME:
JUDGES ARTHUR J. MELLOTT AND DELMAS C. HILL

The preceding few chapters should have made it clear that the Federal District of Kansas has been anything but a judicial backwater since its founding. Kansas federal judges have been notable jurists–albeit sometimes eccentric–and a number of the cases which came before them were of national significance. One trend, which became obvious as the Second World War came to a victorious conclusion, was that the caseload of the court was increasing substantially and that it was too much to expect a single judge to handle. Indeed, by the time of the appointments of Judges Delmas Hill and Arthur Mellott, the annual caseload was close to seven hundred, a burden impossible for a single judge to manage no matter how industrious. Even more to the point, just a few years after the end of the war, the revolution in American civil rights law was beginning, and Kansas and the Federal District Court of Kansas were to be at the heart of this revolution. Thus, the appointments of two singularly well-qualified lawyers to the Federal District Court had enormous importance not only for the court in Kansas but for American jurisprudence and American society as a whole.

Judge Arthur Johnson Mellott

Arthur Johnson Mellott was born on August 30, 1888, in Wallula, Kansas.[1] From 1907 until 1914 Judge Mellott worked as a schoolteacher, and from 1914 until 1917 he was superintendent of schools in Wyandotte County, Kansas.[2] While still teaching, he entered law school as a student in the evening program and graduated in 1917 with an LLB from the Kansas City Law School (now succeeded by the University of Missouri-Kansas City School of Law).[3] Upon graduation he was appointed as an assistant United States attorney for the District of Kansas and served in this role through 1918. He

Judge Arthur Johnson Mellott.

then entered private practice in Kansas City and remained in this practice for several years. During this time, Mellott also served as a professor at the Kansas City Law School, his alma mater. While he surely did not realize it at the time, his years in teaching would prove to be of great significance to his future career because one of his students at the law school was the young Harry S. Truman, later to be president of the United States.

In 1923 Arthur J. Mellott began his long career in public service when he was appointed as a judge of the City Court of Kansas City. In 1925 he resigned his judgeship and successfully ran for county attorney. During these years he also was active in Democratic Party politics, serving as chairman of the Kansas Democratic Club and as chairman of the Democratic Central Committee.[4] In 1934 Judge Mellott was appointed as the deputy commissioner of the Internal Revenue Service in charge of enforcement of the new liquor tax which had been created in the wake of the ending of prohibition.[5] His appointment to this position created a fair amount of amusement in the national press, since Judge Mellott was a "self-described teetotaler" but also because Kansas remained a "dry" state even after federal prohibition laws had been repealed.[6] But his choice was actually reasonable; he was not only from a "dry" state, but he had also gained a reputation as a forceful prosecutor as county attorney in Wyandotte County.[7] This was just the kind of experience needed for the man to direct federal liquor tax

Judge Arthur Johnson Mellott.

laws against the thousands of bootleggers and moonshiners then found nationwide. During his short period as deputy commissioner, Judge Mellott supervised more than three thousand Treasury agents,[8] almost as many as had worked for the agency at the height of prohibition. Their efforts met with success. During the first year of the liquor tax after the repeal of prohibition, the federal government received almost $400 million in new revenue from the tax.[9] By September 1935 the *New York Times* was able to run an article headlined "Bootleggers Knell Seen as Taxes Rise."[10] In August 1935 Judge Mellott, having successfully waged war on bootlegging, was appointed by President Roosevelt as a judge of the United States Board of Tax Appeals, a position in which he remained until 1945.[11]

During Judge Mellott's decade on the tax court he heard a number of important cases. Although tax cases rarely gain much publicity, they are greatly important to the maintenance of the national budget. When Judge Mellott first took his seat on the Board of Tax Appeals, the federal income tax was barely two decades old; at the time, resistance to the tax, as well as outright tax evasion, was still a serious problem. Among the hundreds of tax cases heard by Judge Mellott, one group in particular gained national prominence. In 1937

the U.S. Board of Tax Appeals had come before it a series of prosecutions brought by the IRS and the Treasury against 170 Hollywood celebrities for failure to pay proper taxes.[12] Among the celebrities were some of Hollywood's most famous actors and actresses, including Charlie Chaplin,[13] William Powell,[14] Zasu Pitts,[15] Charles Laughton, and Claudette Colbert. This was the period in which millions of Americans followed every action of their favorite Hollywood stars, and the appearance of so many of these stars in tax court caused a journalistic frenzy. Judge Mellott had the dubious pleasure of presiding over most of these cases.

In 1945 President Truman appointed his old law school professor to a newly created seat on the Federal District Court of Kansas. Judge Mellott's nomination was noncontroversial; he was nominated on November 13, confirmed on November 27, and took his seat on the District Court on November 29.[16] From 1948 until his death in 1957 Judge Mellott served as the chief judge of the district. For the first few years of his judgeship, Judge Mellott heard virtually all of the seven hundred cases which came before the court each year.

Judge Mellott heard a wide variety of cases during his time on the bench. Of course, the most significant was *Brown v. Board*, but not all were of such intrinsic importance. The life of a postwar federal judge in Kansas was that of a generalist on the bench. Among his most notable cases, several, other than *Brown*, merit mention here.

In 1947 Judge Mellott found himself adjudicating a major reorganization of the Aireon Manufacturing Corporation, a manufacturer of radio parts, under the Chandler Act.[17] The corporation's management had performed badly and, as a result, the corporation was put into trusteeship. In order to save the company, Judge Mellott authorized the issuance of a series of bonds and approved the trustees' reorganization plan, thereby saving the company.[18]

Of more national interest, a series of antitrust cases involving major supermarket chains, Safeway Corporation and Kroger Corporation, also found their way into Judge Mellott's court. After a complex and long litigation Safeway was fined $40,000.[19] In the case of Kroger Corp., Judge Mellott imposed a fine of $20,000.[20] These cases were typical of the corporate cases which came before the Federal District Court during Judge Mellott's tenure.

A very different kind of case came before Judge Mellott in 1949. Rex Ingram was one of the most prominent black film actors of the first

Rex Ingram.

half of the twentieth century. He was a remarkable man. He was the first African American to graduate from the medical school at Northwestern University. Rather than practice medicine, however, Ingram went to Hollywood where he was "discovered" and given a small role in the 1918 film, *Tarzan of the Apes*. His big break came in 1936 when he was given a major role in the film *Green Pastures*. He followed this with a series of starring roles in such films as *The Thief of Baghdad*. In the 1930s and early 1940s he also starred in several major Broadway shows. But in 1949 he was arrested and tried for violation of the Mann Act.[21] He was accused and found guilty of transporting a fifteen-year-old girl from Salina, Kansas, across state borders "for immoral purposes."[22] Of course, the prosecution of a prominent African American celebrity under the Mann Act brings to mind the earlier prosecution of the boxer Jack Johnson—symbolic of the use of the Mann Act and other federal statutes to persecute prominent African Americans. It would be wrong, however, to assume that Judge Mellott's decision in the Ingram case was an indicator of the judge's views on race and civil rights. Indeed, a far better indicator of his views, which would become so important during *Brown v. Board*, was Judge Mellott's appointment of Charles Allen Green, a Kansas City musician, as "court crier" in September 1948. Mr. Green was the first African American to be appointed to this post.[23]

Judge Mellott continued to serve as a federal district judge for the District of Kansas until his death on December 29, 1957,[24] and, of course, his greatest case, *Brown v. Board*, was to occur just a few years before.

Judge Delmas Carl Hill

Judge Delmas Carl Hill was born on October 9, 1906, in Wamego, Kansas.[25] His father was a doctor and a loyal Democrat and named his son after a lawyer whom he heard give a stirring speech at the 1904 Democratic National Convention.[26] Delmas Hill was educated in Wamego[27] and then attended Washburn University and Washburn Law School, from which he received the LLB in 1929.[28] After graduation from law school Hill returned to Wamego, where he went into private practice and became active in politics.[29] He was elected city attorney for Wamego in 1929 and served in that capacity until 1934.[30] He was also elected as county attorney for Pottawatomie County in 1931 and served until 1934. In 1934 he was appointed as United States attorney for the District of Kansas and remained in that post for two years.[31] In 1936 Governor Walter Huxman appointed him as general counsel for the State Tax Commission. Upon Governor Huxman's defeat in his attempt at re-election, Hill returned to Wamego and private practice. In 1943 he enlisted in the U.S. Army as a private. He was sent to the Judge Advocate Training Center

Wamego, Kansas, c. 1895. Hometown of Judge Delmas Hill.

and, upon completion of this course, was commissioned as a first lieutenant. Eventually, he was promoted to captain and was awarded a Bronze Star.[32] When the war ended he remained in the army and served as an assistant prosecutor in the war crimes trial of Japanese General Tomoyuki Yamashita,

Delmas "Buzz" Hill, age five.

the infamous officer who ordered the Bataan Death March. In 1946 Hill returned to civilian life and the practice of law in Wamego.[33] He also became chairman of the Kansas Democratic Party in 1946[34] and was a delegate to the Democratic National Convention for Harry Truman in 1948. After the election, in October 1949, President Truman nominated Hill to a newly created seat on the Federal District Court of Kansas.[35] He received his commission in March 1950 and was immediately caught up in the large caseload he now shared with Judge Mellott.

Although he will be best remembered as a federal district judge for his role in *Brown v. Board of Education*, Judge Hill played a major role in one of the most important empirical studies of jury behavior, a role which brought him national attention as well as criticism by the attorney general of the United States, Herbert Brownell, and an investigation by the United States Senate Subcommittee on Internal Security.[36]

In 1952 Dean Edward Levi of the University of Chicago School of Law applied for and received a $400,000 grant from the Ford Foundation to fund a scholarly study of the American

Delmas "Buzz" Hill,
age thirty.

jury system. The study was directed by a young professor at the law school, Harry Kalven Jr. In 1953 Paul Kitch, a graduate of the law school practicing in Wichita, Kansas, contacted the project and suggested that the project secretly record jury deliberations in the Federal District Court in Kansas.[37] The law professors, intrigued by this idea, contacted the chief judge of the Tenth Circuit, Orie Phillips, and District Judge Hill.[38] With their permission, jury discussions in five civil cases heard before Judge Hill in the District Court were secretly audiotaped in 1954. An interesting aspect of this taping was that the researcher sent by the project to be in charge of the taping was Abner Mikva,[39] who later went on to a distinguished career in Congress and on the federal bench.

In 1955 Judge Hill made a presentation about the project and played some of the tapes at the Tenth Circuit's Judicial Conference.[40] Somehow, news of Judge Hill's presentation and of the secret jury taping was leaked to the press. Several months later the *Los Angeles Times* ran a story detailing what

Judge Delmas Carl Hill.

Judge Delmas Hill (center) and his chambers staff: Ned King, Art Johnson, Jack Crawley, and Bill Cahill, in 1949.

had happened. The story became national news and aroused a firestorm of indignation and protest.[41] Herbert Brownell, President Eisenhower's attorney general, condemned all who had been involved in the taping, including Judge Hill.[42] The U.S. Senate Subcommittee on Internal Security (a subcommittee made infamous for its McCarthyite "red-baiting"), chaired by Senators James O. Eastland and William E. Jennings, instituted hearings about the taping, and rumors spread that the judges involved would be impeached, though this never occurred.[43] Eventually, in August 1956, Congress passed legislation making it illegal to tape jury deliberations in federal court.[44]

Although Judge Hill's role in the University of Chicago study was widely criticized at the time, the years have shown the wisdom of his decision to allow jury deliberations to be recorded for study. The research based on the taping was eventually published in 1966 by Professor Kalven and his colleague Professor Hans Zeisel under the title: *The American Jury.*[45] That study is now recognized as one of the most important studies on the civil justice process ever conducted. It was the genesis of the now widely admired field of empirical legal studies and has been the basis for important reforms in jury instructions. Judge Hill played a crucial role in making

Probation/Pretrial Services

The federal probation system was created in 1925, when President Calvin Coolidge signed the Federal Probation Act. The first federal probation officer was hired in 1927. In 1974 the courts added a Pretrial Services component. Currently more than five thousand federal probation and pretrial services officers provide pretrial bond supervision, presentence investigation reports, and community supervision of offenders in the ninety-four districts in all fifty states and the territories. Community supervision services include Probation (1925), Parole (1932), Military Parole (1946), Juvenile (1947), Pretrial (1974), and Supervised Release (1987).

The first federal probation officer in Kansas was appointed in 1931, followed by the first probation clerk in 1932. Currently, the total staff of seventy-two consists of officers, support staff, and consolidated administrative services personnel in three divisional offices – Kansas City (headquarters), Topeka, and Wichita. The district includes all 105 counties in Kansas, with a total area of 82,277 square miles and 2,853,116 residents (2010 Census). All officer positions are classified as hazardous-duty law enforcement. The maximum age for service entry is thirty-seven and the mandatory age for retirement is fifty-seven. Officers are appointed by the chief judge in each district and are sworn in with both the U.S. Courts and the Department of Justice.

Above: District of Kansas United States Probation Officers Phillip L. Messer (deputy chief), Ronald G. Schweer (chief), and Trey W. Burton (assistant deputy chief), 2009. Below: District of Kansas United States Probation Officers Trey Burton, Cassidi Lundell, and Brooke Paulson conducting range practice, 2010.

the study possible.

In 1957, upon the death of Judge Mellott, Judge Hill was appointed chief judge for the Federal District of Kansas and remained as chief judge until he was appointed a judge of the Tenth Circuit Court of Appeals by President John F. Kennedy in 1961.[46] He assumed senior status in 1977 and died on December 2, 1989.

Although any comprehensive analysis of Judge Hill's work on the Tenth Circuit is beyond the scope of this book, a brief mention of two of his most important decisions as a circuit judge must be included. In December 1969 the Tenth Circuit, in an opinion written by Judge Hill, upheld a decision of Federal District Judge Alfred A. Arraj in a case involving a plan by the U.S. government to conduct an underground nuclear test of a forty kiloton bomb at Battlement Mesa, Colorado, just fifty-five miles from the resort city of Aspen.[47] The test was not military; rather, it was part of what was known as Project Plowshares, a program designed to find peaceful uses of atomic energy.[48] Project Rulison itself was designed to test whether an underground nuclear blast could be used to increase productivity of natural gas reserves.

The opposition to Project Rulison made headlines across the U.S. and stories appeared in the *Chicago Tribune* and the *New York Times*.[49] But Judge Hill remained adamant about his decision to let the test go forward, ruling that governmental safety measures were more than adequate and that the possibility of a damaging accident was remote.[50] In the end, the test went forward without any problems. Judge Hill had been right.

The other of Judge Hill's decisions while sitting on the Tenth Circuit which merits mention here was his decision in *Herald v. Seawell* dated December 29, 1972.[51] The case arose from a vote by the stockholders of the *Denver Post* to establish an employee stock ownership plan (ESOP) as a retirement benefit for *Post* employees. The Herald Company, controlled by the Newhouse media empire, owned 18 percent of the *Post*'s stock and was opposed to creation of the ESOP. Having lost the stockholder vote, Herald sued to block the ESOP in federal court. Herald's suit contested that the transfer of stock to the ESOP at a below-market price as voted by the stockholders violated the corporation's duty to act solely as a profit-maximizing entity.

When the case came before Judge Hill in the Tenth Circuit, he surprised many observers by taking the employees' side. He said:

> Basic in that [corporate] rule of law is the profit motive of the corporate entity. In this case, we have a corporation engaged chiefly in the publication of a large metropolitan newspaper, whose obligation and duty is something more than the making of corporate profits. Its obligation is three-fold: to the stockholders, to the employees and to the public.[52]

Hobart Rowan, writing in the *Washington Post*, was excited by Judge Hill's decision, for he saw great potential in it. Rowan believed that this was a decision which would allow suits against large corporations so that "they may spend corporate money to combat pollution, assure safety, or underwrite other worthy causes."[53] Rowan concluded his opinion piece with the following:

> The *Herald*... decision, coming as it does from a circuit court considered rather conservative, is thus an exciting and encouraging landmark.

In his years on both the District and Circuit Courts, Judge Hill was at the center of several landmark cases, an opportunity which comes to few judges. He handled his opportunities with skill, knowledge, and sensitivity. On December 2, 1989, Judge Hill died at the age of eighty-three after living a remarkable life.[54]

Judge Hill with his nephew (now Judge) Thomas Marten and Wichita lawyer Ellis Bever on a fishing trip to the Ozarks, Missouri, in 1960.

Notes to Chapter 4

1. *History of the Federal Judiciary: Mellott, Arthur Johnson,* FED. JUD. CTR., http://www.fjc.gov/servlet/nGetInfo?jid=1615 (last visited Feb. 13, 2011) [hereinafter *FJC: Mellott*].

2. WILLIAM R. DENSLOW, 10,000 FAMOUS FREEMASONS FROM K TO Z, 192 (Richmond, Va.: Macoy Publishing & Masonic Supply Co., 1957).

3. *In Memoriam,* 26 U. Kan. City L. Rev 3, 4 (1957).

4. *Arthur Mellott of U.S. Court Dies,* N.Y. TIMES, Dec. 30, 1957, at 21.

5. *In Memoriam, supra* note 3.

6. *New Liquor War Opens,* N.Y. TIMES, May 2, 1934, at 2.

7. *In Memoriam, supra* note 3.

8. *U.S. Drive Aims to End Bootlegging,* WASH. POST, May 7, 1934, at 1.

9. *13 Dry States To Get Special U.S. Protection,* WASH. POST, Dec. 8, 1934, at 7.

10. *Bootleggers' Knell Seen as Taxes Rise,* N.Y. TIMES, Sept. 14, 1935, at 32.

11. *In Memoriam, supra* note 3.

12. *Tax Hearings Hit Celebrities,* L.A. TIMES, Sept. 28, 1937, at 10.

13. *Film Players to Contest Tax,* L.A. TIMES, Feb. 14, 1941, at 1A.

14. *William Powell Goes to Court in Tax Battle,* L.A. TIMES, Oct. 16, 1945, at 12.

15. *Tax Hearings Hit Celebrities, supra* note 12.

16. *See FJC: Mellott.*

17. *Aireon Trustee Tells Progress,* L.A. TIMES, Jan. 23, 1948, at A12.

18. *Aireon Gets Right to Issue Indebtedness Certificates,* WALL ST. J., Dec. 2, 1947, at 15.

19. *Safeway Suit Ends With $40,000 Fines,* N.Y. TIMES, Mar. 27, 1948, at 21.

20. *Anti-Trust Fine Levied Against Kroger Company,* CHI. DAILY TRIB., May 4, 1948, at A7.

21. *Operation Delays Trial of Ingram,* AFRO-AM, Apr. 16, 1949, at 1.

22. *Actor Sentenced,* PHILA. TRIB., Oct. 4, 1949, at 2.

23. *Texan Named Court Crier,* NEW J. & GUIDE, Sept. 4, 1948, at D2.

24. *History of the Federal Judiciary: Hill, Delmas Carl,* FED. JUD. CTR., http://www.fjc.gov/servlet/nGetInfo?jid=1043 (last visited Feb. 12, 2011) [hereinafter *FJC: Hill*].

25. *FJC: Hill.*

26. Judge Logan, *Presentation of Portrait of the Honorable Delmas C. Hill at the Judicial Conference Tenth Judicial Circuit of the United States* (Sept. 7, 1989), *available at* http://www.10thcircuithistory.org/pdfs/updated_history/portriats/hill_cir_portrait.pdf.

27. *See id. at XCIII.*

28. *Lifetime Achievement Award for 2007 Delmas Hill '29,* WASHBURN UNIVERSITY SCHOOL OF LAW, http://washburnlaw.edu/alumni/association/lifetime/2007/hill-delmas.php (last visited Feb 12, 2011) [hereinafter *Lifetime Achievement Award: Hill*].

29. Logan, *supra* note 26.

30. *FJC: Hill.*

31. *Lifetime Achievement Award: Hill.*

32. Logan, *supra* note 26.

33. *FJC: Hill.*

34. Logan, *supra* note 26.

35. *FJC: Hill.*

36. *Brownell Raps 'Wire Tapping' of Jury Rooms,* CHI. DAILY TRIB., Oct. 6, 1955, at 14.

37. Valerie P. Hans and Neil Vidmar, *The American Jury at Twenty-Five Years,* 16 LAW & SOC. INQUIRY 323, 325 (1991) (book review).

38. *See Brownell Raps 'Wire Tapping' of Jury Rooms, supra* note 36.

39. *Bugging a Jury Needs Congressional Act,* L.A. TIMES, Oct. 6, 1955, at A4, 20.

40. Hans and Vidmar, *supra* note 37, at 325.

41. *Id.* at 325–26.

42. Murrey Marder, *Probers Hint Impeachment of Judges Who Aided Jury Debate Recordings,* WASH. POST & TIMES HERALD, Oct. 14, 1955, at 1.

43. *Jurors Differ on Deliberations 'Tap,'* WASH. POST & TIMES HERALD, Oct. 21, 1955, at 27.

44. *See* 18 U.S.C. § 1508 (1964).

45. Harry Kalven Jr. and Hans Zeisel, *The American Jury,* 1966.

46. *See FJC: Hill.*

47. *Court Denies Move to Halt Nuclear Test,* CHI. TRIB., Sept. 3, 1969, at A7.

48. Anthony Ripley, *Aspen Awaiting Nearby A-Blast,* N.Y. TIMES, Sept. 2, 1969, at 9.

49. *See, e.g., Court Denies Move to Halt Nuclear Test, supra* note 47; Ripley, *supra* note 48.

50. Ripley, *supra* note 48.

51. Hobart Rowan, *Court Case Says Corporate Duties Go Beyond Profit,* WASH. POST & TIMES HERALD, Apr. 8, 1973, at p. G1.

52. *Herald Co. v. Seawell,* 472 F.2d 1081, 1091 (10th Cir. 1972).

53. Rowan, supra note 51.

54. *See FJC: Hill.*

5

BROWN V. BOARD: THE CASE BEGINS

On the twenty-eighth of February 1951, Oliver Brown, whose daughter Linda had been forced to attend a segregated school in Topeka, filed suit in the United States District Court of Kansas. This was the formal beginning of a lawsuit which was to change the social and legal landscape of the United States.

The filing of the suit, which became known as *Brown v. Board of Education of Topeka*, et al., was not, of course, the true beginning of the case. For the beginning of the case, at least in Kansas, one must go back to its early territorial days and the battles, both real and figurative, between the proslavery and Free-State forces. While there were some Kansans who favored equal rights for blacks, this was not the primary social or political ideology of those who opposed the extension of slavery to Kansas. Indeed, the members of the convention that drafted the Wyandotte Constitution rejected granting full equal rights to blacks.[1]

After Kansas became a state, the first constitution of 1861 provided for a "local option" so far as segregated schools were concerned.[2] Of course, the black population of Kansas in its first decades was quite small and so the question of segregation would not have been a practical issue for many Kansas school boards. In 1867, however, the Kansas legislature passed legislation that continued to permit the maintenance of segregated schools by local governments but mandated that, in such cases, there be separate schools for both blacks and whites. In effect, this meant that segregated public schools could exist only in those localities willing to fund two sets of schools.

In the first half of the 1870s there were legislative attempts to mandate both segregation and integration in public schools, but these failed. Of greater significance was legislation in 1879 that permitted segregation in public elementary schools in "cities of the first class," which were then defined as cities with a population greater than fifteen thousand.[3] The reason for this legislation, some scholars argue, was the great increase in the number of black Kansans who came to Kansas as immigrants from the newly unreconstructed South: the Exodusters. In Topeka, for example, the black population doubled between 1875 and 1880.[4] This increase in black population seems to have made some members of the white majority nervous enough to support limited segregation at the elementary-school level.

Although the law of 1879 permitted elementary-school segregation, such segregation was not implemented in every first-class city in Kansas. In Topeka, however, it was. Although several challenges were made to the segregated schools of Topeka over the next several decades, the system continued and spread as Topeka extended its municipal borders.[5]

The school segregation permitted in Kansas' 1879 law gained important legal backing when the Supreme Court of the United States decided the landmark case of *Plessy v. Ferguson*[6] in 1896. The infamous *Plessy* majority decision gave legal recognition to mandatory legal segregation in the United States and gave rise to what became known as "Jim Crow" laws. Under the reign of Plessy, American blacks could be

Facing page: Linda Brown, age nine, stands in front of Monroe Elementary School in Topeka, Kansas, 1953. Above right: An 1878 pamphlet distributed in Nashville, Tennessee, by Exoduster leader Benjamin Singleton to encourage African Americans to move to Kansas. Singleton believed that former slaves would be able to lead happier lives in northern states like Kansas and organized transportation to help them escape discriminatory laws which were being enacted in the South.

Upper right: Monroe Elementary School opened its doors in 1927 as one of four segregated schools for African Americans in Topeka, Kansas. After the school was closed in 1975, ownership passed through various hands before the Trust for Public Land purchased it in 1991. In 1992, it was designated a National Historic Site and now houses the Brown v. Board of Education National Historic Site, which is operated by the National Park Service. Above: Second grade class of Monroe Elementary with their teacher, Edna Vance, March 3, 1949. Below: First-grade class of State Street Elementary School with their teacher, Miss Hunt, shortly after Topeka elementary schools integrated in the wake of Brown v. Board, January 1955.

prohibited from using public facilities such as trains, buses, swimming pools, and, of course, schools, so long as they were provided with "separate but equal" (albeit segregated) facilities of their own. Of course, in many, if not most, American states, "separate but equal" rarely was taken seriously and blacks were assigned to inferior schools, parks, and transportation.

In 1903, William Reynolds, a black man, sued the Topeka school board when his son was denied admission to a segregated white school.[7] The Supreme Court of Kansas, relying on the decision in *Plessy* and citing the Kansas Act of 1879, several Kansas cases that followed, and cases from other states, found that the school board was within its legal rights to operate "separate but equal" elementary schools.[8]

In 1941 the Topeka board was again sued for denying school entrance to another black student in *Graham v. Board of Education*.[9] In this case, however, the question at issue was whether the 1879 act empowered a school board to operate segregated junior high schools.[10] The Kansas Supreme Court ruled that it did not and that Kansas cities of the first class could only rightfully operate segregated elementary schools.

Perhaps the most interesting fact about school segregation in Topeka was that the schools provided for black Topekans were, in fact, often equal to or even better than white schools as far as the quality of the teachers and curriculum. The black population of Topeka was education-minded and proud of the fact that Topeka's segregated schools for blacks were staffed by highly qualified black teachers who implemented a rigorous educational program for their students.[11] Many of the black teachers in the segregated schools held credentials superior to those of teachers in the white schools. But though the schools may have provided a quality segregated education, they were still products of the Kansas Jim Crow law of 1879, and they still reinforced the legal separation of the races.

Thus it was that in 1951, when Oliver Brown filed his lawsuit in the Federal District Court in Topeka, his complaint concerned not the quality of his daughter's education but rather the inconvenience and danger she suffered by the long walk or time-consuming bus ride she experienced twice a day attending a distant elementary school for black students when a white school was closer and reached by a safer route, as well as the per se damage done to black students forced to attend a segregated elementary school.[12]

Though one should not downplay the role played by Oliver Brown in his willingness to be the named plaintiff in a suit challenging the segregation of elementary schools in Topeka, it is also crucial to recognize that the Topeka case was one of a number of similar cases challenging school segregation throughout the United States, a challenge led by the NAACP under the leadership of Charles Houston, a professor at Howard University Law School, and by Thurgood Marshall, the chief strategist and litigator for the NAACP in these cases.[13] One should also not forget the importance of the three judges who sat on the panel which decided Brown in the Federal District Court in Topeka and whose opinion and findings of fact played so crucial a role in the ultimate decision of Brown and its affiliated cases in the Supreme Court of the United States.

The Plaintiffs

Although Oliver Brown was the named plaintiff in *Brown v. Board of Education*, he did not act either alone or without support. The fight against school segregation and other Jim Crow laws in the United States was a fight

The Brown v. Board *plaintiffs in 1953 with their children sitting in front of them: Zelma Henderson with Vicki and Donald, Oliver Brown with Linda, Sadie Emanuel with James, Lucinda Todd with Nancy, and Lena Carper with Katherine.*

dating back to the end of Reconstruction in the South and the decision of the United States Supreme Court in Plessy. Among the many individuals and organizations which fought this great battle, none was more important than the National Association for the Advancement of Colored People (NAACP) founded in 1909.[14] In 1933 Charles Houston, a professor and dean at Howard University Law School, was named as special counsel to the NAACP.[15] In the succeeding two decades, Houston not only litigated cases on behalf of the NAACP, he also used his position at Howard to train several generations of civil rights lawyers dedicated to the end of Jim Crow laws in the United States. Among those he trained were Thurgood Marshall and Robert L. Carter, both important members of the team which litigated Brown and the affiliated cases.[16]

From 1933 until 1950, Houston, his protégés, and the NAACP won a number of court victories against segregation. In 1950, in particular, they won two important cases: *Sweatt v. Painter*[17] and *McLaurin v. Oklahoma State Regents for Higher Education*,[18] which effectively prohibited segregation in higher education. The stage was clearly set for an all-out assault on Plessy. The NAACP team, therefore, began to search for possible plaintiffs and lawsuits which would ultimately bring the question of whether segregation in education was constitutional before the Supreme Court of the United States. This required multiple actions to be brought in courts around the United States. Ultimately, four cases reached the U.S. Supreme Court on appeal: *Briggs, et al. v. Elliott*[19] from the Eastern District of South Carolina; *Davis et al. v. County School Board of Prince Edward County, Virginia*[20] from the Eastern District of Virginia; *Gebhart et al. v. Belton et al.*[21] from the Supreme Court of Delaware; and *Brown v. Board of Education*[22] from the District of Kansas.

The Lawyers in *Brown*

The lawyers who argued in the District Court in Brown were among the best in the United States. Lester Goodell was one of the leading lights of the Topeka and Kansas bars. He had served as a county prosecutor and, for many years, had a successful private practice.[23] The Topeka School Board was one of his clients. He brought all of his expertise and his experience to the defense in Brown. On the plaintiffs' side was one of the most impressive legal teams ever assembled in Kansas. From Topeka there were John and Charles Scott, leading black lawyers in Kansas and the sons and partners of Elisha Scott, the dean of the black legal community in Kansas and a legend.[24] Robert Carter and Jack

Facing page, The Brown family: Linda and Terry Lynn with parents Leola and Oliver in front of their Topeka, Kansas, house in 1954.

Topeka civil rights lawyer Elisha Scott, c. 1950.

Greenberg came from the NAACP in Washington, D.C. Although Thurgood Marshall did not participate in the Kansas District Court trial, Carter and Greenberg represented the next best lawyers the NAACP had on their team.

The Judges

The *Brown* case was heard by a three-judge panel drawn from the Kansas federal judiciary. Having the case heard by a three-judge panel would make it eligible for appeal directly to the United States Supreme Court. The panel's chief was Judge Walter A. Huxman.[25] He was joined by Arthur Johnson Mellott and Delmas Carl Hill. Hill was the most junior of the judges. He had been appointed as a recess appointee by President Truman on October 21, 1949.[26] He was confirmed in his seat by the U.S. Senate on March 8, 1950, and sworn in the next day. Judge Hill graduated from Washburn Law School in1929. Before joining the court, Hill had served as a city attorney in Wamego, a county attorney for Pottawatomie County, and as United States attorney in Kansas for two years. For two years he also served as general counsel to the Kansas Tax Commission. This service coincided with Judge Huxman's term as Kansas governor.[27] At the time of the *Brown* hearing, Judge Hill was forty-four years old and a respected lawyer and jurist.

The second most senior judge on the *Brown* panel was Arthur Johnson Mellott. Judge Mellott was nominated by President Truman in November 1945 and was confirmed by the Senate two weeks later.[28] He was sworn in two days after that. Judge Mellott, at the time of his appointment to the Kansas District Court, was fifty-seven years old and had already had a highly distinguished legal and judicial career. He graduated from law school in 1917 and immediately became an assistant United States attorney for the District of Kansas. He was thereafter in private practice for three years and then became a judge in the Kansas City Court. He then returned

to private pr
commission
U.S. Tax Co
until his ap
    Judge
in Reno Co
Swedenbor
Normal Sch
the Univers
assistant co
private pra
of Kansas i
Huxman o
these two y
clearly fore
immediate
his concer
Kansas Le
free books
the summ
black stud
after the s
race and a
administr
Huxman i

 . . .

to :
as
pu
rig
the
We

The
a Kansas
an enligl
found ar
nominat
Circuit, :
Senate a

The T

T h

history.

Louisa Holt was asked whether attending segregated schools had an adverse effect on black children, a question often asked in Brown and affiliated cases.[43] But of all the answers given to that question by all the distinguished experts, it was Ms. Holt's answer which resonated with both the District Court and, eventually, the U.S. Supreme Court. Louise Holt testified that:

> The fact that it [segregation by race] is enforced, that it is legal … has more importance than the mere fact of segregation itself does because it gives legal and official sanction to a policy which is inevitably interpreted both by white people and by Negroes as denoting the inferiority of the Negro group.

She then went on to explain that once a child was burdened with such a sense of inferiority it would not be erased by later integration.

Although a final expert was called to end the day, the trial was effectively over after Ms. Holt's testimony since she had testified, in effect, that the "separate but equal" doctrine approved in *Plessy* was simply not possible in educational settings. Segregation in and of itself caused damage to the black children subject to it even though the teachers, curriculum, and facilities might be otherwise equal; her testimony was precisely what the NAACP had sought.

The third day of the trial, Lester Goodell put up a competent and predictable defense showing that under *Plessy*, as it was then generally understood, the Topeka School Board had acted wholly within its rights under the 1879 act to segregate its elementary schools.[44]

It took five weeks for the three-judge panel to announce its verdict.[45] The court decided that its judicial hands were bound by the Supreme Court's 1896 decision in *Plessy* and only that court could change the law by reversing itself. But while the plaintiffs lost the case, they may have, in fact, won their ultimate battle because Judge Huxman decided to include in the court's findings of fact — findings which the Supreme Court would have to accept except under very limited circumstances which were not present — that segregation in and of itself, as Louisa Holt had testified, harmed the black elementary students who were forced to attend segregated schools.[46]

Judge Huxman wrote in Finding VIII:

> Segregation of white and colored children in public schools has a detrimental effect upon the colored children. The impact is greater when it has the sanction of the law; for the policy of separating the races is usually interpreted as denoting the inferiority of the Negro group. A sense of

inferiority affects the motivation of a child to learn. Segregation with the sanction of law, therefore, has a tendency to retard the educational and mental development of Negro children and to deprive them of some of the benefits they would receive in a racially integrated school.[47]

The chief judge, who had been a single-term governor, who had demanded the admittance of a black student to medical school, who had demanded that his legislature provide free books to all schoolchildren, stayed true to his progressive principles so many years later and, with the help of a young, obscure KU faculty member, drafted an opinion which left the U.S. Supreme Court little choice but to confront Plessy and, hopefully, overrule it.

In Washington

The subsequent history of the *Brown* case has been the subject of literally hundreds of books and articles and does not need to be discussed at length here. Perhaps, from the perspective of the Kansas participants, the most interesting aspect of the case is that Kansas came very close to accepting a default judgment on appeal.[48] By the time the case reached the U.S. Supreme Court, the composition of the Topeka School Board had changed, there was a new superintendent of schools, and the sentiment in favor of segregation had reversed. The school board decided not to defend its former position. It thus fell to the attorney general of the State of Kansas to decide whether to defend Kansas' position and, from the record, it would appear that had it not been for the prodding of the Supreme Court, the attorney general might well have declined to do so. Finally, the most junior assistant attorney general, a young lawyer named Paul Wilson, was chosen to go to Washington to argue Kansas' position in the U.S. Supreme Court.[49] Not only was this to be Wilson's first appearance before that august tribunal, it was his first appellate argument whatsoever. In fact, Wilson discharged his duties well, but, of course, he was matched against Thurgood Marshall, Robert Carter, and the stellar litigation team fielded by the NAACP. More importantly, society had changed and, eventually, after several years of hearings, re-hearings, and judicial negotiation, the Supreme Court issued its opinion in May 1954, overturning *Plessy*.[50]

Brown Reopened

Although the United States Supreme Court overturned *Plessy* in 1954 and thereby signaled the end of the Jim Crow laws in the U.S., it took a very cautious position on

Justices of the United States Supreme Court: (front row) Felix Frankfurter, Hugo Black, Chief Justice Earl Warren, Stanley Reed, and William O. Douglas; (back row) Tom Clark, Robert H. Jackson, Harold Burton, and Sherman Minton, 1953.

the implementation of its decision. In what has now become a famous phrase, the court ordered that states end segregation "with all deliberate speed."[51] In fact, it took decades for open segregation to end and many would argue that de facto segregation continues in some localities to this day.

Once the U.S. Supreme Court handed down its decision in *Brown*, the Topeka Board of Education proposed a plan to end segregation in its elementary schools and to provide that students would attend neighborhood schools.[52] At the time this plan was proposed it seemed to put an end to the controversy. However, much happened in the next two decades. Congress passed the Civil Rights Act of 1964 and the understanding of what constituted discrimination evolved. The elimination of segregation was not seen as an end, but rather as a milestone on a long road to true racial equality. Gradually, it became clear to many in the civil rights movement that neighborhood schools—as had been adopted in Topeka—would not prevent de facto segregation if neighborhoods themselves were segregated. In Topeka, while neighborhood segregation was not, perhaps, as severe as in some other cities, it was certainly present. Such voluntary segregation was exacerbated in the 1970s by the phenomenon of "white flight" when middle-class whites left inner-city neighborhoods and moved to suburbs which were overwhelmingly white.

Dissatisfaction with the prevailing neighborhood school system and its concomitant de facto segregation in all levels

of Topeka schools led Linda Brown to reopen the Brown case in the U.S. District Court in Topeka in 1979.[53] She employed Topeka attorneys Charles Scott Sr., Charles Scott Jr., Joe Johnson, and Richard Jones to litigate the case.[54] Since no final order had ever been recorded in the case, U.S. District Judge Richard Rogers reopened the case and claimed exclusive jurisdiction in the matter.[55] This case came to be known as Brown III.[56]

It took seven years for the reopened case to come to trial. Finally, in 1986, the litigants came before Judge Rogers. The trial itself took six weeks. At the end of the six weeks, Judge Rogers ruled that the Topeka Board of Education had, indeed, complied with the requirements set by the U.S. Supreme Court in 1954.[57] On appeal, however, the Tenth Circuit Court of Appeals reversed Judge Rogers' decision and sent the case back to Judge Rogers.[58] A petition to the Supreme Court to rehear the case was denied in 1982, and from 1982 until 1999, Judge Rogers worked with the Topeka School Board to find a solution to the problem of de facto segregation. This led, eventually, to a major bond issue; the construction of three new schools, including two magnet schools; changes in school transportation; and the formation of Unified School District 501.[59] Finally, forty-eight years after the case was first filed in the District Court it was officially closed.[60] Its heritage, of course, was a sea change in American education and society as a whole. And it started in Kansas.

Linda and Terry Lynn Brown outside Monroe Elementary School, 1953.

Notes to Chapter 5

1. *See* Richard Kluger, Simple Justice 369 (1975).

2. Jean Van Delinder, Struggles Before *Brown*: Early Civil Rights Protests and their Significance Today 34 (2008).

3. *Id.* at 38.

4. *Id.* at 36.

5. *Id.* at 38–39.

6. *Plessy v. Ferguson,* 163 U.S. 537 (1896).

7. Kluger at 372.

8. Van Delinder at 38–39.

9. *Graham v. Board of Education,* 153 Kan. 840 (1941).

10. Kluger at 379.

11. Rusty Monhollon and Kristen Tegmeier Oertel, *A Century of Struggle for Equality in Kansas,* Kan. History, Spring–Summer 2004, at 117, 131.

12. Kluger at 409–10.

13. Waldo E. Martin, Jr., *Brown v. Board of Education,* A Brief History with Documents 11–12 (1998).

14. Robert J. Cottrol et al., *Brown v. Board of Education:* Caste, Culture, and the Constitution 50 (2003).

15. *Id.* at 56–57.

16. Kluger at 272.

17. *Sweatt v. Painter,* 339 U.S. 629 (1950).

18. *McLaurin v. Oklahoma State Regents for Higher Education,* 339 U.S. 637 (1950).

19. *Briggs, et al. v. Elliott,* 342 U.S. 350 (1952).

20. *Davis, et al. v. County School Board of Prince Edward County, Virginia,* 103 F. Supp. 337 (D. Va. 1952).

21. *Gebhart et al. v. Belton et al.,* 91 A.2d 137 (Del. 1952).

22. *Brown v. Board of Education,* 347 U.S. 483 (1954).

23. Kluger at 403.

24. Cottrol at 129.

25. Kluger at 402.

26. *History of the Federal Judiciary,* Federal Judicial Center, http://www.fjc.gov/servlet/nGetInfo?jid=1043&cid=999& ctype=na&instate=na (last visited Dec. 22, 2010) [hereinafter *History of the Federal Judiciary*].

27. Kluger at 402.

28. *History of the Federal Judiciary.*

29. John Brown to Bob Dole: Movers and Shakers in Kansas History 219 (Virgil W. Dean ed., Lawrence, Kan.: University Press of Kansas, 2006).) [hereinafter Movers and Shakers].

30. *History of the Federal Judiciary.*

31. Movers and Shakers at 220.

32. *Id.* at 221.

33. *Id.* at 222.

34. Kluger at 405.

35. *Id.* at 406.

36. *Id.* at 407.

37. *Id.* at 409–10.

38. *See Id.*

39. *Id.* at 411–15.

40. *Id.* at 419.

41. *Id.* at 420.

42. *Id.* at 419.

43. *Id.* at 421.

44. *See id.* at 422.

45. *Id.* at 423.

46. *Id.* at 424.

47. Movers and Shakers at 224.

48. *See* Kluger at 544.

49. *Id.* at 548.

50. *Brown v. Board of Education,* 347 U.S. 483 (1954).

51. *Brown v. Board of Education,* 349 U.S. 294, 301 (1955).

52. Raymond Wolters, The Burden of *Brown* 253 (1984).

53. *Id.* at 269–70.

54. *See id.* at 270.

55. *See* Wolters at 266.

56. *See Brown v. Board of Education,* 84 F.R.D. 383 (D. Kan. 1979).

57. *See Brown v. Board of Education,* 671 F. Supp. 1290 (D. Kan. 1987).

58. *See Brown v. Board of Education,* 892 F.2d 851 (10th Cir. 1989).

59. *See Brown Timeline,* Topeka Capital-Journal, http://cjonline.com/indepth/brown/archives/timeline.shtml (last visited Feb. 18, 2011).

60. *Brown v. Board of Education,* 56 F. Supp. 2d 1212 (D. Kan. 1999).

District of Kansas Article III judges in 1983: (front row) Patrick Kelly, Richard Dean Rogers, Earl E. O'Connor, Dale E. Saffels and Sam Crow; (back row) George Templar, Wesley Brown, Arthur J. Stanley Jr., and Frank G. Theis.

6

THE POST-*BROWN* COURT: IN MEMORIAM

Although the Kansas decision in *Brown v. Board* will undoubtedly stand as the court's most important ruling of the twentieth century, the court has continued carrying an increasingly heavy caseload and many of its decisions have been of national importance. From 1861 until 1949 Congress had authorized only a single permanent federal district judge for the District of Kansas.[1] In 1949 Congress finally realized the growing inability of a single judge to handle the caseload, and on August 3 authorized a second permanent federal district judge for the district.[2] In 1961 a third judgeship was authorized. [3] In March 1966 another temporary judgeship was approved and made permanent in 1970.[4] In 1978 Congress added another judgeship, bringing the total number to five.[5] In 1990 a sixth judgeship was authorized.[6] In this chapter, we will give short biographies of all of these judges.

Arthur Jehu Stanley Jr.

Judge Arthur J. Stanley Jr. was born on March 21, 1901, in Lincoln County, Kansas.[7] Stanley led an amazing life. He was raised in rural Lincoln County until he was ten years old when his father, a lawyer, moved the family to Kansas City, Kansas.[8] When he was sixteen, he ran away from home and enlisted in the Canadian Army so that he could be sent to fight in World War I. However, Stanley was sent home after the Canadians contacted his father and informed him that Stanley was underage and sent him home. One year later, at seventeen, he again left home, this time to join the United States Army. He joined the Seventh Cavalry and was sent to the Texas border with Mexico to prevent a Mexican invasion.[9] In 1919 his unit engaged the infamous Pancho Villa at Senecu in one of the last horse charges in U.S. military history.[10]

Stanley returned to Kansas City in 1919 and decided to finish high school. In 1920 he graduated from high school and enrolled in the Kansas City School of Law. After only one year of law school, his adventurous spirit prevailed again, and he enlisted in the United States Navy. He requested duty on the

Judge Arthur Jehu Stanley Jr., 1994.

"China Station" and was duly assigned to the U.S.S. *Pidgeon* on Yangtze River patrol. But he didn't give up the law, even while in China. His father sent him, at his request, a copy of Blackstone's *Commentaries*, which he reputedly studied on the Yangtze.[11]

In 1925 Stanley again returned to Kansas City and enrolled as a night student at Kansas City Law School while working as a court clerk in Wyandotte District Court during

Left to right: Judge Stanley in his Canadian Army uniform, 1918; Judge Stanley in his U.S. Army uniform, 1918; Judge Stanley served in the U.S. Navy from 1921 to 1925; From 1941 to 1944, Judge Stanley served in the U.S. Army Air Corps. Below: Letter to Judge Stanley from his mother written on Election Day, 1938.

Judge Stanley: The Persistent American Patriot Son

Judge Stanley was no ordinary teenager. At age sixteen, he wanted to follow his older friends and join the military, with hopes of serving during World War I. His parents wanted him to wait until he was older, but young Stanley repeatedly attempted to enlist in Kansas City, proving far more persistent than his parents anticipated. They hoped a summer on his uncle's farm in southwest Kansas might set him straight. Instead of quashing Stanley's desire to enlist, however, it gave him the opportunity to buy a train ticket to Denver, Colorado, where he attempted to join the Marines. If it wasn't for his youthful looks, he might have succeeded. However, Stanley was recognized from newspaper pictures, and his parents were notified. He finally realized, "There was no use in my going to the U.S. recruiting offices — army or navy. They wouldn't take me." Six months later in January 1918, he ran away to Canada after enlisting in the Canadian Army under an assumed name. His father then traveled to Canada to ensure young Stanley's discharge as an underage American, and the two returned home. Months later, with his parents' reluctant consent, he enlisted in the U.S. Army, where he served in the Seventh Cavalry division. Over the next three decades, he served in the U.S. Army, U.S. Navy, and the U.S. Army Reserves.

Despite his numerous attempts to leave home to join the military while a teenager, Judge Stanley and his parents shared a mutual love and respect throughout their lives. Upon his return from one of those efforts, he changed his name from William Arthur Stanley to Arthur Jehu Stanley Jr., out of respect for his father. The judge later described his father as "thoroughly honest" and attributed his love of reading and learning to his mother's influence. He stressed that he grew up in an intellectual environment where he was exposed to books, ideas, and learning at an early age. "She had a great influence on me."

Exasperated as they may have been by his determination to go against their wishes early on, his parents were equally happy for him and proud of his achievements. On Election Day, 1938, when he ran for county attorney, his mother wrote him the following note which his daughter found among his papers after he died.

Dear Son,

Today I am very proud of you and tomorrow I shall be proud—what the votes decide concerns me only as it affects your happiness—it has nothing to do with my pride which is based on my knowledge of your character and the performance of your official duty. I know I do not have to tell you I love you nor that I have unlimited confidence in you — but I have a desire to write you this morning. In the face of expected victory or the always possible politic(al) defeat that I am and ever shall be proud just to be
Your mother

Written below: "Me too – Dad"

the day. In 1928 he received his LLB and joined his father's law practice. In 1934 he became the Wyandotte county attorney and remained such until he was elected to the Kansas State Senate in 1940. His time in the Kansas State Senate was brief.

Judge Stanley's law school photograph, 1928.

On May 1, 1941, he was recalled to active duty in the U.S. Army at the rank of captain.[12] For the next four years, Stanley was involved in the European theater of war and he was among the group that stormed Omaha Beach on D-Day plus 2. When he was mustered out of the military as the war was ending, he once again returned to Kansas City and private practice. He remained there until 1958.

Arthur Stanley's return to Kansas and law practice also marked his return to politics. He ran as the Republican candidate for the State Senate again in 1948 but was unsuccessful.[13] Although he never again ran for office, he was extremely active in a variety of organizations including the American Legion, the Rotary, the Masons, the American Red Cross, and the Kansas State Historical Society, of which he was a board member and president.[14] In 1958 President Dwight Eisenhower nominated him to be a judge of the Federal District Court of Kansas.[15] He was quickly confirmed and took his seat on the Kansas federal bench. In 1971 he assumed senior status, which he maintained until his death on January 27, 2001.[16]

During his service on the bench, Judge Stanley not only heard the myriad normal cases that fill the life of every modern federal judge, but also heard and decided several cases of great national importance. Judge Stanley presided over the 1966 antitrust case that the government brought against nine oil companies that had been charged with price fixing.[17] Among the defendants were some of the most important regional oil companies, including Phillips Petroleum and Skelly Oil. In 1964 Judge Stanley, who had inherited the Aiuppa case from his

Members of the Stanley law firm in 1948.

predecessor, heard the case and, again, the Chicago gangster, who had been found with 560 frozen birds in the trunk of his car,[18] was convicted and sentenced for his bird massacre.[19] But the case, as we shall see, was not at an end.

Without question, however, Judge Stanley's most famous case was the trial of alleged atomic spy George John Gessner in 1964. [20] This was one of the more bizarre spy cases of the twentieth century.

Judge Stanley shakes hands with his father after being sworn in as a District of Kansas federal judge in 1967.

PFC George John Gessner was a nuclear maintenance technician at Ft. Bliss.[21] His duties included maintenance of a number of missiles, including the Nike, Hercules, and Honest John missiles, all of which were capable of carrying nuclear weapons.[22] Gessner had been in the army for seven years when, in December 1960, he deserted and crossed the border into Mexico.[23] Once in Mexico he went to the Russian Embassy in Mexico City and, apparently, turned over classified information to their intelligence agents. The reasons for Gessner's treason were never clear; he was not a Soviet agent nor did he receive any significant compensation for his treachery. Soon after his meeting in Mexico City, Gessner was apprehended by U.S. military forces, arrested,

Judge Stanley mowing the yard of his Wyandotte County home, 1958.

"I sure hated to do this [release Gessner], but the Atomic Energy Commission classified so much in this case that we just didn't have any evidence. Without that confession, we couldn't do it, and the confession is a secret."

and tried for desertion.[24] This led to one year's incarceration in the disciplinary barracks at Fort Leavenworth. Upon his discharge from Leavenworth, Gessner was arrested on six counts of nuclear espionage, five counts of which were capital and eligible for the death penalty.[25]

Gessner's first plea was one of insanity, but Judge Stanley, after examining psychiatric evidence, ruled that Gessner was competent to stand trial.[26] The second major issue of the trial concerned Gessner's confession to the military authorities. Once again, Judge Stanley ruled that the confession was freely given and admissible at trial.[27] After several days of testimony, Gessner was found guilty but was not sentenced to death. Rather he was sentenced to life imprisonment. This, however, was not the end of the case. Gessner appealed the case to the Tenth Circuit, and in 1965 the Circuit Court ordered that a new trial be held, holding that Gessner's confession had not been freely given but, rather, had been coerced by the army interrogators.[28] At this point, the United States government decided to drop the case and not retry it for fear that another trial would require testimony about nuclear secrets.[29] Judge Stanley was not pleased and told the press:

I sure hated to do this [release Gessner],
but the Atomic Energy Commission classified
so much in this case that we just didn't have any
evidence. Without that confession, we couldn't
do it, and the confession is a secret.[30]

Judge Stanley was not only a superb judge but also a scholar. His years of experience in the military created a lifelong interest in all matters military, an interest evidenced by his years of work with Ft. Leavenworth and efforts to create a frontier fort museum there.[31] He also donated his own military library to the fort.[32]

Judge Stanley's scholarship extended to legal and judicial matters as well. He co-authored several articles, including a history of the Tenth Circuit published in the *Denver Law*

Journal.[33] Perhaps of even more lasting importance, however, were Judge Stanley's efforts, when chief judge of the district, to ensure that the Federal District of Kansas be one of the seven districts in the United States which would establish a federal magistrate judge's position on a trial basis.[34] These efforts were successful and Judge Stanley appointed Robert Miller, a Kansas Supreme Court judge, to serve as the first federal magistrate judge in Kansas City.[35] The experiment, of course, was a great success and federal magistrate judges have been an essential part of the District Court since.

Henry George Templar

Judge Henry George Templar was born in Cowley County, Kansas, in 1901.[36] His family had legal connections: His paternal grandfather had been a court interpreter in Holland, but his parents were farmers in Cowley County.[37] Templar was educated in a one-room schoolhouse and then attended Arkansas City High School, from which he graduated in 1923. He then attended Washburn University on a football scholarship and received the LLB degree from Washburn Law School in 1927.[38] In order to make ends meet, Templar worked part-time as a motorcycle police

Judge Henry George Templar.

officer while attending Washburn. He then returned home to Arkansas City and opened up a law practice. He met with little initial success but was soon appointed as deputy state oil commissioner, which provided him with a steady income. In

Judge Henry George Templar.

Judge Templar presided over a series of appeals by Richard Hickock (above) and Perry Smith, who were convicted of murdering four members of the Clutter family in 1959. Truman Capote interviewed Hickock and Smith while writing In Cold Blood, *a nonfiction account of the murders.*

1933 he was elected to the Kansas House of Representatives, a position he held until 1941.[39] In 1945 he was elected to the Kansas Senate and served there until 1953, when he was appointed United States attorney for the District of Kansas. Less than a year later Templar resigned from this position in order to run as a Republican nominee for governor.

Templar's run for governor attracted national attention. His bid for the Republican slot for governor was backed by the then incumbent Edward Arn and a powerful former senator, Harry Darby.[40] He was challenged for the nomination by the then incumbent lieutenant governor, Fred P. Hall. In an exceptionally close race, Templar was defeated.[41] Upon his defeat he returned to private practice.

In March 1963 President John Kennedy nominated Templar for a seat on the Federal District Court of Kansas.[42] Templar was the second Republican nominated by the Democratic JFK. He was quickly confirmed by the U.S. Senate and on April 12 he took his seat on the District Court.[43]

During Judge Templar's tenure on the District Court he heard a number of high-profile cases. He inherited the Aiuppa case and, finally, after another trial, which featured the

presentation of the dead birds at the core of the case, Aiuppa was again sentenced to prison and this time he went.[44]

Without question, however, the most notorious of Judge Templar's cases were the appeals of Perry Smith and Richard Hitchcock, the cold-blooded murderers of the Clutter family.[45] The two men, who were eventually hanged for their crimes, initiated a series of appeals to the federal courts, and Judge Templar was one of the presiding judges.

Judge Templar spoke at a dedication ceremony for the new Washburn University School of Law building on September 27, 1969.

Judge Templar also presided over one of the cases which arose from the 1954 Supreme Court decision in *Brown v. Board.* In 1973, Marlene Miller filed a case in federal court on behalf of her niece Evelyn Johnson against the Topeka School Board because the board had not yet implemented the changes necessary to comply with the famous 1954 ruling.[46] The case, which was to go to trial before Judge Templar, was settled by the Topeka Board and its insurance company. As part of the settlement approved by the court, Judge Templar agreed to issue a "gag order" preventing the parties from discussing the case. The board feared that should the details of Ms. Johnson's suit and settlement come to light, it would face a rash of additional suits. A reporter from the *Kansas City Star,* however, discovered these facts and the existence of the "gag order."[47] In the face of public criticism of the secrecy order, Judge Templar lifted it and permitted the parties to discuss the case and settlement openly. When interviewed about his decision to issue the original order, he simply commented that he had "stubbed his toe" by agreeing to it in the first place.

Judge Templar, like most of his colleagues on the federal bench, was also brought into the civil rights arena in a number of cases. In one case, he presided at the trial of Joyce Guerrero of Topeka, who was accused of concealing stolen property taken from the Washington office of the Bureau of Indian

Judges Stanley, O'Connor, Brown, Theis, and Templar chatting in 1970.

Affairs when it was occupied during a protest by the American Indian Movement.[48]

In another case, Judge Templar presided over a suit by Private John Thomas Bradley, a soldier at Ft. Riley, Kansas.[49] Bradley, when a private citizen, had participated in a protest at his draft board and had left his draft card and other documents at the board's headquarters. After the protest, the draft board initiated an expedited process by which Bradley was called up for military service before he would normally have been called. Judge Templar, following several other cases in other federal courts, ordered that Bradley be released from military service on the grounds that the Selective Service Act, which instituted the draft, did not permit such expedited processing. Judge Templar's decision in this case, along with those of other courts, eventually forced the Selective Service to abandon these expedited call-ups and drop nearly six hundred draft evasion cases brought on its behalf. Eventually the United States Supreme Court upheld Judge Templar's ruling in this case.

Flier for a debate sponsored by the Gay Liberation Front at the University of Kansas.

In one case, Judge Templar gained national exposure not because of a trial but because of a pretrial ruling. In January 1972 a case was brought before Judge Templar in Topeka. The case was brought by the Gay Liberation Front at the University of Kansas, who claimed that they were the objects of discrimination by the university.[50] Appearing for the plaintiffs was the notorious William Kunstler, the activist lawyer who had represented the defendants in the "Chicago 7" conspiracy trial. When Kunstler went to take his place as the plaintiffs' lawyer, Judge Templar refused to allow him to take his place at counsel's table, stating that Kunstler had shown "disdain and contempt" for the courts "across the country," that Kunstler's "fame" was "notorious," and that Kunstler "had exploited it."[51] Judge Templar allowed Kunstler to remain in the courtroom as a spectator, but the case went ahead with a law student serving as the plaintiffs' counsel. Among the many who criticized this decision was J. Clay Smith, the prominent lawyer, law professor, and government official, who wrote a letter to the *Washington Post* criticizing Judge Templar's decision as based on personal dislike rather than professional considerations.[52]

Judge Templar was also quite active outside the courtroom in many areas and is best known today as the author of what has been the definitive article on the history of the Federal District Court of Kansas.[53] Judge Templar took senior status in 1970, but remained active on the bench until his death on August 5, 1988.[54]

Frank Gordon Theis

Judge Frank Gordon Theis was born in Yale, Kansas, on June 26, 1911.[55] His father was a doctor, and he attended local schools. He enrolled at the University of Kansas and received his BA in 1933. Following graduation he attended the University of Michigan School of Law and received his LLB in 1936. He set up a law practice in 1936, but in 1937 he was appointed to serve as the director of the Inheritance Tax Division of the State Tax Commission and assistant to the commissioner, Delmas C. Hill.[56] He returned to Cowley County and private practice in 1939, and in 1942 also became deputy county attorney, a post he retained until 1946. In 1951 he was appointed by President Truman to serve for two years as the chief counsel for the Kansas Office of Price Stabilization. In 1955 he was appointed as the city attorney for Arkansas City and served in this position for four years. Judge Theis was also active in state Democratic politics beginning soon after his graduation from law school. He was a national delegate to the Young Democrats convention in 1938 and became president of the national group in 1942. In 1950 he was unsuccessful in his bid for a seat on the Kansas Supreme Court.[57] He was elected as chairman of the Kansas Democratic Party in 1955 and served in that position until 1960.[58] He also served as the Kansas member of the Democratic National Committee from 1957 to 1967.[59] He was a Kansas delegate to the Democratic national conventions three times and served as chairman and vice-chairman of the delegation twice.

In 1960 Theis ran as the Democratic candidate for the U.S. Senate against incumbent and former Kansas governor Andrew Schoeppel. In spite of an innovative television campaign which, among other things, stated that Judge Theis

Judge Frank G. Theis, 1994.

Judge Frank G. Theis.

had Eleanor Roosevelt's teeth, Adlai Stevenson's "bald head" and "Lyndon Johnson–size feet" (rather odd claims to say the least), he was unsuccessful in his senatorial bid. After JFK's election, the president indicated that he intended to nominate Theis to a seat on the Federal District Court of Kansas. This appointment was opposed by his former political opponent, Senator Schoeppel, and died. In 1964 Judge Theis chaired Lyndon Johnson's presidential campaign in Kansas; three years later President Johnson nominated Theis for the newly created judgeship in the Federal District of Kansas to be based in Wichita. This time the process went smoothly, and Theis was confirmed by the Senate and took up his seat on the court in March 1967.[60] In 1977 he became chief judge of the District Court until he took senior status in 1981. He stayed active on the court until his death on January 17, 1998.

During his decades on the Federal District Court bench, Judge Theis handled a variety of cases. In 1974 Judge Theis presided over the trial of two Leavenworth prisoners, Armando Miramon and Jesse Lopez, charged with kidnapping and assault in connection with a prisoner uprising at Leavenworth in 1973.[61] In that uprising four prison employees were taken hostage. The prisoners wanted

Judge Theis: Jurist and Sportsman

Not surprisingly, many District of Kansas judges have enjoyed hunting and fishing. One of the district's most dedicated outdoor sportsmen was Judge Frank Theis. Starting with a cane pole in grade school, Judge Theis never stopped fishing, eventually becoming a noted fly fisherman. Much of Judge Theis's success with a fly rod involved his favorite flotation device: a "gondola," a canvas-covered inner tube in which the angler floats along to find a good spot in the stream. He began using a gondola in the Arkansas River area where he grew up, and later rode his gondola in the lakes and streams in many western states, the Ozark region, and near his lodge in Ontario (which he earned as a fee for working on a case in the early 1960s and visited frequently thereafter). Though he caught all kinds of fish, he was probably most noted for fishing for gar. Judge Theis considered the gar to be one of the most neglected Kansas game fish. He even wrote two magazine articles about fishing for gar. In the September/October 1979 issue of *Kansas Fish and Game*, he compared catching Kansas gar to the excitement of a deep-water ocean trip. In the July/August 1994 edition of *Kansas Wildlife and Parks*, Judge Theis explained the proper equipment and technique employed in catching gar on a fly. Over the years Judge Theis also hunted turkey and other game birds with some of his colleagues. He was a true Kansas sportsman.

Judge Theis fishing for gar on the Walnut River in Arkansas City, Kansas, in 1983. Top left: Judge Theis with his daughter-in-law Willena and son, Roger. Top right: Judge Theis. Bottom right: Judge Theis with son Roger, daughter-in-law Willena, and long-time friend and fishing companion Jim Mitchell.

the prison authorities to permit them to have a meeting between a prisoner grievance committee and the media. Much of the trial centered around the defense testimony about conditions at Leavenworth, especially the conditions in solitary confinement, a cell referred to by the prisoners as "the hole." The testimony was devastating, and the description of the cell as overrun by cockroaches as well as the treatment of the

prisoners there — including lack of bedding, sanitary facilities, and daily exercise — deeply affected both the judge and jury. The government's case was also weak, so much so that Judge Theis ordered a direct verdict of innocence for Lopez. The jury also found Miramon innocent of the charges. Since the case involved black inmates and what appeared to be the especially harsh and inhumane treatment they had received at

Above: Rescue workers remove victims from the site of the October 2, 1970, plane crash involving the Wichita State University football team. The team was en route to Logan, Utah, for a game against Utah State University when the plane crashed near Silver Plume, Colorado, killing thirty-one of the forty people on board. Left: A charred football helmet photographed at the crash scene.

A memorial service for Karen Silkwood at Kerr Park in Oklahoma City on November 13, 1978, four years after she died in a car crash.

Leavenworth, it attracted great attention nationally.

Judge Theis also presided in the suit brought by survivors of members of the Wichita State University football team who died in a tragic airplane crash in 1970.[62] The survivors claimed that the federal government was at fault for the crash, which had killed thirty-one people, through the negligence of the Federal Aviation Authority, which had failed to adequately inspect the charter airplane.[63] Judge Theis, in response to a government motion to be dismissed from the case, ruled that the government could, in fact, be sued by the survivors.

Perhaps the two most notorious cases over which Judge Theis presided were the trial of publisher Al Goldstein for obscenity and the suit by the heirs of Karen Silkwood against Kerr-McGee Corporation and others over her contamination by plutonium and her mysterious death in an automobile

accident, one week after she had gone to the media with reports of negligence at a nuclear plant operated by Kerr-McGee.

Al Goldstein, a New York resident, was the publisher of several sexually explicit magazines including the infamous *Screw* magazine. Goldstein was indicted in Federal District Court in Wichita in December 1974 for sending obscene materials through the mail to recipients in Wichita.[64] Goldstein's defense was that these subscriptions had been ordered by federal postal inspectors to entrap Goldstein and his publishing company and enable prosecutors in Kansas to file charges against him. He argued that the federal authorities had chosen Wichita as the venue for the entrapment and subsequent indictment because they believed that a Wichita jury would almost certainly find Goldstein, his

Gerald Spence, attorney for the Silkwood estate, after the two and a half-month trial concluded on May 18, 1979.

partner, and his company guilty. Whether these allegations were true is difficult to determine, but they were prophetic. Goldstein and his fellow defendants were found guilty of the charges against them by a jury in the Wichita Federal District Court in June 1974. In December, Judge Theis set aside this verdict on grounds that the prosecution had made prejudicial statements to the jury and ordered a new trial.[65]

Goldstein's subsequent trial not only attracted national attention but was complicated by Goldstein's multiple requests for delays on the basis of claimed medical problems, including sleep apnea.[66] Goldstein also sought a change of venue for the trial, which Judge Theis denied. Finally, Goldstein made a deal with the prosecution and agreed that his company would plead guilty in exchange for having the charges brought against him and his partner personally dropped. Judge Theis ordered Goldstein's company to pay $30,000 in damages, and the affair was over.[67]

Judge Theis's actions in the Goldstein trial, especially his setting aside the first conviction and ordering a new trial, won him praise both from Goldstein's lawyer, Herald Fahringer, and from the eastern press.[68] Fahringer praised Judge Theis and said that he was "surprised that a judge would have the courage and fortitude" to set aside the conviction. Judge Theis was not as sympathetic as Fahringer wanted to suggest. After accepting Goldstein's company's guilty pleas, he stated that "he never had any doubt about the obscene nature of the material" and that he believed "as a jurist, the public has the right to set its own standard of morality."[69]

Karen Silkwood was a laboratory worker in a Kerr-

McGee plutonium production facility in Crescent, Oklahoma.[70] She had organized employees at the plant and was concerned that the plant's safety measures were inadequate. In 1974 she claimed that she had been contaminated by plutonium from the plant.[71] Significant traces of the deadly material were found in her apartment and in her urine.[72] One week after going public with this information, she died in a car crash. Kerr-McGee claimed that Silkwood had contaminated herself deliberately as a ploy to force the company to make the changes she advocated.[73] They also claimed to know nothing of the cause of her car crash.[74] Silkwood's heirs believed that she had been the subject of harassment by Kerr-McGee and by FBI agents investigating her contamination.[75] Doubts about her fatal crash spread through media across the U.S. Some believed that she had been murdered. Her heirs brought suit against Kerr-McGee in the Federal District Court in Oklahoma City. Jerry Spence, the flamboyant and famous trial lawyer, was retained to represent the heirs.[76]

The Silkwood trial was difficult from the beginning. The federal government was deeply concerned about national security at the trial.[77] Kerr-McGee and the rest of the U.S. nuclear industry were concerned that should Silkwood's heirs be successful, vast and expensive changes to procedures and plants would be necessary.[78] The plant had been operating, so the company claimed, in accord with all federal regulations. The first judge assigned to the case was excused when his ties to Robert Kerr, one of the founders of Kerr-McGee, were made public. The second federal judge assigned to the case was excused after he made rude remarks about the Silkwood legal team. By this point, it was clear to everyone involved that this case was a "hot potato" and whoever was assigned to preside over the case next had to be a judge of great character, intelligence, and probity. As a result, they asked Judge Theis to come to Oklahoma City and preside.[79] And so he did.

The trial lasted more than eight weeks. Kerr-McGee presented dozens of witnesses, including plant officials, experts, and even the chairman of Kerr-McGee. Both sides were constantly at each other's throats and civility was strained. Spence referred to the defense team as "the men in gray."[80] The defense team submitted motions to dismiss on the grounds that the jury could not avoid being prejudiced against Kerr-McGee because of the recent Three Mile Island nuclear accident.[81] To make matters worse, the film *The China Syndrome*, starring Jane Fonda and detailing a fictionalized version of the Three Mile Island incident, was released nationally during the trial. Judge Theis did a remarkable job of keeping the trial proceedings going, although a variety of anti-nuclear protestors surrounded the courthouse each day. He was also criticized by Spence and the Silkwood legal team for conducting a secret "meeting" with officials to hear evidence that the government believed was too sensitive to be heard publically — a meeting from which Silkwood's lawyers were excluded.[82] Finally, after eight grueling weeks, the six-person jury returned a verdict in favor of Silkwood's heirs and awarded them $10.5 million, including $10 million in punitive damages.[83] Kerr-McGee asked Judge Theis to set aside the jury verdict and award. In a fifty-four-page opinion Judge Theis refused.[84]

Judge Earl Eugene O'Connor

Judge Earl Eugene O'Connor was born on his family's farm near Paola, Kansas, on October 6, 1922.[85] The son of farmers, he attended school, as he liked to tell people, in a one-room schoolhouse for his elementary education.[86] In 1936 he enrolled at Paola High School, from which he graduated in 1940.[87] After graduation, he attended the University of Kansas, but his university education was interrupted by war. On campus he had enlisted in both the ROTC and the Enlisted Reserve Corps. The latter contingent was called to active duty in March 1943.[88] O'Connor's eyesight prevented him from being sent to the infantry along with his buddies and, instead, he became a member of the Operations Division of the army. He was rapidly promoted to sergeant and then picked for Officer Training School. Upon finishing there, he was commissioned as a second lieutenant and was assigned to the transport ships ferrying the army across the North Atlantic to fight in the European theater of war. He spent two years at this perilous task and was not mustered out of the army until a year after the war had officially ended. In August 1946, the now First Lieutenant O'Connor returned home to Kansas and KU.

Judge Earl Eugene O'Connor.

Judge O'Connor: The Road to a Career in Law

How lawyers came to be interested in law school often makes for interesting stories, and Judge Earl O'Connor's experience is no exception. Judge O'Connor grew up on a farm in rural Miami County, Kansas, near the prominent dairy farm of Montie and Hazel Martin. During that time, the Martins were sued by a former employee who alleged that a bull from their dairy farm had attacked and gored him. When the case went to trial, there was significant publicity about it. Indeed, many local farmers, including Judge O'Connor's father, attended the trial, which featured noted trial lawyers Barney Sheridan and Karl V. Shawver Sr. Earl O'Connor even skipped school for closing arguments and became entranced. During his portrait-hanging ceremony, Judge O'Connor talked about how he could still see the Martins' lawyer "demonstrating to that jury how that hired man had stood out behind a tree with a pitchfork and goaded that bull until he became more angry than ever. Apparently the jury was convinced by that

argument because the bull won the case."

After the trial, Judge O'Connor's mother became determined that he would go to law school. She worked very hard to raise money for an education fund. At one point during his second year in law school, Judge O'Connor decided that he should give up school and return home to work on the family farm. When he got there and announced his plan, his mother listened and then refused to feed him dinner. She gave him some money and his father drove him to Ottawa to catch the bus back to Lawrence. Judge O'Connor later thanked his parents for their input in determining his career. He also developed a lifelong friendship with the Martins' son, Keith, who became a consummate trial lawyer in his own right.

O'Connor quickly completed his undergraduate business degree and then, with the help of the G.I. Bill, enrolled in the School of Law at KU.[89] He graduated with his LLB in January 1950 and, in partnership with his classmate George Lowe and Lowe's father, set up a practice in Mission, Kansas.[90] His time in private practice was short. In July 1951 he went to work for John Anderson (later to be governor) as an assistant county attorney in Johnson County.[91] Once again, his time there was short. O'Connor, after switching political party membership, was elected as a Republican as a juvenile and probate judge in Johnson County and took his seat on the court in January 1953.[92] He was then elected district judge for Johnson County just two years later and assumed his seat on that court in January 1955.

Judge O'Connor spent ten years as a Kansas district judge. During this decade he established the pattern which would be characteristic of his life. He became deeply involved with court matters outside as well as inside the courtroom. He became the co-author of the first published *Pattern Jury Instructions* for use in Kansas. He served as president of the Kansas District Judges Association and of the Johnson County Bar Association. The rest of his career would demonstrate his belief that a judge must work not only in the courtroom, but also for the betterment of the bar and the bench.

In 1965, at the age of forty-two, Judge O'Connor became Justice O'Connor when he was appointed as an associate justice of the Kansas Supreme Court.

Judge Earl Eugene O'Connor, 1994.

The court at this time was vastly burdened with work since there was no intermediate level appellate court in Kansas until 1977.[93] When Justice O'Connor accepted his appointment, it meant taking on an unmanageable case load of appellate cases. In spite of the difficulties, Judge O'Connor acquired a stellar reputation as a judge. One of his later colleagues on the Federal District Court, Judge Tom VanBebber, referred to him as a "judge's judge."[94] Indeed, his reputation had grown to national proportions and his name was mentioned as a possible replacement for Supreme Court Justice Abe Fortas in 1969.[95] That did not happen, but when Judge Stanley, on the Federal District Court of Kansas, assumed senior status in 1971, Judge O'Connor was nominated for the seat by President Richard Nixon and was quickly confirmed by the Senate.[96]

During a long career on the court, Judge O'Connor tried hundreds of cases, but he stated that he believed that the most important case that came before him was the Kansas

Judge O'Connor at the dedication of the Kansas City, Kansas, United States Courthouse on June 10, 1994. In 1998, the courthouse was re-named the Robert J. Dole United States Courthouse.

City School desegregation case.[97] The U.S. Department of Justice filed the case against the Kansas City, Kansas, School Board in 1973. The allegations were that Kansas City, Kansas, had failed to comply with the U.S. Supreme Court ruling in *Brown v. Board* and that its schools remained segregated. The government sought, as a remedy, a multidistrict desegregation order.

It took four years for the case to come to trial before Judge O'Connor. When it finally did come before him, Judge O'Connor held that the school district had failed to make adequate progress in desegregation and found that six schools were particularly problematic. He refused to order a multidistrict desegregation plan, as the government had requested, but he crafted a desegregation order that required the closure of some segregated schools; the bussing of children among schools; and, most important for the future, that the Sumner High School, which was an all-black high school, be transformed into a "magnet school" focused on academic excellence and college preparatory work.[98] This was the creation of Sumner Academy, now one of the most important and academically successful high schools in Kansas.

As part of his desegregation order, Judge O'Connor required that the KCK Board of Education and the superintendant of schools report annually to him on their progress towards compliance with *Brown* and Judge O'Connor's order.[99] In effect, Judge O'Connor took control of the KCK school system. He remained in control for two decades. It was not until August 1997 that the Justice Department and the KCK Board of Education reached agreement that judicial oversight of the school system was no longer necessary.[100] In his order ending the twenty-year-old case, Judge O'Connor found that the school district had had "excellent results" and that "all vestiges of segregation... have been removed to the extent practicable." Judge O'Connor's twenty-year supervision over the schools of Kansas City, Kansas, had transformed the system and had changed the lives of thousands of young men and women for the better. He had done something quite remarkable.

As important as the KCK school desegregation case was, it was only one case out of a lifetime caseload of nearly seven hundred.[101] Other important cases over which Judge O'Connor presided were the multiple cases arising from a toxic chemical leak at a U.S. Titan Missile base near Rock, Kansas, the Topsy's securities cases, and the highly publicized criminal prosecutions brought against many of the major Kansas road building companies for bid-rigging in the 1980s.[102] In all of these cases Judge O'Connor proved his mettle as a trial judge.

It would be misleading, however, to suggest that every case that came before Judge O'Connor was of national importance. There were lighter moments, such as in the prosecution of Robert S. Lyons.

When Robert Lyons found himself in Judge O'Connor's court he was thirty-five years old and selling water purification systems.[103] But that was only his day job. Robert Lyons was a con man. He had constructed a false identity for himself. He told women that he was a spy for the CIA, an army major general, and a hero who had rescued POWs in Vietnam. He even claimed to be close friend of Elvis. He must have been convincing, since several women fell under his spell, and one, Hannah Cohen, even married him. But when he confessed to his lies, Cohen divorced him and the process that would end in Judge O'Connor's courtroom on charges of falsely claiming to be in the army had begun. In October 1989, Judge O'Connor sentenced Lyons to a $500 fine and placed him on probation for a year. As Shakespeare stated, "the quality of mercy is not strained, it droppeth as the gentle rain from Heaven," or in this case from Judge Earl O'Connor.

Judge O'Connor was rightly proud of the leadership roles he took among his fellow judges. He became chief judge of the Federal District of Kansas in 1981 and remained in the post until 1992, when he took senior status.[104] He co-founded the National Conference of Federal Trial Judges and was appointed by Chief Justice Warren E. Burger to be a member of the Court Administration Committee of the Judicial Conference in 1975.[105] In 1988 Judge O'Connor was chosen by the judges of the Tenth Circuit to be their representative to the Judicial Conference. During his years serving on these committees Judge O'Connor labored tirelessly to improve judicial pay.[106] When this finally happened in 1989, he was deservedly given much of the credit for it.[107] In 1990 Chief Justice William Rehnquist appointed Judge O'Connor to the Executive Committee of the Judicial Conference, the first time a federal district judge was appointed to so lofty a position.

Among all of Judge O'Connor's administrative accomplishments, he rated his successful campaign to get a new Federal Courthouse for Kansas City, Kansas, as the most important and satisfying. The courthouse that Judge O'Connor entered in 1971 as a newly appointed federal district judge was dilapidated, too small, and unsafe from a security perspective.[108] For much of his career on the federal bench, Judge O'Connor worked to convince the government to replace it. After twenty years he succeeded, and the ground-breaking for the new courthouse took place in 1991 and it officially opened as the Robert Dole Federal Building in 1994. Judge O'Connor proudly presided at both ceremonies, since without his efforts neither would have taken place and no new building would have been built.

Judge O'Connor died on November 29, 1998, with a full caseload.[109]

Judge Patrick F. Kelly

Judge Patrick F. Kelly was born in Wichita, Kansas, on June 25, 1929.[110] He attended Wichita schools and Wichita State University. In 1953 he received his LLB degree from

Judge Patrick F. Kelly.

Washburn Law School. Upon graduation he became a first lieutenant in the U.S. Air Force as a member of the Judge Advocate General's Corps and served until 1955.[111] In 1955 he joined the Wichita law firm Kahrs & Nelson. In 1959 he set up his own practice and remained in private practice until 1980. In 1960 he ran unsuccessfully for a seat in the Kansas State Senate, and in 1968 he was unsuccessful in his bid for the U.S. congressional seat from his district. Beginning in 1975, he helped form a Kansas steering committee for candidate Jimmy Carter, and his office served as the first

Kansas headquarters for Carter's campaign.[112] In April 1980 he was nominated for the vacant seat on the Federal District Court in Wichita, opened when Judge Wesley Brown took senior status.[113] Judge Kelly took his place on the District Court on May 23, 1980. In 1992 Judge Kelly became chief judge of the district and served in this position until June 1995, when he assumed senior status. Judge Kelly retired from the bench in March 1996. He died on November 16, 2007.

Judge Kelly had a remarkable judicial career. Whether it was as a result of his independence of spirit or simply a matter of luck and timing, Judge Kelly found himself in the national spotlight several times in his career on the bench. In case after case, Judge Kelly took positions that required bravery and judicial independence rarely seen on the bench. No one, not the attorney general of the United States nor his own bishop, was safe from his wrath if he felt that they had behaved improperly.[114]

Judge Kelly presided over several major cases, as well as hundreds of lesser fame. He presided over one of the toxic shock syndrome cases in which a woman had died after using a Playtex tampon.[115] The jury awarded her estate and heirs $10 million in punitive damages, but Judge Kelly, in what was an extremely unusual ruling, offered to reduce the damages award if Playtex would take the tampons off the market.[116] Playtex did so. Judge Kelly's ruling was praised by many in the nation, but condemned by just as many. His own comment about his ruling was characteristic: "I don't know if I have the authority to do it. But I'm going to try."[117] In another statement about his ruling he said: "I'm the first to admit I didn't have the authority to do it and there's no legal precedent. But I did it anyhow because I think it was right."[118]

Judge Kelly always stood up for what he thought was right. In another unusual move, Judge Kelly appeared as a defense witness in a Kansas Supreme Court disciplinary proceeding against an attorney from Hays, Kansas.[119] The lawyer had been charged for abusing legal process, including bringing groundless cases. Judge Kelly appeared as a witness for the defense, stating that the defendant was "an interesting person as it relates to his sensitivity to stated cases."[120] He went on to say that in many of the cases which the defendant had brought to his court, the defendant was "on the edge of breakthrough of some kind of a theory or claim or a new extension of a doctrine or something…." Judge Kelly admired legal creativity, even when, as he stated in this case, he "could not always see" the legal argument.[121]

Although Judge Kelly presided over many cases during his sixteen years on the federal bench, he will always be remembered for one case arising from the so-called "summer of mercy," a weeks-long protest and blockade of two abortion clinics in Wichita by the antiabortion group Operation Rescue in 1991.[122]

On July 15, 1991, Operation Rescue, a prominent prolife

Judge Patrick F. Kelly.

organization, began a series of protests against abortion providers in Wichita, Kansas.[123] These protests, planned long in advance, were to be the basis for a national campaign to change abortion laws not only in Kansas but throughout the United States. Members of the group and other sympathizers gathered together to blockade entrance to two Wichita clinics. The owners of the two clinics sought a preliminary injunction from the Federal District Court in Wichita to stop the blockades.[124] Judge Kelly granted the injunction and stated that he would use federal marshals to enforce the injunction and, if necessary, order the arrest of those who defied it. Within two weeks more than one thousand arrests had been made and the Operation Rescue leadership—including New Yorker Randall Terry, its founder— and several others, including Catholic priests, had been jailed.[125] On August 6, in the face of continuing disturbances, Judge Kelly announced that he would order the arrest of any protestors in defiance of his injunction, including then governor Joan Finney, if she were to join the protest.[126]

Abortion protesters blocking the entrance to George Tiller's clinic during the Summer of Mercy protest in 1991.

Throughout early August the rhetoric continued to increase and the battle in Wichita between Judge Kelly and Operation Rescue became the focus of national attention. Both sides were highly critical of the other. Judge Kelly called Mr. Terry "a hypocrite" and Mr. Terry responded that Judge Kelly was "out of control." Judge Kelly also became the target of death threats and was forced to stay away from his own church for fear of violence.[127]

Operation Rescue appealed Judge Kelly's injunction to the Tenth Circuit Court of Appeals.[128] In a remarkable twist, the United States government entered the case on

Judge Kelly in his courtroom, 1995.

the side of Operation Rescue.[129] U.S. Attorney General Richard Thornburgh, however, stated that the government position should not be taken as support for the protestors' goals or policies but, rather, was narrowly crafted simply to argue against the basis for Judge Kelly's decision and the applicability of a Reconstruction-era statute which formed its core. In response Judge Kelly went to the media and appeared on national television to criticize the government's intervention.[130] By this point, the legal battle had become the focus of national media attention and the basis for newspaper and magazine articles and editorials throughout the country.

The legal battle was finally settled when the Tenth Circuit ruled in favor of Operation Rescue and against Judge Kelly's interpretation of the law.[131] By this time, however, the protests were dying down, the Operation Rescue leaders had returned home to New York and other states, and the "summer of mercy" was at an end; Wichita was once again calm, and Judge Kelly had become one of the best known federal judges in the United States.

Judge Dale Emerson Saffels

Judge Dale Emerson Saffels was born in Moline, Kansas, on August 13, 1921.[132] He was educated in local schools and joined the U.S. Army in 1942 on his twenty-first birthday.[133] He was commissioned as a second lieutenant in January 1943 and assigned to the Signal Corps. He was sent to the European theater and served as the commander of the 1373rd Signal Corps. He was discharged in 1946 as a major. Upon his return he enrolled at Emporia State Teachers College and received his BA in 1947. He then enrolled at Washburn Law School and received his LLB in 1947. Upon graduation he settled in Garden City, Kansas, and began practice.[134] In the early 1970s he joined a Topeka law firm, and in 1975 a Wichita firm: Gott, Hope, Gott and Young. In 1950 he was elected as county attorney for Finney County on the Democratic ticket and served two terms.[135] In 1956 he was elected to the Kansas House from Garden City and served there until 1963. In 1962 he was the Democratic candidate for governor but was defeated by John

Dale Saffels (left) with his brother Harold, c. 1925.

Anderson.

Saffels's judicial career began in 1967, when the newly elected Democratic governor, Bob Docking, appointed him to a seat on the Kansas Corporation Commission (KCC).[136] He served on the commission until 1975 and as chairman from 1968. In 1968 he was appointed chairman of the Federal Home Loan Bank in Topeka. Judge Saffels's years on the KCC and as chairman of the Federal Home Loan Bank were crucial to his later career on the federal bench. As a member and then chairman of the KCC, Judge Saffels exercised quasi-judicial power over regulated industries in Kansas. As chairman of the Federal Home Loan Bank in Topeka, he exercised regulatory oversight over Kansas savings and loan associations. The experience and expertise he gained in these positions served him well in later years as a federal district judge.

In May 1979 Judge Saffels was nominated by President Jimmy Carter to the newly created judgeship in the Federal District of Kansas. He sailed through the confirmation process and took his seat on the court in November 1979.[137] He was assigned at that time to the court in Kansas City, Kansas, and remained there until he was relocated to Topeka in 1989.[138]

Judge Saffels was an amazingly hardworking judge. He heard every habeas corpus petition before the District Court. Between 1980 and 1995 he heard 3,754 such petitions which, if not a record in the U.S. judiciary, is close.[139] He also heard regular cases, many of them concerned with intricate points of corporate law. Of these, the most nationally important was the trial *SEC v. George Platt*, a case involving multiple defendants charged by the government with trading on insider information.[140] While such cases are not unusual, the Platt case was because one of the defendants was Barry Switzer, the beloved football coach at the University of Oklahoma. Judge Saffels found, to the profound relief of OU football fans, that there was insufficient evidence against Mr. Switzer.

Judge Saffels also decided a number of cases of great importance to the then growing Native American sovereignty movement. In one case, Kansas had begun to issue traffic tickets to Native Americans who refused to obtain valid Kansas license plates for their cars and instead used plates issued by their tribes, even off the tribal reservations.[141] The Native American defendants claimed that their tribes were sovereign nations and, as such, had the ability to issue automobile license plates and that tribal members were not required

Judge Saffels served in the U.S. Army from 1942 to 1946 during World War II.

Judge Dale Emerson Saffels.

Judge Saffels and Governor Bob Docking.

to obtain Kansas plates. In a series of rulings Judge Saffels agreed, bolstering the nascent sovereignty movement. In other cases, Judge Saffels held that Native American tribes were not subject to Kansas state taxes on gasoline, once again bolstering tribal sovereignty and presaging both legislation and case law

Above: Judge Saffels (center) in a hearing. Below left: Judge Saffels with his wife, Elaine, and Senator Bob Dole; below right: with President John F. Kennedy in 1962.

for decades to come.[142]

Without question, the most important case over which Judge Saffels presided, at least from the national perspective, was the Franklin Savings & Loan Association case.[143] In 1989, in the midst of the national panic over the solvency of savings and loan associations, accelerated by the activities of Charles Keating and his ties with several U.S. senators, the U.S. Office of Thrift Supervision (OTS) declared that the Franklin Savings & Loan Association (FS&L) of Ottawa, Kansas, was insolvent and took over the bank.[144] FS&L had been acquired by an investor group led by Ernest Fleisher in 1973 and was not an ordinary S&L.[145] Instead, Franklin engaged in a series of complex financial hedge transactions.[146] The issue in the takeover and the case was whether Franklin had a loss. Franklin claimed that they did not under generally accepted accounting principles (GAAP). The OTS claimed that they did. Franklin sought relief in the Federal District Court and the case came before Judge Saffels. The business press was delighted that Judge Saffels, with his experience on the KCC and Federal Home Loan Bank, was the presiding judge.[147] The case took eighteen days and pitted two major accounting firms against each other.[148] Judge Saffels, in a ninety-four page opinion, decided that OTS was in the wrong

and excoriated the OTS inspectors as inexperienced and ignorant about the financial transactions in which Franklin had been engaged.[149] In an exceptionally unusual decree, he ordered the OTS to return Franklin to its owners and took control of the bank for ninety days to prevent the OTS from attempting another takeover of the bank.[150] His decision gained national attention. The *Wall Street Journal*, in a series of articles, praised the decision and lauded Judge Saffels for his expertise and understanding of the complex transactions involved in the case.[151] *Time* magazine also viewed Judge Saffels's decision in a positive light.[152] Judge Saffels was hailed nationally as a lone voice of reason in a time of unreasonable panic. In May 1991 the Tenth Circuit reversed Judge Saffels's decision on the grounds that the OTS did not have to follow GAAP but had the right to seize the bank solely upon its own accounting analysis.[153] Although reversed, Judge Saffels remained convinced that he was correct.[154] Many accounting and banking experts agreed.

Judge Saffels remained on the District Court until his death on November 14, 2000.[155] Like so many of his colleagues on the Federal District Court of Kansas, he remained independent until the very end.

Judge Tom VanBebber

Judge George Thomas VanBebber was born October 21, 1931.[156] He attended public schools in Troy, Kansas, where his widowed mother served as postmistress and raised her four children.[157] A childhood bout of polio left him dependent on crutches for the rest of his life, a fact that did little to deter his career path.

As a high school student, he was hired by Charles Calnan, the editor of the local newspaper, the *Kansas Chief*, the oldest continuously published newspaper in Kansas.[158] He learned to set type, and he became the paper's sportswriter and its police and court reporter. Calnan was an early mentor and helped instill in VanBebber a love of American history that lasted throughout his life.[159] The job also left him with a keen interest in law enforcement and the law, as well as great respect for journalism as a good basis for objective thinking and clear legal writing.

In 1949 VanBebber began his college education as a prelaw student at the University of Kansas in Lawrence.[160] He was in the last KU class allowed to earn a "combined degree," which provided a Bachelor of Arts degree and a law degree after three years of undergraduate study and three years of law school.[161] In later years, Judge VanBebber refused the opportunity to pay $25.00 and have his LLB converted to a JD, because "in my mind it didn't give me any more knowledge than I had and it didn't give me any more prestige." Upon graduation in 1955, VanBebber returned to Troy. He was a

full-fledged member of the Kansas bar at age twenty-three.[162]
He had a job waiting there as an associate with Robert Reeder,
who had a general practice and was the elected county
attorney for Doniphan County. He often wondered what new
clients must have thought about his youthful abilities. One
of his duties was to serve as assistant county attorney. That
work provided him with a new interest in public service and
politics.

In 1956, Reeder decided not to run again for county
attorney and recruited VanBebber to run.[163] He lost that
election to Jack Euler, who became a prominent Kansas
attorney, a member of the Kansas legislature, and president
of the Kansas Bar Association. Later, Judge VanBebber
thought that loss was an important benefit, because it enabled him to pursue the career path that led to his judicial appointment. The district judge then serving in Doniphan County was Chet Ingels.[164] In 1959, there was an opening for an assistant United States attorney in Topeka. Judge Ingels recommended VanBebber, and he was hired by Wilbur Leonard, the U.S. attorney. VanBebber joined a staff of three other attorneys and Leonard, and he moved to Topeka. As an AUSA, VanBebber obtained significant trial experience in both civil and criminal litigation.

Campaign card from Judge VanBebber's run for state representative in 1972.

Judge VanBebber speaking before the Kansas House of Representatives.

At the time, there was no federal judge sitting in Topeka.
Judge Arthur Stanley, who sat in Kansas City, Kansas, and
Judge Delmas C. Hill, who sat in Wichita, would travel to
Topeka and other places then designated as official court sites,
such as Leavenworth and Fort Scott. In addition, Judge Walter
Huxman, then a member of the United States Court of Appeals
for the Tenth Circuit, had his office in Topeka and would
occasionally handle district court cases there.

Among the usual run of federal criminal prosecutions,
VanBebber handled stolen car cases brought under the Dyer
Act and prosecutions for transporting brucellosis-infected

Judge George Thomas VanBebber.

cattle over state lines. He also was assigned civil cases, such
as a lawsuit filed by Topeka residents who wanted to stop the
noise caused by military jet planes flying in and out of Forbes
Field. In hundreds of cases, he represented the United States
Army Corps of Engineers as it proceeded to condemn land for
the Tuttle Creek Reservoir near Manhattan and the Toronto
Reservoir in southeastern Kansas.[165]

In the fall of 1959, VanBebber moved to the Kansas
City, Kansas, office of the U.S. attorney, to replace an AUSA
who had been appointed to the state court bench. It was a
one-lawyer branch office. That was the beginning of a long,
close relationship with Judge Arthur Stanley, who became
VanBebber's second mentor and his judicial role model.

After the change to a Democratic administration in
1960, VanBebber had the unusual opportunity to stay on as
an AUSA, even though he was a Republican.[166] He did so
for several months and then, in August 1961, he moved back
to Troy, because he had decided to open his own office as a
sole practitioner.[167] He purchased office space from his old
mentor, Charles Calnan, in the building next to the newspaper

Above: District Judges Thomas Marten, Kathryn Vratil, and Tom VanBebber and Magistrate Judge David Waxse at a naturalization ceremony at the Fort Scott National Historic Site in Fort Scott, Kansas on May 22, 1998. Left: Judge VanBebber with his wife, Alleen, on their wedding day in 1986.

legislator to be a great work experience and a great place to make lifelong friendships. He was elected to a second term, but newly elected Governor Robert Bennett soon asked him to become chairman of the Kansas Corporation Committee, the state agency that regulates Kansas utilities.[170] He took the position and succeeded Dale E. Saffels, who was soon to be his judicial colleague. He left the KCC when his four-year term expired in April 1979 and went back home to Troy to practice law.[171]

In 1981, Judge Frank Theis took senior status, which created an opening for a U.S. district judge in Wichita.[172] VanBebber applied for the position, but it went to Judge Sam Crow, who was then serving as U.S. magistrate in Topeka. In turn, the district judges appointed VanBebber to take the magistrate's position, and Judge VanBebber closed his Troy law office and once again moved to Topeka. In 1989, he was selected by President George H. W. Bush to fill the vacancy in Topeka created when Judge Richard Rogers took senior status.[173] However, Judge Saffels wished to return to Topeka, and the vacancy was moved instead to Kansas City, Kansas.[174]

Cases more often went to trial in 1990, and Judge VanBebber tried twenty-five jury trials in his first year as district judge.[175] His national profile was probably highest when he was assigned by the Tenth Circuit Court of Appeals to sentence Michael Fortier, after all of Oklahoma's district judges were recused.[176] Fortier was an accomplice in the 1995 bombing of the Murrah Federal Office Building in Oklahoma City. Judge VanBebber had to

Michael Fortier, accomplice in the 1995 bombing of the Alfred P. Murrah Federal Building in Oklahoma City.

decide whether, after weighing the cooperation Fortier had given prosecutors, he should be sentenced within the federal sentencing guidelines or receive either a lighter or heavier sentence.[177] Judge VanBebber departed upward from the guidelines sentence, adding five years to the seven provided in the guidelines, for a total of twelve years in prison. Fortier appealed the sentence to the Tenth Circuit and the case was remanded for resentencing.[178] Judge VanBebber applied a different analysis and again sentenced Fortier to twelve years in prison, the sentence served by Fortier.[179]

Two other cases involved Judge VanBebber's well-

office. In 1962, Jack Euler decided not to run again for county attorney, so VanBebber ran for the office and was elected without opposition. He served three terms as county attorney, dealing mostly with small crimes: worthless checks, burglaries, and arson, and just one homicide in six years.

VanBebber's first appointed state service was in 1967, when the Kansas Judicial Council asked him to join a special committee appointed to rewrite the state's Criminal Code and Code of Criminal Procedure, which were adopted by the legislature in 1971.[168] At that time, Doniphan County had been represented in the legislature for ten years by Jack Euler. On June 20, 1972, the last day for filing for office, Euler called, informed him that he would not seek re-election, and suggested that VanBebber file for election. He drove to Topeka, filed in the secretary of state's office, and was finally elected with 60 percent of the vote.[169] Although being a part-time lawyer was a financial hardship, VanBebber found being a recognized, strong support of the First Amendment. The first was *Case v. Unified School District No. 233.*[180] A national LGBT organization, Project 21, provided free copies of the book *Annie on My Mind* to forty-two high schools in the Kansas City metropolitan area. Because the book included a homosexual theme, some parents in the Olathe, Kansas, School District complained, and the controversy included a book-burning event.[181] The Olathe superintendent of schools refused to accept the gift, and he further ordered that the book be removed from the shelves, although some copies had actually been there for some ten years without controversy.

Cover of Annie on My Mind, *a 1982 novel about a romantic relationship between two seventeen-year-old girls. The book was banned by the Olathe Public Schools and a lawsuit ensued.*

In response, several students, parents, and a teacher filed suit, supported by the American Civil Liberties Union and represented by pro bono attorneys from the Shook, Hardy, and Bacon law firm.[182] The case went to trial in September 1995. Judge VanBebber ruled that, while a school district is not obligated to purchase any given book, the First Amendment and the corresponding parts of the Kansas State Constitution preclude removing a book from circulation unless it is deemed educationally unsuitable.[183] He ruled *Annie on My Mind* to be educationally suitable, based on expert testimony. He found that the school board officials' testimony showed the book was removed because of their disapproval of its ideology, and that the school board had violated its own materials selection and reconsideration policies.[184] He called the book's removal an unconstitutional attempt to "prescribe what shall be orthodox in politics, nationalism, religion, or other matters of opinion." The decision was not appealed, and the book was restored to library circulation.

In 2003, Judge VanBebber again decided a publicized First Amendment case in *O'Connor v. Washburn University.*[185] The Topeka campus has a number of permanent outdoor sculptures located on green space between the student union and the main administration building.[186] It also provides there an additional annual temporary display of five artworks chosen by a citizens' committee. One of the loaned artworks on annual display in 1993 was a small bronze statue that appeared to be a bishop wearing a miter and stole and titled "Holier Than Thou." A student and a faculty member brought suit, alleging that it was intentionally offensive to Roman Catholics and violated the Establishment Clause.[187] Judge VanBebber, in denying injunctive relief, found: "In an environment of higher learning on a college campus, the court cannot conclude that a reasonable observer would perceive the university's display of 'Holier Than Thou' as an attack on Catholics."[188] He found that the plaintiffs presented no evidence that the outdoor sculpture garden was intended to support a religious theme or message or to express religious hostility, and he found no violation of the First Amendment.

In 1995, Judge VanBebber became chief judge upon the retirement of Judge Patrick Kelly, and he served in that capacity until he took senior status in 2001.[189] He took pride in two accomplishments during his tenure.[190] One was a commitment to long-range planning for staffing needs and dealing with budget restraints. The other was early implementation of the electronic filing system now used extensively in the federal courts. He continued to carry a full caseload after taking senior status, including the screening of all civil cases brought without assistance of counsel by inmates incarcerated in federal and state prisons in Kansas.[191] Between six hundred and seven hundred cases per year were being filed by prisoners, most of them legally frivolous. Judge VanBebber, assisted by two law clerks, enjoyed taking the burden of initial screening from the active judges and being able to sort out and give serious consideration to those with arguable legal merit.[192] He stayed fully active and engaged in judicial work until his death on May 26, 2005.

Notes to Chapter 6

1. George Templar et al., *Kansas: The Territorial and District Courts, in* THE FEDERAL COURTS OF THE TENTH CIRCUIT: A HISTORY 30 (James K. Logan ed., U.S. Court of Appeals for the Tenth Circuit, 1992).

2. Act of Aug. 3, 1949, ch. 387, 63 Stat. 493.

3. Act of May 19, 1961, Pub. L. No. 87-36, 75 Stat. 80.

4. Act of March 18, 1966, Pub. L. 89-372, 80 Stat. 75; Act of June 2, 1970, Pub. L. No. 91-272, 84 Stat. 294.

5. Act of Oct. 20, 1978, Pub. L. 95-486, 92 Stat. 1629.

6. Judicial Improvements Act of 1990, Pub. L. No. 101-650, 104 Stat. 5089.

7. *History of the Federal Judiciary: Stanley, Arthur Jehu Jr,* FED. JUD. CTR. http://www.fjc.gov/servlet/nGetInfo?jid=2272&cid=999&ctype=na&instate=na (last visited Feb. 4, 2011).

8. James F. Duncan, *Arthur J. Stanley, Jr.,* 10TH CIRCUIT HISTORICAL SOCIETY, 1, http://www.10thcircuithistory.org/pdfs/Stanley_Article.pdf (last visited Feb. 5, 2011).

9. *Id.* at 2.

10. *Id.* at 2.

11. *Id.* at 3.

12. *Id.* at 3.

13. ROBERT W. RICHMOND, ARTHUR JEHU STANLEY, JR: SENIOR UNITED STATES DISTRICT JUDGE 36 (2d ed. 1996).

14. *Id.* at 43–45.

15. *Id.* at 51.

16. Duncan, *supra* note 8, at 7.

17. *Federal Court Accepts 9 Oil Firms' No Contest Pleas in Price Rigging,* WALL ST. J., Nov. 22, 1966, at 9.

18. *Aiuppa v. United States,* 338 F. 2d 146, 147 (10th Cir. 1964).

19. *Killed Doves to Be Shown at Aiuppa Trial,* CHI. TRIB., Aug. 22, 1963, at 1.

20. *See generally Gessner v. United States,* 354 F.2d 726 (10th Cir. 1965).

21. *Trial Opens for Deserter Accused as Soviet Spy,* N.Y. TIMES, May 27, 1964, at 5.

22. D. J. R. Bruckner, *Confession Too Hot So Ex-GI Convicted as Spy Is Set Free,* L.A. TIMES, Mar. 9, 1966, at 10.

23. *Ex-Soldier Arraigned on Spy Charge,* L.A. TIMES, Oct. 3, 1962, at 9.

24. Duncan, *supra* note 8, at 4.

25. *Death Verdict Asked for GI in Spy Trial,* CHI. TRIB., May 29, 1964, at 9.

26. *Ex-Soldier Arraigned, supra* note 22.

27. *Spy Confession Allowed at Trial,* WASH. POST, May 31, 1964, at A8.

28. *Gessner v. United States,* 354 F.2d 726 (10th Cir. 1965).

29. Brucker, *supra* note 21, at 1.

30. *Id.* at 10.

31. Richmond, *supra* note 13, at 44

32. Duncan, *supra* note 8, at 6.

33. Arthur. J. Stanley and Irma S. Russell, *The Political and Administrative History of the United States Court of Appeals for the Tenth Circuit,* 60 DENV. L.J. 119 (1982–1983).

34. Duncan, *supra* note 8 at 5–6.

35. *Id.* at 6.

36. *History of the Federal Judiciary: Templar, Henry George,* FED. JUD. CTR., http://www.fjc.gov/servlet/nGetInfo?jid=2354&cid=999&ctype=na&instate=na (last visited Feb. 4, 2011) [hereinafter Templar History].

37. COWLEY COUNTY HERITAGE BOOK COMMITTEE, THE HISTORY OF COWLEY COUNTY, KANSAS, 304 (1990).

38. *Id.* at 305.

39. Templar History.

40. Seth S. King, *G.O.P. Control Put to Kansas Voters,* N.Y. TIMES, Aug. 2, 1954, at 10.

41. *Free Swinging Rival Defies Sen. Kefauver,* CHI. DAILY TRIB., Aug. 5, 1954, at A3.

42. *2d Republican Out of 96 Gets U.S. Judgeship,* CHI. DAILY TRIB., Mar. 22, 1962, at C11.

43. Templar History.

44. *Joey Aiuppa Sentenced in 2d Dove Trial,* CHI. TRIB., Aug. 20, 1966, at B3.

45. Templar et al., *supra* note 1, at 33.

46. Joe Mattox, *Topeka Board of Education and Us,* AFRO-AMERICAN, May 26, 1979, at 4.

47. *Americana: Topeka's Secret,* TIME, May 7, 1979.

48. *Topeka Woman Is Guilty of Concealing U.S. Property,* N.Y. TIMES, May 24, 1973, at 41.

49. Ronald J. Ostrow, *U.S. Quietly Dropping Draft Evasion Cases,* L.A. TIMES, May 28, 1970, at 21.

50. *The Nation,* L.A. TIMES, Jan. 28, 1972, at A2.

51. Albin Krebs, *Kunstler Incurs a Judge's Wrath,* N.Y. TIMES, Jan. 28, 1972, at 69.

52. J. Clay Smith, *Barring of Kunstler,* WASH. POST, Feb. 10, 1972, at A19.

53. *See* Templar et al., *supra* note 1, at 15.

54. Templar History.

55. *History of the Federal Judiciary: Theis, Frank Gordon,* FED. JUD. CTR., http://www.fjc.gov/servlet/nGetInfo?jid=2360&cid=999&ctype=na&instate=na (last visited June 16, 2011) [hereinafter Theis History].

56. JOHN A. PRICE, 10TH CIRCUIT HISTORICAL SOCIETY, FRANK G. THEIS 1, http://www.10thcircuithistory.org/pdfs/Theis article.pdf (last visited Feb. 7, 2011).

57. H. Con. Res. 5038, 1998 Leg., 10th Sess. (Kan. 1998).

58. Price, *supra* note 55, at 1.

59. *Id.* at 2.

60. Theis History.

61 *Two Leavenworth convicts cleared,* AFRO-AMERICAN, Dec. 7, 1974, at 6.

62. *See In re* Air Crash Disaster near Silver Plume, Colo., on Oct. 2, 1970, 445 F.Supp. 384 (D. Kan. 1977)

63. *Judge Says U.S. Can Be Sued In Air Crash,* WASH. POST,

Apr. 30, 1976, at A2.

64. *Judge Frank G. Theis, 86; Presided Over Silkwood Case,* N.Y. TIMES, Jan. 24, 1998, at A13.

65. *Publisher Goldstein Goes on Trial Again,* WASH. POST, Oct. 31, 1977, at A6.

66. *Al Goldstein Denied Trial Delay,* N.Y. TIMES, July 24, 1977, at 16.

67. *Goldstein Pays $30,000, Ending Obscenity Trial,* N.Y. TIMES, Mar. 16, 1978, at B6.

68. Ted Morgan, *United States Versus The Princes of Porn,* N.Y. TIMES MAGAZINE, Mar. 16, 1977, at 38.

69. *Goldstein Pays $30,000, Ending Obscenity Trial, supra* note 67.

70. William K. Stevens, *Silkwood Radiation Case is Ready for Jurors Today,* N.Y. TIMES, May 15, 1979, at A14.

71. Myrna Oliver, *Silkwood Nuclear Trial Reaches Midpoint,* L.A. TIMES, Apr. 4, 1979, at B16.

72. Myrna Oliver, *Silkwood Trial Told of Plutonium Particles in Kitchen,* L.A. TIMES, Apr. 11, 1979, at A17.

73. Myrna Oliver, *Kerr-McGee Chairman Defends Firm's Safety at Silkwood Trial,* L.A. TIMES, May 4, 1979, at B18.

74. Howard Kohn, *Justice for Radiation Victim,* CHI. TRIB., May 27, 1979 at A1.

75. William Worthy, *After Assassinations, See Who Stands to Gain,* AFRO-AMERICAN, Oct. 7, 1978, at 5.

76. Myrna Oliver, *Issues Narrowed in Silkwood Plutonium Contamination Suit,* L.A. TIMES, Apr. 6, 1979, at B21.

77. CHARLES G. PEARSON, BIOGRAPHY OF THE HONORABLE FRANK G. THEIS, SENIOR UNITED STATES DISTRICT JUDGE 77 (Mennonite Press, Inc.) 1999).

78. Bill Curry, *Nuclear Power Producers Are Watching Radioactive Contamination Trial,* WASH. POST, Mar. 7, 1979, at A3.

79. Pearson, *supra* note 77, at 75.

80. Beverly Beyette, *Ideas: Gerry Spence: For the Defense,* L.A. TIMES, Sept. 1, 1982, at F12.

81. Pearson, *supra* note 76, at 78.

82. Seymour M. Hersh, *Dispute Over National Security Emerges in Bitter Suit on Role of Dead Laboratory Worker,* N.Y. TIMES, May 7, 1978, at 34.

83. Myrna Oliver, *$10.5 Million Awarded in Silkwood Trial,* L.A. TIMES, May 19, 1979, at 1.

84. *Silkwood,* 485 F. Supp. at 591.

85. *History of the Federal Judiciary: O'Connor, Earl Eugene,* FED. JUD. CTR., http://www.fjc.gov/servlet/nGetInfo?jid=179 4&cid=999&ctype=na&instate=na (last visited Feb. 9, 2011) [hereinafter O'Connor History].

86. Tenth Circuit Historical Society, Earl E. O'Connor 1, http://www.10thcircuithistory.org/pdfs/O'Connor_bio.pdf (last visited Feb. 9 2011).

87. *Id.* at 2.

88. *Id.* at 3.

89. *Id.* at 4.

90. *Id.; See also* O'Connor History.

91. Tenth Circuit Historical Society, *supra* note 86, at 4.

92. *Id.* at 5.

93. *Id.* at 6.

94 *Id.* at 1.

95. *Id.* at 6.

96. *Id.* at 6–7.

97. *Id.* at 7.

98. Karen Dillon, *Federal Judge in Kansas Says He Will Retire in March,* KAN. CITY STAR, December 19, 1991, at C2.

99. John T. Dauner, *Schools Have Seen Much Change Since Desegregation,* KAN. CITY STAR, Apr. 10, 1997, at 4.

100. John T. Dauner, *Segregation Case Closed, Judge Rules KCK School District Met and Exceeded the Order He Issued in 1977,* KAN. CITY STAR, Aug. 7, 1997, at A1.

101. Tenth Circuit Historical Society, *supra* note 86, at 7.

102. *Id.* at 8.

103. *Con Man Sentenced After Wooing Women with Elvis, CIA Tales,* LEXINGTON HERALD-LEADER, Oct. 11, 1989, at A8.

104. O'Connor History.

105. Tenth Circuit Historical Society, *supra* note 86, at 9.

106. Judith Havemann, *A Federal Pay Raise "Wish List,"* WASH. POST, Jan. 28, 1989, at A11.

107. Tenth Circuit Historical Society, *supra* note 86, at 9.

108. ROBERT W. RICHMOND, EARL E. O'CONNOR: SENIOR UNITED STATES DISTRICT JUDGE (Mennonite Press, Inc.) 1997).

109. O'Connor History.

110. *History of the Federal Judiciary: Kelly, Patrick F.,* FED. JUD. CTR., http://www.fjc.gov/servlet/nGetInfo?jid=1250&cid=99 9&ctype=na&instate=na (last visited Feb. 12, 2011) [hereinafter Kelly History].

111. Guide to Papers of Patrick F. Kelly, http://specialcollections.wichita.edu/collections/ms/2004-01/2004-1-a.html.

112. Letter from Patrick Kelly to James Gammil, Jr., Director of Personnel Office, President Carter White House (Jan. 16, 1978) (on file with the Jimmy Carter Library).

113. Kelly History.

114. *See Judge Criticizes Bishop Over Abortion Protest,* N.Y. TIMES, Aug. 14, 1991, at A16.

115. *O'Gilvie v. Int'l Playtex, Inc.,* 609 F.Supp. 817 (D. Kan. 1985).

116. *Id.* at 818.

117. *Tampon-Maker Offered Trade on Damage Award,* N.Y. TIMES, Mar. 22, 1985, at A10.

118. Michael Siconolfi, *Novel Punitive-Damage Approach Raises Consumer-Protection Fears,* WALL ST. J., Sept. 17, 1985, at 31.

119. *In re* Boone, 7 P.3d 270 (Kan. 2000).

120. *Id.* at 282.

121. *Id.* at 283.

122. *Women's Health Care Services, P.A. v. Operation Rescue-National,* 773 F.Supp 258 (D. Kan. 1991).

123. *Judge Frees Leaders of Abortion Protests at Wichita*

Clinics, N.Y. Times, Aug. 30, 1991, at A19.

124. Don Terry, *U.S. Judge in Abortion Case Is Target of Death Threats*, N.Y. Times, Aug. 8, 1991, at A16.

125. *Abortion Protest Brings Jail Term*, N.Y. Times, Aug. 13, 1991, at A13.

126. *Judge Threatens Wichita Abortion Protestors*, N.Y. Times, Aug. 6, 1991, at A14.

127. Terry, *supra* note 124.

128. *Women's Health Care Services, P.A. v. Operation Rescue, Inc.*, 24 F.3d 107 (D. Kan. 1994).

129. Anthony Lewis, *Thornburgh Puzzle*, N.Y. Times, Aug. 12, 1991, at A15.

130. *U.S. Backs Wichita Abortion Protesters*, N.Y. Times, Aug. 7, 1991, at A10.

131. *Women's Health Care Services, P.A.*, 24 F.3d at 110.

132. *History of the Federal Judiciary: Saffels, Dale Emerson*, Fed. Jud. Ctr., http://www.fjc.gov/servlet/nGetInfo?jid=2088&cid=999&ctype=na&instate=na (last visited Feb. 10, 2011) [hereinafter Saffels History].

133. Jim Garner, 10th Circuit Historical Society, Dale E. Saffels, U.S. District Judge, District of Kansas 1, http://www.10thcircuithistory.org/pdfs/Saffels 20Bio.pdf (last visited Feb. 10, 2011).

134. Garner, *supra* note 133.

135. *Id.* at 2.

136. *Id.* at 2.

137. Saffels History.

138. Garner, *supra* note 133, at 2.

139. *Id.* at 4.

140. *Id.* at 3.

141. Carl Manning, *Judge Puts Indian Tribe in Driver's Seat*, Topeka Capital-Journal, Sept. 24, 1999.

142. Robert Boczkiewicz, *State Seeks Ability to Tax Fuel*, Topeka Capital-Journal, Jan. 19, 2000.

143. *Franklin Sav. Ass'n et al. v. Office of Thrift Supervision, et al.*, 742 F. Supp. 1089 (D. Kan 1990) *rev'd.* 934 F.2d 1127 (10th Cir 1991), *cert. denied* 503 U.S. 937 (1992).

144. *See Sheep and Goats*, Wall St. J., Sept. 19, 1990, at A22.

145. *Federal Takeover of Franklin Savings Upheld*, N.Y. Times, May 30, 1991, at D26.

146 Floyd Norris, *Thorny Issues in S. & L. Seizure*, N.Y. Times, Sept. 7, 1990, at D1.

147 Eric N. Berg, *S. & L. Judge is Adept at Complicated Data*, N.Y. Times, Sept. 10, 1990, at D2.

148 Linda Greenhouse, *Court Takes Home-Office Tax Case*, N.Y. Times, Mar. 24, 1992, at D1.

149. Susan Schmidt, *Regulators Ordered to Return S&L*, Wash. Post, Sept. 6, 1990, at E1.

150. Stephen Labaton, *U.S. is Told to Return Big S. & L.*, N.Y. Times, Sept. 6, 1990, at D1.

151. *The Franklin Fiasco*, Wall St. J., Sept. 7, 1990, at A14.

152. *THRIFTS: Give Me Back My S&L*, Time, Sept. 17, 1990.

153. *Federal Takeover, supra* note 143.

154. Robert Richmond, The Honorable Dale Emerson Saffels, Senior United States District Judge 35 (1996).

155. Saffels History.

156. Steve Fry, *Judge Dies in His Sleep at 73*, Topeka Capital-Journal, May 27, 2005, at A5.

157. Lew Ferguson, *Biography of the Honorable George Thomas VanBebber*, 6–7 (2006).

158. *Id.* at 17.

159. *Id.* at 18.

160. *Id.* at 21.

161. *Id.* at 25.

162. *Id.* at 26.

163. *Id.* at 27.

164. *Id.* at 29.

165. *Id.* at 30.

166. *Id.* at 31.

167. *Id.* at 33.

168. *Id.* at 37.

169. *Id.* at 37–38.

170. *Id.* at 43.

171. *Id.* at 45.

172. *Id.* at 49.

173. *Id.* at 57.

174. *Id.* at 59.

175. *Id.* at 61.

176. Steve Fry, *Judge Dies in His Sleep at 73*, Topeka Capital-Journal, May 27, 2005, at A5.

177. Ferguson, supra note 157 at 76–77.

178. *U.S. v. Fortier*, 180 F. 3d 1217 (10th Cir. 1999).

179. Ferguson, supra note 157, at 77.

180. *Case v. Unified School District No. 233*, 908 F. Supp. 864 (D. Kan 1995).

181. Ferguson, supra note 157 at 77.

182. Joe Lambe, *Lawyers Celebrate First Amendment Program that Grew from Flap Over "Annie,"* Kansas City Star, October 3, 2009.

183. *Case*, supra note 180.

184. *Id.* at 875–76.

185. *O'Connor v. Washburn*, 305 F. Supp. 2d 1217 (D. Kan. 2006).

186. *Id.* at 1219.

187. *Id.* at 1218.

188. *Id.* at 1220.

189. *Judge Who Sentenced Fortier in OKC Plot Dies Suddenly*, Wichita Eagle, May 27, 2005, at 4B.

190. Ferguson, supra note 157 at 79.

191. *Id.* at 78.

192. Steve Fry, *Judge Dies in His Sleep at 73*, Topeka Capital-Journal, May 27, 2005 at A5.

District of Kansas Article III judges in 2010: (front row) Sam Crow, Richard Rogers, Wesley Brown, and Monti Belot; (back row) Eric Melgren, Carlos Murguia, John Lungstrum, Kathryn Vratil, Tom Marten, and Julie Robinson.

7

THE TWENTY-FIRST CENTURY JUDGES

The Federal District Court for the District of Kansas has the distinction of having some of the wisest and most experienced district judges in the United States. Together the three oldest and most senior judges have over a century of combined experience on the bench. They are more than senior judges; they are "Super Seniors." The two newer senior judges continue to carry on the tradition of exceptional service after normal retirement age.

The Senior Judges
Judge Wesley Brown

As of the date of this writing, Senior Federal District Judge Wesley Brown is the oldest living sitting federal judge.[1] He has won virtually every award Kansas has to offer to lawyers and jurists. He is, simply put, a phenomenon. He was born on June 22, 1907, in Hutchinson, Kansas. His was not an easy childhood. Due to his father's illness, his family found itself in difficult financial straits, a situation which led Wesley Brown to spend much of his childhood working to assist his family. In spite of this, Brown graduated from high school and enrolled at the University of Kansas in the fall of 1925. He supported himself by working at Weaver Dry Goods (now Weaver's Department Store) in Lawrence.[2] His grades that first year were not good, and he left KU and returned home, where he took a job at a bank. In 1927, having saved enough to pay his tuition and expenses, he returned to KU.[3] This time his grades were acceptable. In 1929 he left KU to enroll at the Kansas City School of Law. To support himself at law school he worked in the local Model A plant on the assembly line.[4] After two years, however, he was laid off and again returned to Hutchinson to save money.[5] Finally, he returned to law school in 1932 and received his LLB in 1933.[6]

After graduation, Wesley Brown again returned to Hutchinson and entered the practice of law, but found that his salary as a lawyer was inadequate to support a family. He decided to run on the Democratic ticket for Reno County

Top: Wesley Brown, a freshman at the University of Kansas. Below: Judge Brown in his U.S. Navy uniform, 1945.

attorney, a position which paid the then princely sum of $3,000 per year. He remained in this office for four years and then returned to private practice, this time with his name on his firm's letterhead.

In 1944 Brown enlisted in the United States Navy. He was thirty-seven, and he was sent to the Philippines. In one of those coincidences that can change lives, he met Delmas Hill there and, according to Brown, it was this chance encounter and the conversations he had with the future Judge Hill that first gave him the idea that he might like to be a judge someday.

Brown returned to Hutchinson and rejoined his firm when he was discharged from the navy in 1946. He remained in the private practice of law until 1958, when Judge Hill again helped to change his life. Judge Hill asked him to become a United States referee in bankruptcy. After much thought, Brown consented. Four years later President John F. Kennedy nominated Judge Brown for a federal district judgeship—a vacancy created by Judge Hill's appointment to the Tenth Circuit Court of Appeals. Judge Brown's nomination met with bipartisan support in the U.S. Senate, and he took his seat on the Federal District Court of Kansas, a seat he

Above: Judge Wesley E. Brown.. Top right: Judge Brown has been featured in numerous publications throughout the years. This photograph appeared in the Wichita Eagle *on June 22, 2000, his ninety-third birthday. Bottom right: Judge Brown holds his gavel.*

still occupies—albeit in senior status—to this day.[7] In 1971 Judge Brown became chief judge of the district and served in that role until 1977.[8] In 1979 he took senior status. During his career, Judge Brown was appointed by Chief Justice Earl Warren to serve on a panel organized in 1968 to hear a backlog of cases in the Southern District of New York.[9]

Throughout his long career Judge Brown has decided thousands of cases, many of which were of national significance. The range of Judge Brown's juristic learning as reflected in the diversity of the cases he has decided is amazing. In 2006, for instance, Judge Brown decided the case of *Via Christi Regional Medical Center v. Blue Cross and Blue Shield of Kansas.*[10] His decision interprets complex and little understood provisions of ERISA, the federal retirement and health benefits statute. In 1966, forty years before, Judge Brown was the first federal judge in the United States to permit an applicant for U.S. citizenship to omit that part of the oath which deals with the obligation to bear arms.[11] The immigrant cited religious objections. Indeed, Judge Brown has made it clear throughout his long judicial tenure that he enjoys naturalization proceedings more than virtually any other part of his job.[12]

In 1967, while sitting on a panel with Judges Stanley and Hill, Judge Brown examined the constitutionality of the Kansas loyalty oath, which required state employees to pledge

that they did not belong to a political party or organization which advocated overthrowing the federal or state government.[13] A professor of psychiatry at the KU School of Medicine refused to sign the oath on the basis of principle and asked the court to declare the statute unconstitutional, which it did.[14] In 1968 Judge Brown presided over a landmark twelve-week trial adjudicating the royalty rights of helium producers and royalty owners.[15] In 1982 Judge Brown presided over another case of national importance, one in which he ruled that seventy-one black former train porters had been unfairly compensated by their union.[16] Indeed, it has been reported that during his career so far, Judge Brown has decided more than five thousand cases in which the opinions were not published,[17] in addition to all of those he decided that may be found in almost half a century's worth of *Federal Reporters.*

Judge Richard Rogers

Judge Richard Dean Rogers was born in Oberlin, Kansas, in 1921.[18] He received his BS from Kansas State University in 1943 and his LLB from the University of Kansas School of Law in 1947. From 1943 until 1945 Rogers served in the U.S. Army Air Corps as a bombardier. In 1947 he entered private practice in Manhattan, Kansas. In 1950, he was elected as a Republican to the Manhattan City Commission, and in 1952 he was elected mayor of Manhattan. From 1954 until 1958 Judge Rogers served as county attorney for Riley County, and in 1960 he returned to the Manhattan City Commission and served until 1964, when he was again elected mayor of Manhattan. He served as the general counsel to the Kansas Farm Bureau from 1960 to 1975.

From 1964 until 1968 Rogers served in the Kansas House of Representatives, and in 1968 he was elected to the Kansas Senate. In 1975 he became the president of the Kansas Senate. On July 15, 1975, President Gerald R. Ford nominated Rogers to replace retiring Judge George Templar on the Kansas Federal District Court. He was confirmed quickly by the U.S. Senate and took his place on the bench on August 5, 1975. He took senior status on January 1, 1989.

In his thirty-six years on the federal bench, Judge Rogers has presided over many significant cases and has won multiple awards for his many activities on and off the bench.[19] In 1975 Judge Rogers presided over a suit by a young Kansas

Top: Richard Dean "Dick" Rogers played halfback for Kansas State University, 1940. Below: Judge Rogers served as a bombardier in the U.S. Army Air Corps from 1943 to 1945.

Judge Richard Rogers: A Noble and Effective Politician

Before his appointment to the federal bench in 1975, Judge Richard Rogers enjoyed a long and storied political career in Kansas. In 1950, at age twenty-eight, he was elected to the newly created Manhattan City Commission after working to pass legislation that implemented the city commission/mayor form of government. Two years later, he was elected mayor of Manhattan. An integral part of his mayoral term involved dealing with the aftermath of the disastrous Great Flood of 1951, in which the Manhattan downtown business district had been deluged with eight feet of water.. In fact, while the city was focused on dealing with major issues resulting from the flood, fluoridation of the water supply, a hot topic for many years, passed easily during his tenure as mayor. Under his leadership Manhattan was named an All-American City, one of only eleven in the country in 1952.

Judge Rogers ran for city commission again in 1960 and was elected to a four-year term. He became the state chairman of the Republican Party in 1962. In 1964, he was elected to the State House of Representatives and re-elected mayor of Manhattan. Perhaps his proudest accomplishment during his second term as mayor involved the establishment of the Human Relations Board to ensure civil rights for all Manhattan citizens. Later, this experience led to the passage of a public accommodations bill by the Kansas legislature. In 1968, Judge Rogers was elected to the Kansas Senate, where he served until his appointment to the bench.

Judge Rogers speaking on the Kansas Senate floor.

Judge Richard Dean Rogers.

District of Kansas judges, 2010.

University sprinter, Clifford Wiley, whose eligibility had been withdrawn pursuant to NCAA rules on scholarship limits.[20] Mr. Wiley was from a poor family in Baltimore, Maryland, and had run afoul of NCAA rules because he had received both a scholarship under the federal government's Basic Educational Opportunity Program and a track scholarship from KU. He needed both in order to pay for his education and living expenses. Judge Rogers first issued an injunction prohibiting the NCAA from taking away Riley's eligibility and then ruled that the method of computing scholarship limitations used by the NCAA was unconstitutional. This helped poor collegiate athletes across the United States.

In 1980 Judge Rogers took on the federal government and its decision to hold indefinitely at Leavenworth Cuban refugees who had committed crimes prior to immigrating to the United States as part of what was then known as the "Freedom Flotilla."[21] In a case brought by refugee Pedro Rodriguez, Judge Rogers ruled that Mr. Rodriguez could not be held in prison at Leavenworth without a hearing or any date set for a hearing.[22] In his opinion, Judge Rogers was explicitly critical of the United States attorney general and stated that the practice of indefinite incarceration of refugees "amounts to an abuse of discretion on the part of the Attorney

General and his delegates."[23] In commenting on Judge Rogers's decision, the *Chicago Tribune* noted: "It adds to one's pride in being an American that here the rule of law is so strong that a Pedro Rodriguez can win a suit against the United States."[24] Judge Rogers's decision caused a national debate on the problem of some eighteen hundred Cuban refugees and eventually brought about changes in the way they were treated by the federal government.[25]

As significant as many of the cases decided by Judge Rogers were during his career, there is probably none that has attracted as much national attention as the revival of *Brown v. Board* in 1979. In that year, on the twenty-fifth anniversary of the U.S. Supreme Court's landmark decision, a group of Topeka citizens, including Linda Brown Smith, whose father was the original plaintiff in the 1954 suit,[26] alleged that the Topeka School Board had not complied with the Supreme Court's ruling in *Brown* and that the original case remained open. The case was pending before Judge Rogers's court for eight years until April 1987, when Judge Rogers issued a fifty-page decision holding that the Topeka School Board had, in fact, complied with the Supreme Court's 1954 order, even though it had not achieved a complete integration of the city's schools.[27]

Judge Rogers's 1987 decision met with considerable resistance from the civil rights community.[28] Others, such as an editorial writer in the *Wall Street Journal* for April 16, 1987, lauded Judge Rogers's opinion.[29] But the Tenth Circuit Court of Appeals disagreed, reversed Judge Rogers's decision and sent the case back.[30] From 1987 until 1999 Judge Rogers, in effect, supervised the Topeka school system and worked with it to achieve full compliance with *Brown*.[31]

Judge Sam Crow

Judge Sam Crow was born in Topeka, Kansas, in 1926.[32] In 1944 he joined the United States Navy. When he returned, he enrolled at the University of Kansas and received his BA in 1949. He then enrolled at the Washburn Law School, from which he received the JD in 1952.[33] After graduation, Crow entered private practice in Topeka, but, almost immediately, he enrolled in the U.S. Army Judge Advocate Generals Corps. He graduated from the JAG School and completed numerous other JAG training programs.[34] In 1953 he returned to private practice in Topeka and was a partner in Rooney, Dickinson, Prager & Crow until 1963, and with successor firms until 1975.

In 1973 Judge Crow was appointed as a part-time federal magistrate judge.[35] In 1975 he was appointed to serve as a full-time federal magistrate judge. In 1981 President Ronald Reagan appointed Judge Crow as a federal district judge for the District of Kansas with his chambers and court located in Wichita.[36]

Even after his appointment as a federal magistrate judge, Judge Crow continued to be active in the armed forces, attending courses both in 1975 and 1977.[37] In 1986 Judge Crow retired from the U.S. Army Reserve with the rank of colonel. He has been the recipient of numerous awards from the military, from the bar, and from educational institutions.[38] In 1997 the Topeka Inn of Court changed its name to the "Sam A. Crow" Inn in his honor.

Judge Sam A. Crow.

Judge Crow has presided over countless civil and criminal cases during his years on the federal bench. Like so many of his colleagues through the years in the District of Kansas, he has shown an independent streak and been willing to challenge other courts and other judges. One of his most notable cases in this regard was his 2002 opinion in *U.S. v. Cline.*[39] The *Cline* case presented one of the most difficult problems faced by federal judges after the U.S. Supreme Court's rulings in the *Daubert*[40] and *Kumho*[41] cases, cases which revolutionized the admissibility rules for scientific evidence in federal courts.[42] These new rules forced judges to make complex decisions about whether only particular techniques which were "tested" and found to be good science or whether a technique, albeit untested

Above: Sam Crow, age five, with his dog, Buttons. Right: In 1944, Judge Crow joined the U.S. Navy.

or incompletely tested but still deemed reliable, might still be admissible. The dilemma was of special concern with fingerprint evidence. Judge Crow, in *Cline*, ruled that fingerprint evidence "has withstood the scrutiny and testing of the adversarial process" and would be admissible.[43] In this case Judge Crow stood up to the U.S. Supreme Court and reaffirmed the power of federal district judges to make these evidentiary calls without rigorous "scientific" tests.

Another side of Judge Crow became manifest in the trial before him of Kendal Lee Warkentine, a young Mennonite. Warkentine had refused to register for the draft on the grounds that the registration form did not permit him to state that he was a conscientious objector on religious grounds.[44] Warkentine was prosecuted for this failure. Although many other federal judges across the country were handing out prison sentences to men who refused to register, Judge Crow showed his sympathy for this young man, stating that he knew that his refusal was based purely on his religious beliefs. Instead of prison, Warkentine signed a modified registration form and was ordered to serve two years' probation.[45]

Of all of the cases over which Judge Crow presided during his years on the bench, none attracted so much national attention nor tried the judge's patience as did *Koch v. Koch*. This epic case, which pitted brother against brother and brothers against mother, arose from a dispute as to the proper valuation given to the stock of Koch Corporation, a privately held company, when Charles and David Koch bought out the interests of William and Frederick Koch.[46] The litigation stretched out for twelve years and occupied the time of countless lawyers and judges.[47] Judge Crow found himself presiding over the last major litigation on *Koch v. Koch*. In the midst of a hard-fought trial, Judge Crow issued a "gag order" against all the parties involved so that the publicity campaigns he perceived to be disrupting the state and the trial would cease.[48] The gag order was effective, albeit controversial, and the jury finally returned a verdict in favor of Charles and David Koch, a verdict which was affirmed by the U.S. Court of Appeals for the Tenth Circuit.[49] Thus Judge Crow was able to bring to conclusion a massive case worthy of Charles Dickens.

Judge Crow also gained national attention for less judicial reasons. In 1993 Gary McKnight was to appear in federal court in Topeka to be sentenced on drug and tax charges.[50] But the sentencing never happened. Instead, McKnight, according to one news report: "was a man on a mission, he had a plan. He was going to go to war ...." His enemy was the federal court in Topeka and all those who worked there, including Federal Magistrate Judge Ronald Newman and Judge Crow and their staffs.

McKnight entered the Frank Carlson Federal Building from the underground parking lot. He was armed for a war: two semiautomatic pistols, a revolver, and pipe bombs. First, he killed a security guard, Gene Goldsberry, who was stationed by the elevators. He also shot and wounded a passerby, Terry Lee Morrow. As this was going on Judge Crow heard what he knew was gunfire. Judge Crow and his assistant went into the corridor and saw Goldsberry lying wounded. Under instructions from federal marshals, Judge Crow and his assistant returned to his chambers and locked the entry doors. Explosions followed. The siege lasted for hours. Several other federal employees were injured. Finally, McKnight ended the attack by committing suicide.

After the attack, Judge Crow told reporters that McKnight's attack had been the first attack inside a federal courthouse. As a result of that attack, security at federal courthouses throughout the United States was given far more attention and modifications and additions to security were implemented.

Judge Monti Belot.

Judge Monti Belot

Judge Monti Belot was born in 1943 in Kansas City, Missouri.[51] He received his BA degree from the University of Kansas in 1965 and his JD degree from the University of Kansas School of Law in 1968. From 1968 to 1971 Belot served as a JAG Corps officer in the United States Naval Reserve. From 1971 until 1973 he served as law clerk to Kansas Federal District Judge Wesley E. Brown in Wichita. From 1973 until 1976 he served as an assistant United States attorney in Topeka, Kansas. From 1976 to 1983 he was in private practice in Kansas City, Kansas, and from 1983 until 1991 he was in private practice in Coffeyville, Kansas. In July 1991 President George H. W. Bush appointed Judge Belot to a newly created seat on the Kansas Federal District Court. He was confirmed by the U.S. Senate and took his seat on the court in November 1991. He took senior status in March 2008.

Like his senior peers on the Federal District Court of Kansas, Judge Belot has had and continues to have a remarkable career on the bench. During his tenure as a federal district judge he has presided over a wide range of important cases. It is difficult, as it is with all judges currently on the federal bench, to pick among their many cases those that are most noteworthy. In Judge Belot's career, several cases have certainly attracted much media attention. For instance, Judge Belot presided over the prosecution of a nurse and her husband who were accused of "enslaving" the patients in the nursing home that the couple operated and of horrible practices, such as the "nude therapy," that they conducted with some patients.[52] The pair was found guilty of the charges and was sentenced to prison by Judge Belot. Interestingly, on appeal, the Tenth Circuit not only upheld the convictions but remanded the sentencing portion of the case to Judge Belot for reconsideration as to whether the sentence should be longer.[53]

Another case in 2009 decided by Judge Belot was one that set an important constitutional precedent.[54] During a meeting held by the city of Mulvane, Kansas, to discuss the possibility that a new casino might be constructed near Mulvane, an opponent of the casino was told that she might not speak at the public meeting and was escorted out of the room by Mulvane police.[55] She sued the City of Mulvane for violating her constitutionally protected right of free speech.[56] Judge Belot ruled in favor of the protester and held that the city's and the mayor's actions were constitutionally prohibited.[57]

At the time of the writing of this book, Judge Belot continues not only to hear cases but to hear cases of great import. In August 2010, James Bopp Jr., a lawyer resident in Terre Haute, Indiana, filed a lawsuit on behalf of four Kansans that challenges the process by which Kansas selects its Supreme Court justices.[58] This suit is a step in the several year-long quests by certain groups in Kansas, led by Americans for Prosperity, to force a change to give the Kansas Legislature a greater say in the current selection process.[59] The case is crucial to the constitutional and governmental structure of the Kansas judiciary and Judge Belot will play a major role in its resolution.

Judge John Watson Lungstrum

Judge John Watson Lungstrum was born in Topeka, Kansas, in 1945.[60] He attended Yale University as a "scholar of the house" and received his BA degree from Yale in 1967.[61] He then returned to Kansas and enrolled at the University of Kansas School of Law, where he served as editor-in-chief of the *Kansas Law Review* before receiving a JD degree.[62] After graduation he moved to California to begin the practice of law, but his fledgling practice was interrupted by his service in the U.S. Army as a lieutenant. In 1972 he returned to Lawrence, Kansas, and remained there in the private practice of law until he was nominated in 1991 by President George H. W. Bush to succeed Judge Dale Saffels on the Federal District Court of Kansas. He took his seat on the bench in November 1991. He served as chief judge of the Kansas District from 2001 to 2007.

Judge Lungstrum at his desk in Korea while serving in the army, 1972.

During his years on the bench, Judge Lungstrum has gained a national reputation as a brilliant jurist capable of handling a wide variety of cases. Among the many in which he participated, a couple merit discussion. For instance, Judge Lungstrum mediated a complex and newsworthy case involving the J. C. Nichols Company in the mid-1990s. The lawsuit, brought by

Judge John Watson Lungstrum.

shareholders and ESOP (Employee stock ownership plan) participants (and ultimately joined by the company), alleged breaches of fiduciary duty concerning deals entered into by management. Although the case was pending in the Western District of Missouri, Judge Lungstrum was asked by the parties and that court to mediate the matter. The *Kansas City Star* reported that secret settlement talks among all the parties and their lawyers (including involved insurance companies) lasted for three days with one session lasting until nearly 2 a.m. Judge Lungstrum successfully resolved the case with impressive doses of forceful diplomacy and determination.

Judge Lungstrum also presided over a major tobacco case against R. J. Reynolds by a plaintiff whose legs had to be amputated as a result of his smoking.[63] Judge Lungstrum awarded the plaintiff $15 million in punitive damages and characterized the tobacco company's deliberate concealment of the dangers of smoking as "nefarious."[64]

In addition to bearing the many burdens of a federal district judge, including seven years as chief judge, Judge Lungstrum also taught for more than two decade at the University of Kansas School of Law.[65] Every semester, Judge Lungstrum would arrive at the law school before eight in the morning to teach generations of law students.[66]

Active District Judges

Judge Kathryn Hoefer Vratil

Chief Federal District Judge Kathryn Hoefer Vratil was born in 1949 in Manhattan, Kansas.[67] She received her BA from the University of Kansas in 1971 and her JD in 1975. After graduation she became law clerk for Judge Earl O'Connor and served in that capacity until 1978. From 1978 until 1992 Vratil was in the private practice of law in Kansas City, Missouri. In addition, from 1990 to 1992 she served as a municipal court judge for the City of Prairie Village, Kansas. In July 1992 she was nominated by President George H. W.

Judge Kathryn Hoefer Vratil.

Bush to succeed Judge O'Connor on the Federal District Court of Kansas and took her seat in October 1992. In 2008 Judge Vratil became Chief Judge Vratil and holds this post today.

Judge Vratil was a pioneer in law school and a pioneer on the bench. She was one of only

Judges O'Connor, Stanley, and Vratil.

fourteen women in her law school class.[68] Upon graduation she became the first woman law clerk for Judge O'Connor. When she joined the District Court in 1992 she became the first woman to sit on that court in Kansas. Her ascension to the chief judgeship likewise was a first. In a life of so much accomplishment and so many "firsts," it is notable that she highlights an early case over which she presided as especially memorable.[69] The case was a suit brought by NCAA member school coaches against the NCAA's policy which "capped"

salaries for most of the coaches, allegedly in violation of federal antitrust laws.[70] The case, not surprisingly, gained national attention and one of the witnesses in the case was none other than Roy Williams, the great KU basketball coach.[71] Chief Judge Vratil is proud—and rightfully so—of the fact that her decision in this case has become a standard in law school textbooks.[72] It is a model of clear writing and precise analysis and was a harbinger of more such decisions to come.

Judge J. Thomas Marten

Judge J. Thomas Marten was born in Topeka, Kansas, in 1951.[73] He was born into a judicial family: his great uncle was Judge Delmas C. Hill.[74] Marten remembers that his uncle would bring him to his chambers as a small boy. He received his BA degree from Washburn University in 1973 and his JD from the Washburn Law School in 1976.[75] From 1976 to 1977 he clerked for Justice Tom Clark of the United States Supreme Court, the highest honor any law school graduate can achieve. He entered private practice in Omaha, Nebraska, in 1977. From 1980 to 1981 he practiced in Minneapolis, Minnesota, and then moved to McPherson, Kansas, where he remained in private practice for fifteen years.

Judge J. Thomas Marten.

Judge Marten (back row, fourth from right) is pictured in this group photograph of the United States Supreme Court clerks for the 1976-77 term of court.

Judge Marten was nominated by President Bill Clinton to succeed Judge Patrick Kelly in October 1995 and received his commission as a federal judge in January 1996.

Judge Marten is a perfect example that federal judges can be highly creative people. His first aspiration professionally was not the law, but songwriting, an activity he continues to embrace.[76] But his creativity is not limited to music. Judge Marten has also been creative in his courtroom. He has adopted a practice pioneered in Arizona of having litigants' attorneys make their opening statements before jury selection in voir dire begins.[77] Judge Marten finds this technique to make for more efficient voir dire and to raise the "comfort level" of the jury.[78] Judge Marten has used this technique for thirteen years and it has attracted national attention.[79] Indeed, Judge Marten teaches a one-week trial procedure course at Harvard Law School every other year.[80] Trial efficiency—and costs to litigants—are very much a concern of Judge Marten. It is his fear that the cost of justice has meant a "loss of accessibility" to the courts over the years. His efforts at increasing trial efficiency and lowering litigation costs have influenced his innovative jury selection procedures and also led him to serve on the court's Bench-Bar Committee and to champion Rule 1's mandate to federal judges to increase court efficiency and lessen the time needed for litigation in the federal court system.[81]

Judge Marten plays guitar with his band, "The Shoes."

Judge Carlos Murguia.

Judge Carlos Murguia

Judge Carlos Murguia was born to immigrant parents in Kansas City, Kansas, in 1957.[82] Carlos Murguia attended the University of Kansas and received his BS in 1979 from the university and his JD from the law school in 1982.[83] He was in private practice from 1982 until 1987. He also served as a hearing officer in Wyandotte County from 1984 to 1990 and as the coordinator for immigration amnesty programs for El Centro from 1985 until 1990. In 1990 he was appointed as a District Court judge in Wyandotte County, Kansas, a position he retained until 1999. In March 1999 President Bill Clinton nominated Judge Murguia to succeed Judge Sam Crow on the Federal District Court of Kansas. He was confirmed on September 8, 1999, and assumed his place on the court on September 22, 1999. Judge Murguia was the first federal district judge for the District of Kansas of Hispanic origins.

Of the many cases presided over by Judge Murguia during his tenure on the federal bench, one of the most fascinating—and colorful—was the trial and sentencing of Michael C. Cooper, founder and head of Renaissance, the Tax People, a company that specialized in giving tax advice to and

The Murguia Family

Judge Carlos Murguia belongs to a remarkably successful immigrant family from Mexico, who settled in the Argentine neighborhood of Kansas City, Kansas. Of Alfred and Amalia Murguia's seven children, four hold law degrees –three from KU and one from Harvard—and two are federal judges. While Carlos sits in the District of Kansas, his sister, the Hon. Mary Murguia, served as a federal district judge in Arizona for ten years and in 2010 was appointed to a seat on the Ninth Circuit Court of Appeals. The Murguias are the only brother and sister federal judges in the United States. Mary's

The Murguia family.

twin sister, Janet Murguia, is president of the National Council of La Raza, a national Hispanic civil rights and advocacy organization, and their brother, Ramon Murguia, is a successful businessman and attorney in Kansas City, Kansas. The three nonlawyer siblings have all been successful in their own right. Five of the Murguia siblings, as well as their mother, Amalia, still reside in Argentine, where the close-knit family has maintained a strong presence for over sixty years. In fact, Carlos's wife, Ann Brandau-Murguia, is a member of the Board of Commissioners for the Unified Government of Wyandotte County and Kansas City, Kansas, representing Argentine, Rosedale, and the surrounding area.

filing tax returns for the wealthy.[84] Mr. Cooper had a colorful career before the courts.[85] In a February 2001 hearing he claimed Fifth Amendment protection fifty-five times.[86] He was jailed for contempt of court in May 2003 in Shawnee County, Kansas.[87] Later freed, he was again arrested while at the Mexican border in October 2004.[88] His 2008 trial in federal court lasted seven weeks and resulted in conviction on seventy-three counts and acquittal on seventy-five counts.[89] In April 2008, Mr. Cooper was sentenced by Judge Murguia, after a dramatic four-hour hearing, to twenty years in prison, $10,670,000 in restitution to the Internal Revenue Service, and forfeiture of approximately $75 million in property.[90]

Judge Robinson testifies before Congress on courthouse usage as chair of the Committee on Court Administration and Case Management in 2010.

Judge Julie Robinson.

Judge Julie Robinson

Judge Julie Robinson was born in Omaha, Nebraska, in 1957.[91] She received her undergraduate degree from the University of Kansas in 1978 and her law degree in 1981. From 1981 to 1983 she clerked for Judge Benjamin Franklin of the United States Bankruptcy Court and in 1983 became an assistant United States attorney in the District of Kansas.

Judge Julie Robinson.

She remained at the U.S. Attorney's Office until she was appointed as a United States bankruptcy judge in 1994. In September 2001 Judge Robinson was nominated by President George W. Bush to succeed Judge Thomas VanBebber as a federal district judge. She received her commission and began her judgeship in December 2001.

Judge Robinson was the first African American and the second woman to serve as a federal district judge in Kansas. Her career has been meteoric and, as she relates, always filled with the unexpected.[92] An example Judge Robinson likes to cite is the time a rancher brought his cattle to the courthouse as part of a bankruptcy proceeding. Her appointment to the Federal District Court was also not routine. She was nominated by President George W. Bush on September 10.[93] At that time, the president would generally telephone the judicial nominee the next day to congratulate her.[94] But, in Judge Robinson's case, the next day was 9/11 and the president was, of course, unable to call. When she went to Washington, D.C., for her confirmation hearings, the U.S. Senate was in the middle of the anthrax crisis and senators had evacuated their offices. Nonetheless, Judge Robinson managed to get confirmed.

Like all federal district judges in Kansas, Judge Robinson carries a heavy and diverse caseload. Of the many cases she has heard in her decade on the bench, none, perhaps, has garnered so much local and national attention as the prosecution of David Wittig, former CEO of Westar Energy.[95] In April 2006 Judge Robinson sentenced Mr. Wittig to eighteen years in prison and $19,500,000 in fines and restitution.[96] The conviction was overturned in 2007 and a new trial was set for September 2010.[97] However, before the trial could take place, the United States Supreme Court issued its decision in *Skilling v. United States*, in which the court limited the application of the "honest services law," which had been critical not only in Skilling's prosecution but also in Wittig's.[98] As a result the case against Wittig was dropped before it went to trial.

Judge Eric Melgren

Judge Eric Melgren is the most recent appointee to the Federal District Court of Kansas. Judge Melgren was born in Minneola, Kansas, in 1956.[99] He grew up there and decided in the fifth grade that he wanted to become a lawyer.[100] He received his BA from Wichita State University in 1979 and his JD from the Washburn University School of Law in 1985.[101] From 1985 to 1987 he was law clerk to Judge Frank Theis on the Kansas Federal District Court. From 1987 until 2002 he was in private practice in Wichita, Kansas. In 2002 Judge Melgren was appointed the United States attorney for the District of Kansas and served in that position until he was nominated by President George W. Bush to succeed Judge Monti Belot on the Federal District Court. His appointment came in the waning days of the Bush administration but the unanimous support of the Kansas senators and his receipt of the highest possible recommendation by the nonpartisan American Bar Association's Committee on Judicial Qualifications ensured an easy confirmation.[102] He took his seat on the Federal District Court on October 6, 2008.[103]

Judge Melgren lecturing at Washburn University Law School.

While Judge Melgren's stay on the Federal District Court has been short, it has not been idle. Among the most important cases over which he has presided so far must rank the age discrimination suit filed in 2005 against Boeing Co. and AeroSystems.[104] Ninety former Boeing workers sued the company, alleging that they had been fired because of their age, a violation of the Age Discrimination in Employment Act.[105] Judge Melgren ruled against the workers in June 2010.

In 2009 Judge Melgren found himself in the midst of the great controversy between Sunflower Electric Power Co., which wished to build new coal-fired utility plants in Western Kansas, and the Kansas state government, which, through the rulings of the secretary of the Department of Health and Environment, had banned construction.[106]

Judge Melgren has also not been without the more unusual cases. In a case that highlights the dangers of Internet exposure, a young woman and her mother sued the young woman's former boyfriend.[107] She had allowed him to photograph her while she was engaged in various sexual activities. The young man later sent copies of these

Judge Eric F. Melgren.

photographs via email to his former lover's family and co-workers. The young woman and her mother sued for invasion of privacy and infliction of emotional distress. Judge Melgren found himself presiding over this suit, which resulted in a jury verdict for plaintiffs.

The Caseload of the Court Yesterday and Today

The work of the Federal District Court of Kansas has never been easy, but if one studies the history of the court's workload over time, it becomes absolutely clear that the burden on each judge and on the court staff has grown astronomically since its founding a century and a half ago. In the earliest days of the court, the number of cases that would be decided by the federal district judge in a year tended to stay well below one hundred.[108] By its centennial in 1951, the court's caseload was up to about seven hundred cases, for which there were only two judges. Today, that number has again increased substantially. In 2006 there were 2,300 case filings in the Federal District Court of Kansas.[109] There were also 2,426 case terminations and 1,896 cases pending in 2006. To accomplish all of this work, there were six federal district judges, three senior district judges, and seven federal magistrate judges. Today, one hundred and fifty years after its founding, the Federal District Court of Kansas is a complex judicial organization composed of federal district judges, federal magistrate judges, federal bankruptcy judges, law clerks, and other staff who provide a forum for dispute adjudication for over two million Kansans.

Leadership

There is another role that has been filled by many of the judges in the Federal District for Kansas that is not so public. Kansas federal judges have provided leadership in a large number of ways to the federal judiciary as a whole. This type of service—quiet, time-consuming, unrewarded—is essential for the proper functioning of the federal courts. Kansas federal judges have been involved in some of the most significant judicial committees and exercised leadership thereon. Judge Wesley Brown has served on the Judicial Conference of the United States and on the Committee on the Administration of the Bankruptcy System. Judge Sam Crow has served on the Advisory Committee on Criminal Rules. Judge John Lungstrum has sat on the Committee on the Budget, and was both a member of and chair of the Committee on Court Administration and Case Management. Judge Thomas Marten

has sat on the Committee on Information Technology for the federal courts. Bankruptcy Judge Robert Nugent sits on the Committee on Federal-State Jurisdiction.

During his lifetime, Judge Earl E. O'Connor sat on the Executive Committee, the Judicial Conference of the United States, the Committee on the Judicial Branch, and the Committee on Court Administration. Federal Magistrate Judge James O'Hara sits on the Committee on Judicial Resources. Judge Julie Robinson has been a member and chair of the Committee on Court Administration and Case Management. Judge Richard Rogers has sat on the Committee on Space and Facilities, and Judge Dale Saffels sat on the Committee on Financial Disclosure. Judge Arthur Stanley sat on the Judicial Conference of the United States and on the Committee on the Operation of the Jury System. Judge Tom VanBebber sat on the Committee on the Administration of the Magistrate Judges System. Chief Judge Kathryn Vratil sits on the Judicial Panel on Multi-District Litigation, the Committee on the Administrative Office, and the FJC Committee for District Judge Education. Federal Bankruptcy Judge Dale L. Somers sits on the Committee for Judicial Resources. Considering how much else these federal judges must do as part of their job, their voluntary service in leadership positions that maintain and improve the federal judiciary is all the more remarkable.

Notes to Chapter 7

1. *The Hon. Wesley E. Brown*, WESLEY E. BROWN INN OF COURT, www.webinnofcourt.org/the-hon-wesley-e-brown (last visited Jan. 23, 2011).

2. *See id*; Mark Fagan, *150 Years of Style*, LJ WORLD, (Sept. 30, 2007), http://www2.ljworld.com/news/2007/sep/30/150_years_style.

3. *See The Hon. Wesley E. Brown, supra* note 1.

4. H.R. Res. 512, 110th Cong. (2007).

5. *The Hon. Wesley E. Brown, supra* note 1.

6. *Id*; *History of the Federal Judiciary: Brown, Wesley Ernest*, FED. JUD. CTR., http://www.fjc.gov/servlet/nGetInfo?jid=289 (last visited Jan. 23, 2011) [hereinafter *FJC: Brown*].

7. *The Hon. Wesley E. Brown, supra* note 1; *FJC: Brown*.

8. *FJC: Brown*.

9. Edward Ranzal, *Speed-Up Starts In Federal Court*, N.Y. TIMES, Mar. 12, 1968, at 1.

10. Case No. 04-1253-WEB, 2006 U.S. Dist. LEXIS 87194 (D. Kan. Nov. 29, 2006).

11. *See Man Becomes U.S. Citizen Without Oath to Bear Arms*, N.Y. TIMES, Sept. 6, 1966, at 21.

12. *See Seven Decades of Justice*, KAKE NEWS, (May 19, 2006), http://www.kake.com/news/headlines/2833541.html.

13. *Federal Court Voids Loyalty Oath*, N.Y. TIMES, Sept. 12, 1967, at 51.

14. *Ehrenreich v. Londerholm*, 273 F. Supp. 178, 180 (D. Kan. 1967).

15. *Judge Rules Helium Producers in Gas Field Needn't Share Profit With Royalty Owners*, WALL ST. J., Sept. 11, 1968, at 5.

16. *Black Rail Porters Win $6 Million From Union*, N.Y. TIMES, Dec. 3, 1982, at A16.

17. *Seven Decades of Justice, supra* note 12.

18. *History of the Federal Judiciary: Rogers, Richard Dean*, FED. JUD. CTR., http://www.fjc.gov/servlet/nGetInfo?jid=2042 (last visited Jan. 23, 2011) [hereinafter *FJC: Rogers*].

19. Awards include, Warren W. Shaw Distinguished Service Award (2007). *Topeka Bar Association Awards*, TOPEKA BAR ASS'N, (last viewed July 22, 2010), http://www.topekabar.com/awards.html. KU Law Society Distinguished Alumni Award (1980). *Distinguished Alumni*, KU SCHOOL OF LAW, (last accessed June 1, 2010), http://www.law.ku.edu/~kulaw/alumni/distinguished.

20. *See Court Ruling Hits NCAA*, CHI. TRIB., Aug. 11, 1976, at C4.

21. *Federal Judge Asserts U.S. Cannot Imprison Refugees Indefinitely*, N.Y. TIMES, Jan. 2, 1981, at A1.

22. 505 F. Supp. 787 (D. Kan. 1980).

23. *Id* at 792.

24. *The Winner, Pedro Rodriguez*, CHI. TRIB., Jan. 8, 1981, at B2.

25. Jeff Prugh, *Debate Rises Over Cuban Refugees Still*

Imprisoned, L.A. TIMES, June 14, 1981, at A1.

26. *See Brown v. Board of Education*, 84 F.R.D. 383 (D. Kan. 1979). *See also Landmark Segregation Case Revived to Probe Compliance After 25 Years*, L.A. TIMES, Nov. 30, 1979, at B4.

27. *Brown v. Bd. of Educ.*, 671 F. Supp. 1290 (D. Kan. 1987).

28. *See, e.g., Judge Rules Topeka Schools Are Not Segregated*, N.Y. TIMES, Apr. 10, 1987, at A19; *Segregation Ruling "Incredible," Says ACLU*, NEW J. & GUIDE, Apr. 22, 1987, at 11.

29. *See Topeka's Redemption*, WALL ST. J., Apr. 16, 1987, at 30.

30. *Brown v. Bd. of Educ.*, 892 F.2d 851 (10th Cir. 1989).

31. *See Brown v. Unified School District No. 501*, 56 F. Supp.2d 1212 (D. Kan. 1999) (dismissing the case).

32. *History of the Federal Judiciary: Crow, Sam A.*, FED. JUD. CTR., http://www.fjc.gov/servlet/nGetInfo?jid=538 (last visited Jan. 23, 2011) [hereinafter *FJC: Crow*].

33. *FJC: Crow*.

34. *Honorary Doctor of Law*, WASHBURN UNIV. SCH. OF LAW, http://www.washburnlaw.edu/alumni/honorarydegrees/pastrecipients/index.php (last visited Jan. 23, 2011).

35. *Id.*

36. *FJC: Crow*; Steve Henry, *Judge Sam A. Crow Discusses Federal Judicial Appointment Process*, WASHBURN UNIV. SCH. OF LAW (Apr. 21, 2004), http://www.washburnlaw.edu/news/2004/2004-04pdp-crow.php; *See also Judge Sam Crow Moving to Topeka*, 61 J. KAN. B. ASS'N 3 (Jan. 1992).

37. *Honorary Doctor of Law, supra* note 34.

38. Kansas Bar Association Phil Lewis Medal of Distinction. *Hon. Sam A. Crow Receives Kansas Bar Association Phil Lewis Medal of Distinction*, KAN. BAR ASS'N, (June 14, 2010), http://www.ksbar.org/public/kba/2010_news/crow.shtml. Warren W. Shaw Distinguished Service Award (2000). *Topeka Bar Association Awards*, TOPEKA BAR ASS'N, (last viewed July 22, 2010), http://www.topekabar.com/awards.html. 2000 Distinguished Service Award from Washburn Law School. *Recipients*, WASHBURN UNIVERSITY SCHOOL OF LAW, http://www.washburnlaw.edu/alumni/association/awards/distinguished.php. (Other awards include: Who's Who in America, 2005 Shriner of the Year.)

39. 188 F. Supp. 2d 1287 (D. Kan. 2002).

40. 509 U.S. 579 (1993).

41. 526 U.S. 137 (1999).

42. *See, e.g.,* David L. Faigman, *Is Science Different For Lawyers?* 297 SCI. 339 (July 19, 2002).

43. *U.S. v. Cline*, 188 F. Supp. 2d 1287, 1294 (D. Kan. 2002).

44. *Protester Gets "New" Draft Status*, CHI. TRIB., Mar. 9, 1983, at 3.

45. *Id; Mennonite Ends Draft Ordeal*, CHI. TRIB., (Mar. 11, 1983).

46. *See* Leslie Wayne, *The Very Private Energy Giant Opens Up, Thanks Largely to an Ugly Family Fight*, N.Y. TIMES, Nov. 20, 1994, at F1.

47. Leslie Wayne, *Brother Versus Brother*, N.Y. TIMES, Apr. 28, 1998, at D1.

48. *See Koch v. Koch Indus.*, 6 F. Supp. 2d 1185 (D. Kan. 1998).

49. *See Koch v. Koch Indus.*, 203 F.3d 1202 (10th Cir. 2000).

50. Steve Fry, *Man on a Mission*, TOPEKA CAPITAL-J., (Aug. 05, 2003), *available at* http://cjonline.com/stories/080503/loc_mcknight.shtml.

51. *History of the Federal Judiciary: Belot, Monti L.*, FED. JUD. CTR., http://www.fjc.gov/servlet/nGetInfo?jid=152 (last visited Jan. 23, 2011) [hereinafter *FJC: Belot*].

52. *Nurse Convicted for "Nude Therapy,"* TOPEKA CAPITAL-J., Oct. 27, 2009, *available at* http://cjonline.com/news/state/2009-10-27/nurse_convicted_for_nude_therapy; Ron Sylvester, *Sentence for Arlan Kaufman…*, THE WICHITA EAGLE, Jan. 24, 2006, at 1.

53. *U.S. v. Kaufman*, 546 F.3d 1242 (10th Cir. 2008); *Id.*

54. *See Fansworth v. City of Mulvane*, 660 F. Supp. 2d 1217 (D. Kan. 2009).

55. *Id* at 1222-23; *Judge: Mulvane Violated Rights*, TOPEKA CAPITAL-J., Sept. 16, 2009, *available at* http://cjonline.com/news/state/2009-09-16/judge_mulvane_violated_rights.

56. *Fansworth*, 660 F. Supp. 2d at 1223.

57. *Id* at 1229.

58. Verified Complaint for Declaratory and Injunctive Relief, *Dool v. Burke*, No. 10-1286 (D. Kan. Aug. 25, 2010); Ron Sylvester, *Lawsuit Seeks to Change How Kansas Supreme Court Judges are Appointed*, WICHITA EAGLE, Aug. 26, 2010, *available at* http://www.kansas.com/2010/08/26/1464343/lawsuit-seeks-to-change-how-kansas.html.

59. *See, e.g.,* David Hanna, *Kansans Deserve Better Judicial Selection*, AFP KS. BLOG (Feb. 13, 2006), http://www.americansforprosperity.org/kansans-deserve-better-judicial-selection.

60. *History of the Federal Judiciary: Lungstrum, John Watson*, FED. JUD. CTR., http://www.fjc.gov/servlet/nGetInfo?jid=1439 (last visited Jan. 23, 2011) [hereinafter *FJC: Lungstrum*].

61. *Two distinguished alumni earn law school's highest honor*, http://www.news.ku.edu/2010/may/19/lawalumni.shtml (last visited July 27, 2011).

62. Hon. John W. Lungstrum, THOMSON REUTERS, http://pview.findlaw.com/view/2152407_1?channel=LP (last visited Jan. 23, 2011).

63. *See Burton v. R.J. Reynolds Tobacco Co.*, 205 F. Supp. 2d 1253 (D. Kan. 2002). *See also* Myron Levin, *R.J. Reynolds Ordered to Pay Smoker $15 Million*, L.A. TIMES, June 22, 2002, *available at* http://articles.latimes.com/2002/jun/22/business/fi-smoke22.

64. *Burton*, 205 F. Supp. 2d at 1255-56.

65. Interview by Jessica McCloskey with Hon. John Watson Lungstrum, Judge, U.S. Dist. Court, Dist. of Kan., in Kan. City, Kan. (July 30, 2010) [hereinafter Interview with Hon. John Watson Lungstrum]. *See also FJC: Lungstrum*.

66. Interview with Hon. John Watson Lungstrum.

67. *History of the Federal Judiciary: Vratil, Kathryn Hoefer*, FED. JUD. CTR., http://www.fjc.gov/servlet/nGetInfo?jid=2469 (last

visited Jan. 23, 2011) [hereinafter *FJC: Vratil*].

68. Interview by Ryan Schwarzenberger with Hon. Kathryn Hoefer Vratil, Judge, U.S. Dist. Court, Dist. of Kan., in Kan. City, Kan. (July 20, 2010) [hereinafter Interview with Hon. Kathryn Hoefer Vratil].

69. Interview with Hon. Kathryn Hoefer Vratil.

70. *Law v. NCAA*, 902 F. Supp. 1394, (D. Kan. 1995).

71. Interview with Hon. Kathryn Hoefer Vratil. *See also* Kirk Johnson, *Colleges; Assistant Coaches Win N.C.A.A. Suit; $66 Million Award*, N.Y. TIMES, May 5, 1988.

72. Interview with Hon. Kathryn Hoefer Vratil.

73. *History of the Federal Judiciary: Marten, John Thomas*, FED. JUD. CTR., Marten, John Thomas, http://www.fjc.gov/servlet/nGetInfo?jid=1490 (last visited Jan. 23, 2011) [hereinafter *FJC: Marten*].

74. Interview by Ryan Schwarzenberger & Jessica McCloskey with Hon. J. Thomas Marten, Judge, U.S. Dist. Court, Dist. of Kan., in Wichita, Kan. (June 23, 2010) [hereinafter Interview with Hon. J. Thomas Marten].

75. *FJC: Marten.*

76. Interview with Hon. J. Thomas Marten.

77. Interview with Hon. J. Thomas Marten. *See also* Hon. J. Thomas Marten, *A Few Thoughts And Reminders On Trial Practice*, PRAC. LITIGATOR, Sept. 2009, at 11, 12.

78. Interview with Hon. J. Thomas Marten.

79. *FJC* Marten.

80 Interview with Hon. J. Thomas Marten.

81. *Id. See also*, FED. R. CIV. P. 1.

82. *History of the Federal Judiciary: Murguia, Carlos*, FED. JUD. CTR., http://www.fjc.gov/servlet/nGetInfo?jid=2832 (last visited Jan. 23, 2011) [hereinafter *FJC: Murguia*]; see also, Manny Lopez, *Raising the Bar: Murguia Family has Deep Roots in the Argentine Neighborhood of Kansas City*, Kansas City Bus. J., (Feb. 9, 2001).

83. *FJC: Murguia.*

84. *See U.S. v. Cooper*, 2007 WL 1201460 (D. Kan. Apr. 23, 2007), 2009 WL 1010221 (D. Kan. Apr. 14, 2009), 2010 WL 2737136 (D. Kan. Apr. 21, 2010); Steve Fry, *Tax People Head to be Sentenced*, TOPEKA CAPITAL-J, (Mar. 16, 2010), http://cjonline.com/news/local/2010-03-16/tax_people_head_to_be_sentenced.

85. Steve Fry, *Federal Agents Raid Renaissance*, TOPEKA CAPITAL-J., (Oct. 12, 2000), http://cjonline.com/indepth/renaissance/stories/101200_irsraid.shtml.

86. Steve Fry & Jonna Lorenz, *Witness Mum; Invokes Fifth*, TOPEKA CAPITAL-J., (Feb. 14, 2001), http://cjonline.com/indepth/renaissance/stories/021501_carterrenaissance.shtml.

87. Steve Fry, *Pyramid Scheme Suspect Sent to Jail for Contempt*, TOPEKA CAPITAL-J, (May 15, 2003), http://cjonline.com/stories/051503/bus_renaissance.shtml.

88. Michael Hooper, *Renaissance Leader Arrested*, TOPEKA CAPITAL-J, (Oct. 27, 2004), http://cjonline.com/stories/102704/loc_renaissance.shtml.

89. *See Tax People Head to be Sentenced, supra* note 84.

90. Steve Fry, *Cooper Sentenced to 20 Years*, TOPEKA

CAPITAL-J., Apr. 20, 2010, *available at* http://cjonline.com/news/local/2010-04-20/cooper_sentenced_to_20_years.

91. *History of the Federal Judiciary: Robinson, Julie A.*, FED. JUD. CTR., http://www.fjc.gov/servlet/nGetInfo?jid=2908 (last visited Jan. 23, 2011) [hereinafter *FJC: Robinson*].

92. Interview by Ryan Schwarzenberger with Hon. Julie Robinson, Judge, U.S. Dist. Court, Dist. of Kan., in Topeka, Kan. (June 30, 2010) [hereinafter Interview with Hon. Julie A. Robinson].

93. *FJC: Robinson.*

94. Interview with Hon. Julie A. Robinson.

95. *See, e.g., Retrial Planned for Westar Officials*, N.Y. TIMES, Feb. 2, 2005.

96. *U.S. v. Lake*, 472 F.3d 1247, 54 (10th Cir. 2007).

97. *Id*; Steve Fry, *Lake-Wittig Case Dismissed*, TOPEKA CAPITAL-J. (Aug. 19, 2010), http://cjonline.com/news/local/2010-08-19/lake_wittig_case_dismissed.

98. *United States v. Lake*, No. 03-40142-02-JAR, slip op. at 1-2 (D. Kan. Jan. 6, 2011); *U.S. v. Skilling*, 130 S. Ct. 2896 (US 2010).

99. *History of the Federal Judiciary: Melgren, Eric F.*, FED. JUD. CTR., http://www.fjc.gov/servlet/nGetInfo?jid=3195 (last visited Jan. 23, 2011) [hereinafter *FJC: Melgren*].

100. Interview by Ryan Schwarzenberger & Jessica McCloskey with Hon. Eric F. Melgren, Judge, U.S. Dist. Court, Dist. of Kan., in Wichita, Kan. (June 23, 2010).

101. *FJC: Melgren.*

102. Interview with Hon. Eric F. Melgren.

103. *FJC: Melgren.*

104. *Apsley v. Boeing*, 722 F. Supp. 2d 1218, 1225 (D. Kan. 2010); *see also Judge Drops Age Lawsuit Against Boeing, Sprint*, MANUFACTURING.NET (June 30, 2010), http://www.manufacturing.net/News-Judge-Drops-Age-Lawsuit-Against-Boeing-Spirit-063010.aspx.

105. *Apsley*, 722 F. Supp. 2d at 1225.

106. *See* David Lisi, *Kansas Judge Takes Sunflower Arguments Under Advisement*, GLOBAL CLIMATE LAW BLOG, Feb. 23, 2009, http://www.globalclimatelaw.com/2009/02/articles/climate-change-litigation/kansas-judge-takes-sunflower-arguments-under-advisement-legislature-may-moot-ruling.

107. Kashmir Hill, *Women Sues Ex-Boyfriend for Sending Sex Photos to her Family and Co-Workers*, TRUE/SLANT, (Oct. 14, 2009) http://trueslant.com/KashmirHill/2009/10/14/75000-sex-photos-lawsuit-piper-peterson-michael-moldofsky.

108. *See* Paul E. Wilson, *The Early Years: The Bench and Bar Before 1882, in* REQUISITE LEARNING AND GOOD MORAL CHARACTER: A HISTORY OF THE KANSAS BAR, 27, 35 (Robert W. Richmond, ed., 1982); James K. Logan, *The Federal Courts and Their Judges-The Impact on Kansas History, in* THE LAW AND LAWYERS IN KANSAS HISTORY 57, 63 (Virgil W. Dean ed., 1993).

109. *Judicial Caseload Profile – Kansas*, U.S. DISTRICT COURT, http://www.uscourts.gov/cgi-bin/cmsd2006.pl (last visited Feb. 16, 2011).

District of Kansas magistrate judges in 2010: (front row) Donald W. Bostwick and K. Gary Sebelius; (back row) James P. O'Hara, Gerald Cohn, Karen M. Humphreys, Gerald L. Rushfelt, and David J. Waxse.

8

THE MODERN COURT: FEDERAL MAGISTRATE AND BANKRUPTCY JUDGES

Since the 1790s, federal district judges have always had staff to assist them in their many tasks. Among these staff were "commissioners" whose appointments, emoluments, and duties carried from court to court.[1] When it became apparent after the Second World War that judicial caseloads were growing rapidly and the complexity of many of these cases was also increasing, the federal judiciary realized that it would be helpful to transform the position of commissioner into a quasi-judgeship and expand their jurisdiction.

In 1968 Congress passed and the president signed into law the Federal Magistrates Act of 1968, which permanently established the position of federal magistrate.[2] In 1990 by act of Congress, the title was changed to federal magistrate judge.[3] In 1976 Congress provided that federal magistrate judges had the authority to conduct evidentiary hearings in response to a 1974 Supreme Court decision that such hearings were not permitted under the 1968 Federal Magistrates Act.[4] The Federal Magistrates Act of 1979 expanded the jurisdiction and authority of federal magistrate judges to include all civil trials so long as the parties involved consented.[5] The act also authorized federal magistrate judges to conduct misdemeanor criminal trials so long as the defendant waived the right to a jury trial. Finally, the act clarified the process for the appointment of federal magistrate judges and authorized the creation of merit selection panels to assist in the process.

Today federal magistrate judges have the authority and jurisdiction to conduct much of the business of federal district courts except for felony criminal proceedings.[6] Federal magistrate judges do not have life tenure; instead full-time magistrate judges are appointed for a term of eight years, and part-time federal magistrate judges are appointed for a term of four years.[7] The terms may be renewed.[8]

Unlike the selection process for federal district judges, federal magistrate judges are appointed by the federal district judges of each district with the advice of a merit selection panel.[9] Federal magistrate judges do not require presidential nomination or senatorial approval.[10] The total number of federal magistrate judges is determined by the Judicial Conference of the United States.[11] Currently, more than five hundred federal magistrate judges hold office full time and approximately forty are part time.[12] Federal magistrate judge positions are allocated on the basis of each district's caseload and other local conditions of each judicial district.[13]

The significance of federal magistrate judges in the administration of the federal judicial system cannot be overstated. According to data collected by the Federal Magistrate Judges Association, during the period from September 2007 to September 2008, federal magistrate judges performed 968,921 "judicial activities."[14] This number included 269,071 civil pretrial duties, hearing 175,241 motions, 21,602 settlement conferences, and 49,915 other pretrial activities. Federal magistrate judges performed 164,937 felony pretrial duties and concluded 10,814 civil cases with parties' consent. Federal magistrate judges also submitted 22,745 recommendations to federal district court judges on habeas corpus and prisoner civil rights cases. The list could go on. What these statistics make eminently clear is that without federal magistrate judges and the enormous number of duties they fulfill, the federal judiciary could not function.

The Federal District Court of Kansas has been a leader in utilizing federal magistrate judges since the inception of the office. Kansas was one of the first federal district courts to appoint magistrates. The federal district judges for the District of Kansas appointed two of the first federal magistrates in 1969 as part of the trial program that began after passage of the 1968 act.[15] Since then a number of distinguished, highly competent lawyers have served as federal magistrate judges.

Kansas Federal Magistrate Judges 1969–2011

	Last Name	First Name	Middle Initial	Commission Date	Active Service Terminated	Succession	Type	Location
1	Bannon	F.C.		6/1/1969	5/31/1980	New Position	PT	Leavenworth
2	Calihan	Ray	H	6/1/1969	4/30/1973	New Position	PT	Garden City
3	Chalfant	Michael	E	6/1/1969	10/5/1972	New Position	PT	Hutchinson
4	Flood	Steven	P	6/1/1969	8/13/1975	New Position	PT	Hays
5	Hannah	Jerry	W	6/1/1969	5/31/1973	New Position	PT	Topeka
6	Lord	David	S	6/1/1969	7/1/1972	New Position	PT	Salina
7	Markham	John	B	6/1/1969	1/31/1977	New Position	PT	Parsons
8	Miller	Robert	H	6/1/1969	10/30/1975	New Position	FT	Kansas City
9	Phillips	Donald	D	6/1/1969	9/30/1984	New Position	PT	Colby
10	Robertson	Walter	P	6/1/1969	4/9/1973	New Position	PT	Junction City
11	Wilson	Paul	E	6/1/1969	5/31/1973	New Position	PT	Lawrence
12	Wooley	John	B	6/1/1969	9/30/1993	New Position	FT	Wichita
13	Barta	Ronald	D	2/1/1973	1/31/1977	vice - Lord	PT	Salina
14	Brown	E.	Edward	5/2/1973	9/30/1984	vice - Calihan	PT	Garden City
15	Crow	Sam	A	6/1/1973	9/14/1975	vice - Hannah	PT	Topeka
16	Davis	Victor	A	6/4/1973	11/30/1987	vice - Robertson	PT	Junction City
17	Crow	Sam	A	9/15/1975	12/20/1981	New Position	FT	Topeka
18	Sullivant	J.	Milton	11/17/1975	9/8/1985	vice - Miller	FT	Kansas City
19	Wichman	Ross	J	10/1/1975	5/8/1978	vice - Flood	PT	Hays
20	Tillotson	John	C	6/10/1981	12/7/1997	New Position	PT	Leavenworth
21	VanBebber	G.	Thomas	6/14/1982	12/7/1989	vice - Crow	FT	Topeka
22	Reid	John	T	10/31/1984	11/16/2008	New Position	PT/FT	Wichita
23	Rushfelt	Gerald	L	9/9/1985		vice - Sullivant	FT	Kansas City
24	Newman	Ronald	C	3/26/1990	8/21/1999	vice - VanBebber	FT	Topeka
25	Humphreys	Karen	M	11/1/1993		vice - Wooley	FT	Wichita
26	Walter	Catherine	A	12/8/1997	2/20/2003	New Position	PT	Topeka
27	Bostwick	Donald	W	7/22/1999		vice - Reid	FT	Wichita
28	Waxse	David	J	10/4/1999		vice - Rushfelt	FT	Kansas City
29	O'Hara	James	P	4/17/2000		vice - Newman	FT	Topeka/ Kansas City
30	Sebelius	K.	Gary	2/21/2003		New Position	FT	Topeka
31	Cohn	Gerald	B	6/14/2009	9/1/2010	Temporary Position	PT	Wichita
32	Gale	Kenneth	G	8/2/2010		vice-Bostwick	FT	Wichita

Brief Biographies of Full-time Kansas Federal Magistrate Judges

Justice Robert H. Miller

In 1969 the judges of United States District Court for the District of Kansas appointed Robert H. Miller as one of the district's first two full-time federal magistrates.[16]

Justice Miller was born in Columbus, Ohio, in 1919 and grew up there and in Pittsburgh, Pennsylvania.[17] He attended college and law school at the University of Kansas, receiving a BA in 1940 and an LLB. in 1943. Miller served as a security and intelligence officer in the U.S. Army until 1946, when he returned to Kansas and settled in Miami County, where he practiced law and served as Miami County attorney and Paola city attorney. In 1960, he was elected to the bench, becoming a district court judge for Kansas' Sixth Judicial District.[18] He served in that capacity until his appointment as a federal magistrate in 1969. In 1975, he returned to the state court bench when he was appointed to the Kansas Supreme Court, becoming chief justice in 1988. In 1990, Justice Miller retired from the bench, and he died September 9, 2009.

Judge John B. Wooley

Also appointed in 1969 as one of the district's first two full-time federal magistrates was John B. Wooley.[19] John B. Wooley was born in 1926 in Wichita, Kansas, where he

grew up and attended school.[20] After graduating from high school, Wooley enlisted in the U.S. Navy, serving in the South Pacific theater.[21] After decorated service and an honorable discharge in July of 1947, he enrolled at Wichita State University, receiving a bachelor's degree 1952. Wooley then attended law school at Washburn University, receiving his law degree in 1956. After law school, he returned to the Wichita area, where he practiced from 1956 through his appointment to the federal bench on June 1, 1969. During his time in private practice, he served three years as a deputy prosecuting attorney in the Sedgwick County Attorney's office (1958–1961). Judge Wooley remained a federal magistrate judge until his retirement on October 1, 1993.[22] Throughout his career, he also participated in the active U.S. Army Reserve as both a member and officer, retiring in 1982 from the JAG Corps with a rank of colonel.[23] He spends his retirement in Wichita.

Judge Sam A. Crow

Judge Sam A. Crow was appointed the district's third full-time magistrate judge on September 15, 1975, after serving as a part-time magistrate for two years. Judge Crow was appointed a federal district judge in 1981; for a more detailed biography of Judge Crow, please see Chapter 7.

Judge J. Milton Sullivant

The district appointed J. Milton Sullivant as its fourth full-time magistrate judge in 1975. Sullivant was born on October 27, 1917, in Waverly, Kansas.[24] He attended Fort Scott

Junior College and then the University of Kansas, where he played football and captained the 1939 team. Sullivant received his law degree from KU in 1942 and then practiced briefly in Paola, Kansas, before joining the U.S. Navy. After his discharge at the end of the war, he settled his family in Kansas City, Kansas, where he was active in the bar, serving as president of both the Wyandotte and Miami County Bar Associations and as assistant county attorney for Wyandotte County for four years. In 1971, Sullivant was appointed as a federal bankruptcy judge and served in that capacity until his 1975 appointment as a federal magistrate judge. Judge Sullivant retired from the bench on September 8, 1985, and moved to Baldwin City, Kansas, where he operated a cattle ranch until his death on March 22, 2000.

Judge George Thomas VanBebber

On June 14, 1982, the judges of the district appointed George Thomas VanBebber to fill the federal magistrate judge vacancy created when Judge Crow assumed the federal district bench. Judge VanBebber himself became a federal district judge on December 8, 1989; for a more detailed biography of Judge VanBebber, please see Chapter 6.

Judge John Thomas Reid

On October 31, 1984, the judges of the district appointed John Thomas Reid to fill a newly created federal magistrate judgeship.[25] Reid was born in Newton, Kansas, in 1929.

He received a BA from Wichita State University in 1955 and an LLB from Washburn Law School in 1958. Following graduation from law school, he returned to Newton, where he opened his own law office and served as a municipal judge. In 1961 he became a probate judge for Harvey County. He served in this capacity until 1967, when he returned to private practice until 1971, at which time he became district attorney for Harvey County. In 1975 he again returned to private practice, where he remained until his federal magistrate judge appointment in 1984. After fifteen years, Judge Reid retired from active service in 1999 but remained on the federal bench as a recalled magistrate judge until his death on November 16, 2008.[26]

Judge Gerald L. Rushfelt

In 1985, Gerald L. Rushfelt was selected to fill the vacancy created when Magistrate Judge J. Milton Sullivant retired from the bench.[27] Rushfelt was born in Kansas City,

Kansas, in 1929. He received an associate's degree from Graceland College in 1949 and a Bachelor of Arts degree from the University of Kansas in 1953. After graduating from KU, he served two years in the U.S. Army and then returned to KU to attend law school. In 1958, after receiving his law degree, Rushfelt entered private practice with the Kansas City firm of Sullivant & Smith. He practiced there (with various successor firms) and also served as a Leawood Municipal Court judge pro tempore until his appointment to the federal bench in 1985. From 1980 until 1983 he served as critique instructor in Trial Advocacy at the University of Kansas School of Law. He is a fellow of the American College of Trial Lawyers, belongs to the American Board of Trial Advocates, International Society of Barristers, Kansas Bar Foundation, and Kansas Inn of Court. He retired from active service in 1999, but remains on the bench as a recalled magistrate judge.

Judge Ronald C. Newman

In March of 1990, Ronald C. Newman was appointed to fill the magistrate judge vacancy created when Judge VanBebber took a seat on the federal district court bench.[28] Judge Newman was born in Louisville,

Kentucky, in 1943. He graduated from William Jewell College in 1965 and received his law degree from the University of Kansas School of Law in 1970. He then practiced law with two Kansas City, Kansas, law firms: Weeks, Thomas, Lysaught and Mustain from 1970 to 1980 and Mustain and Newman from 1980 to 1990, becoming managing partner at both.[29] During his time on the bench, Judge Newman became renowned for his skill as a mediator. He served on the bench until his untimely death on August 21, 1999.

Judge Karen Mitchell Humphreys

The judges of the District of Kansas appointed Karen Mitchell Humphreys as U.S. magistrate judge in Wichita, on November 1, 1993, to fill the vacancy created when Judge

Wooley retired. Humphreys was born in Ashland, Kansas, in 1948.[30] She attended the University of Kansas, earning a BA degree in 1970 and a JD in 1973. Humphreys then practiced in both state and federal courts, including an eight-year stint as an assistant U.S. attorney for the District of Kansas in Topeka and Wichita.[31] In 1987, the governor of Kansas appointed Judge Humphreys to the state district court bench in Sedgwick County, Kansas.

She served in this role as a trial judge until her appointment to the federal bench in 1993. Judge Humphreys has completed two eight-year terms and was reappointed for a third term in 2009. She is currently chief magistrate judge for the district. Judge Humphreys has served as adjunct faculty at Washburn Law School and Wichita State University.[32] She also belongs to numerous nonprofit organization boards and regional and national committees, including the Federal Magistrate Judges Association and Advisory Group.

Judge Donald W. Bostwick

On July 22, 1999, Donald W. Bostwick was appointed as a federal magistrate judge in Wichita to succeed Judge Reid.[33] Bostwick was born in Augusta, Kansas, in 1943. He attended

the University of Kansas, receiving a BS in 1965 and a JD in 1968. Upon passing the Kansas Bar, he entered private practice in Wichita, Kansas, with the firm Adams, Jones, Robinson & Malone, where he remained until his appointment to the federal bench in 1999. Judge Bostwick retired from active service on August 1, 2010, and currently serves as a recalled magistrate judge in the District of Kansas. He belongs to the Wichita, Kansas, and American Bar Associations, and served as president of the Wichita Bar Association from 1990 to 1991. He is a fellow in the American College of Trial Lawyers, the American Bar Foundation, and the Kansas Bar Foundation.

Judge David J. Waxse

In 1999, David J. Waxse was selected by the judges of the District of Kansas to fill the vacancy created when Judge Gerald Rushfelt retired.[34] Judge Waxse was born in Oswego, Kansas, in 1945.[35] He received a BA from the University of Kansas in 1967 and a JD from Columbia Law School in 1971. Waxse then returned to Kansas, where he entered private practice with Payne & Jones and served as city attorney for De Soto, Kansas. In 1984, he joined the Overland Park office of Shook, Hardy & Bacon, where he was a partner from 1986 to 1999 and served as assistant general counsel of the firm until his appointment to the federal bench. Judge Waxse completed his first eight-year term as a U.S. magistrate judge and was reappointed to a second term in 2007. He has lectured at the University of Kansas and belongs to and has held various leadership positions with the American Bar Association, American Bar Foundation, American Judicature Society, Earl E. O'Connor Inn of Court, Federal Magistrate Judges Association, Johnson County Bar Association, Kansas Bar Foundation, Kansas Bar Association, Kansas City Metropolitan Bar Association, and the Midwest Bioethics Center. He served as president of the Kansas Bar Association in 1997-98.

Judge James P. O'Hara

On April 17, 2000, James P. O'Hara was appointed as a federal magistrate judge for the District of Kansas, succeeding Judge Newman.[36] O'Hara was born in 1955 in Detroit, Michigan. He attended the University of Nebraska, receiving a Bachelor of Arts degree in 1977. He then enrolled at the Creighton University School of Law, receiving a JD in 1980.[37] After law school, he clerked for two federal judges in the District of Nebraska: Robert V. Denny and C. Arlen Beam. In 1982 after completing his clerkships, O'Hara moved to the Kansas City area, where he entered private practice with the firm of Shugart, Thomson & Kilroy. He remained with the firm until his appointment to the federal bench in 2000, having served on the executive, hiring, and associates committees and as managing partner of its Overland Park office. In 2008, Judge O'Hara was appointed to a second eight-year term as magistrate judge. He currently serves as the district's ADR (Alternative Dispute Resolution) administrator and the magistrate judge representative on the Judicial Conference's Committee on Judicial Resources. He teaches trial advocacy as a member of the adjunct faculty at the University of Kansas

School of Law, belongs to and has held various leadership positions with the Earl E. O'Connor American Inn of Court and serves on the Board of Editors of the *Journal of the Kansas Bar Association.* Judge O'Hara has also served on the Ethics and Grievance Committee of the Johnson County Bar Association, Kansas Board for Discipline of Attorneys, Bench-Bar Committee of the U.S. District Court of Kansas, and the boards of several civic and church organizations.

Judge K. Gary Sebelius

On February 21, 2003, the district judges appointed K. Gary Sebelius to fill a newly created magistrate judge position, which brought the number of full-time, active magistrate judges in the district to five.[38] Sebelius was born in Norton, Kansas, on November 8, 1949.[39] He received a bachelor's degree in 1971 from Kansas State University and a JD from Georgetown University Law Center in 1974.[40] After graduating from law school, he returned to Kansas, where he entered private practice with the Topeka firm of Eidson, Lewis, Porter and Haynes. He remained there until 1989, when he joined the firm of Davis, Wright, Unrein, Hummer and McCallister, where he practiced until 1993. He then joined the firm Wright, Henson, Somers, Sebelius, Clark and Baker, where he remained until his appointment to the federal bench.[41] Judge Sebelius belongs to the Topeka, Kansas, and American Bar Associations and the Association of Trial Lawyers of America. He also served in various leadership roles with Kansas Legal Services.[42]

Judge Kenneth G. Gale

On August 2, 2010, Kenneth G. Gale was appointed to fill the vacancy created by the retirement of Magistrate Judge Donald Bostwick. Judge Gale was born in 1955 at Ft. Huachuca, Arizona.[43] He received a BA from Loyola University in 1977 and then both entered the army and enrolled in Washburn University School of Law. He graduated from law school in 1980 and continued his military career, serving in the U.S. Army Judge Advocate Generals Corps until 1984.[44] He then joined the Wichita firm Matlack & Foote and Focht while remaining with the U.S. Army Reserve. In 1990, he joined the firm Focht, Hughey & Calvert and began serving in the National Guard. He then joined the Adams Jones law firm in 1997, where he remained until his appointment to the bench in 2010. In 2008, he retired from the National Guard with the rank of colonel.[45] Judge Gale belongs to and has served in various leadership positions with the Wichita and Kansas Bar Associations.

Notable Achievements of Kansas Federal Magistrate Judges

While by the very nature of their jurisdiction and assigned tasks federal magistrate judges do not usually garner the same degree of public acknowledgment as their colleagues the federal district judges, federal magistrate judges handle some of the most difficult parts not only of run-of-the-mill litigation but also of cases with great national importance. Federal magistrate judges have been key players in many crucially significant cases, such as the R. J. Reynolds products liability case,[46] a number of employment law cases, the first case in the federal courts seeking the return of a child kidnapped and taken to Mexico pursuant to the Hague Convention on the Civil Aspects of International Child Abduction Remedies Act,[47] requirements for producing email in discovery, and the application of the "Sedona Rules" on electronic discovery.[48]

Kansas federal magistrate judges have also been leaders in a number of areas of "cutting-edge" federal law. Chief Magistrate Judge Karen Humphreys was one of the first to introduce a drug re-entry court in the federal courts.[49] Although only a few years old, the program already shows great promise for reducing recidivism among high-risk federal prisoners upon release from prison. Federal Magistrate Judge David Waxse has been at the forefront of providing solutions for the many problems now arising in regard to the application of federal discovery rules in the context of new digital technologies. His 2005 and 2006 decisions in *Williams v. Sprint/United Management Company*[50] have been hailed as breakthroughs in this difficult area of jurisprudence and have been discussed nationally as well as followed in many other courts. Magistrate Judge Waxse, along with Kansas District Judge J. Thomas Marten, sits on the advisory board of the Sedona Conference, the leading forum for discussion of electronic discovery in the United States.

Federal Bankruptcy Judges

Article 1, Section 8, Clause 4 of the United States Constitution gives Congress power to create a system for the adjudication of bankruptcies. The first statute to do so was the Bankruptcy Act of 1800, which authorized federal district judges to appoint commissioners to hear bankruptcy cases in their districts.[51] The Bankruptcy Act of 1867 declared that federal district courts were also courts for the adjudication of bankruptcy and established the office of register.[52] Registers were required to fulfill minimum requirements and post a security bond but were not given judicial authority. Judicial authority remained with the federal district court that had appointed the register.

The inadequacies of the existing system for adjudicating bankruptcies, combined with the effects of several economic panics in the latter part of the nineteenth century, convinced Congress to pass a comprehensive Bankruptcy Act in 1898.[53] The position of register was replaced by that of referee, although the powers and duties of the successor were very little changed from the former. Federal district judges continued to permit referees to handle most aspects of bankruptcy litigation and referees continued to have, at best, quasi-judicial authority.

In 1938 the Chandler Act became law, largely in response to the economic turmoil of the Great Depression.[54] This act made significant improvements in the administration of bankruptcy jurisdiction but, again, made few structural changes to the system. The appointment of referee continued to vary from district to district and the majority of referees' compensation came from court fees paid by litigants.[55]

Finally, in 1978 Congress passed and the president signed legislation creating a new "Bankruptcy Code" and made significant changes to the office of referee.[56] Indeed, there were to be no more referees, but, instead, there were to be federal bankruptcy judges with broad authority to decide cases in bankruptcy. The authority conveyed upon the new bankruptcy judges was challenged in the Supreme Court of the United States in the case of *Northern Pipeline Construction Co. v. Marathon Pipeline Construction Co.*[57] In this case, the U.S. Supreme Court ruled that federal bankruptcy judges had judicial authority only to adjudicate bankruptcy issues and not other matters that might arise in the course of a case.[58] In 1984 Congress passed and the president signed the Federal Judgeship Act of 1984.[59] This act made bankruptcy courts "units" of the federal district courts and placed the power to appoint bankruptcy judges in the hands of the U.S. circuit courts.

District of Kansas bankruptcy judges in 2004: Dale L. Somers, Robert E. Nugent, Robert D. Berger, and Janice M. Karlin.

Federal Bankruptcy Referees and Judges 1923–2011

	Last Name	First Name	Middle Initial	Commission Date	Active Service Terminated	Succession	Type	Location
1	Porter	Silas		1923	1932	New position	Referee	Topeka
2	Fisher	Harry	W	1924	1932	New position	Referee	Fort Scott
3	Todd	Arnold	C	1927	1932	New position	Referee	Wichita
4	Adams	E.	R	1928	1930	New position	Referee	Kansas City
5	Bistow	Frank	B	1930	1945	New position	Referee	Salina
6	Gates	Louis	R	1930	1944	vice-Adams	Referee	Kansas City
7	Jochems	W.	D	1931	1934	vice-Todd	Referee	Wichita
8	Hatcher	E.	H	1932	1944	vice-Porter	Referee	Topeka
9	Ratner	Payne	H	1932	1936	New position	Referee	Parsons
10	Fleeson	Howard	T	1933	1944	vice-Jocherns	Referee	Wichita
11	Keene	A.	M	1936	1948	New position	Referee	Fort Scott
12	Bukaty	John	J	1944	1946	vice-Gates	Referee	Kansas City
13	Castor	Harry	C	1944	1948	vice-Fleeson	Referee	Wichita
14	Sloan	Edward	R	1944	1962	vice-Hatcher	Referee	Topeka
15	Miller	Harry	J	1946	1948	vice-Bukaty	Referee	Kansas City
16	Young	John	I	1946	1948	New position	Referee	Salina
17	Brown	Wesley	E	4/1/1958	4/4/1962	New position	Referee	Wichita
18	Dawes	Joseph	J	3/16/1961	12/31/1970	vice-Sloan	Referee	Topeka
19	Morton	Robert	B	4/27/1962	5/2/1986	vice-Brown	Judge	Wichita
20	Sullivant	J.	Milton	1/1/1971	10/31/1975	New position	Referee	Kansas City
21	Franklin	Benjamin	E	2/9/1976	4/7/1993	vice-Sullivant	Judge	Kansas City
22	Pusateri	James	A	12/17/1976	5/31/2003	New position	Judge	Topeka
23	Pearson	John	K	5/22/1986	5/21/2000	vice-Morton	Judge	Wichita
24	Flannagan	John	T	10/16/1989	10/15/2003	New position	Judge	Topeka
25	Robinson	Julie	A	2/15/1994	12/24/2001	vice-Franklin	Judge	Topeka
26	Nugent	Robert	E	6/14/2000		vice-Pearson	Judge	Wichita
27	Karlin	Janice	M	10/16/2002		vice-Robinson	Judge	Topeka
28	Somers	Dale	L	9/19/2003		vice-Pusateri	Judge	Topeka
29	Berger	Robert	D	10/16/2003		vice-Flannagan	Judge	Kansas City

Brief Biographies of Kansas Federal Bankruptcy Judges

Judge Robert B. Morton

In 1962 Robert B. Morton became the first U.S. bankruptcy judge in the District of Kansas. Morton was born in Webb City, Missouri, on October 26, 1912, and moved at a young age to Wichita, Kansas, where he grew up.[60] He received undergraduate and law degrees from the University of Kansas and was admitted to the bar in 1935. He then entered private practice in Wichita, joining the firm Kidwell, Darrah, Ball & Morton, and later Aley, Morton, Darrah and Mellor. In 1942, Morton joined the United States Marine Corps and served three years in the South Pacific, receiving the Bronze Star before retiring with the rank of lieutenant colonel. In 1962 Judge Morton was appointed U.S. bankruptcy judge, serving as president of the National Conference of Bankruptcy Judges from 1975 to 1976 and participating in a ten-year effort to rewrite a revision to the code, which Congress approved in 1978. Judge Morton retired from the bench in 1986 and then joined the Wichita firm Morris, Laing, Evans, Brock and Kennedy. He served on the Board of Regents of Wichita University for eight years and as chair in 1956 and 1962. Judge Morton passed away on June 25, 2005, at the age of ninety-two.

Judge Benjamin E. Franklin

Benjamin E. Franklin was appointed the district's second bankruptcy judge on February 9, 1976.[61] Franklin was born on September 5, 1922, and grew up in Mobile, Alabama. He joined the U.S. Army in 1943 and served two years in Europe, earning four Bronze Stars. He received a bachelor's degree in 1947 from Xavier University in New Orleans, Louisiana, and then attended law school at the University of Detroit, earning his LLB in 1952. In 1953, Franklin relocated to the Kansas City area, where he entered private practice in Wyandotte County. From 1957 to 1961, he served as assistant county counselor and practiced with the firm of Meeks, Gray, Franklin, Smith & Whyte. Franklin served as assistant U.S. attorney for the District of Kansas from 1961 to 1968, when he was appointed U.S. attorney, becoming the first African American to hold that position in Kansas and the second nationwide. In 1969, he left the U.S. attorney's office and entered private practice in Kansas City, Kansas, serving as counsel for the Board of Public Utilities of Kansas City and lecturing at the University

of Kansas School of Law from 1973 to 1976. Upon his appointment to the bench in 1976, he became the first African American U.S. bankruptcy judge in Kansas, and only the third nationwide. Throughout his career, he belonged to and held leadership positions in various organizations, including Alpha Phi Alpha and Sigma Pi Phi fraternities; the Kansas City, Kansas, and Wyandotte County Bar Associations; the Kansas, Federal, American and National Bar Associations; and the NAACP. Judge Franklin remained on the bench until his death on April 7, 1993.

Judge James A. Pusateri

On December 17, 1976, James A. Pusateri was appointed to fill a new bankruptcy judgeship in the District of Kansas.[62] Pusateri was born in Kansas City, Missouri, in 1938.[63] He attended the University of Kansas, where he earned both bachelor's and law degrees.[64] He then entered private practice in Johnson County, Kansas, serving on the Prairie Village city council from 1967 to 1969.[65] In 1969, he became an assistant United States attorney for the District of Kansas and served in this capacity until his appointment to the bench in 1976.[66] Judge Pusateri presided over the bankruptcy court in Topeka until he retired in May of 2003 at age sixty-five.[67] He spends his retirement in Florida.[68]

Judge John K. Pearson

In 1986 the Tenth Circuit judges selected John K. Pearson to fill the vacancy created when Judge Morton retired.[69] Pearson was born in 1945. He received a BA from the University of Wisconsin at Madison in 1968 and served as a lieutenant in the United States Navy from 1968 to 1969 [70] He enrolled at the University of California-Hastings College of Law, earning a JD in 1973. Pearson then moved to Kansas to clerk for United States District Judge Arthur Stanley.[71] After his clerkship, he became associated with the Wichita firm of Kahrs, Nelson, Fanning, Hite and Kellogg, where he remained until 1977[72] when he joined the Federal Intermediate Credit Bank as a staff attorney.[73] From 1979 until 1982 Pearson served as an assistant United States trustee in Wichita.[74] He then returned to private practice with McDowell, Rice and Smith, where he remained until his appointment to the bench in 1986. Judge

Pearson served as a bankruptcy judge until he retired from the bench in 2000 and joined the Hinkle, Elkouri law firm in 2000.[75] In 2010, he joined the Adorno & Yoss law firm in Lawrence, Kansas.[76] He has authored numerous publications, taught at the University of Kansas School of Law, the President's College School of Law, and Wichita State University, and belongs to and has held leadership positions in the Wichita and Kansas Bar Associations, the American Bankruptcy Institute, the American College of Bankruptcy, and the National Conference of Bankruptcy Judges.[77]

Judge Julie A. Robinson

The judges of the Tenth Circuit appointed Julie A. Robinson to the United States Bankruptcy Court for the District of Kansas on February 15, 1994, succeeding Judge Benjamin E. Franklin, for whom she had clerked after receiving her law degree from the University of Kansas School of Law. Judge Robinson became a federal district judge on December 1, 2001; for a more detailed biography of Judge Robinson, please see Chapter 7.

Judge John T. Flannagan

On October 16, 1989, the judges of the Tenth Circuit appointed John T. Flannagan to a fourteen-year term on the United States Bankruptcy Court for the District of Kansas.[78] Flannagan was born in Fremont, Nebraska, and graduated from high school in Scott City, Kansas.[79]

He received a BS from the University of Kansas and then attended Washburn University Law School, earning a JD in 1964. He then joined the Olathe firm Payne & Jones and practiced there until 1983, when he established a solo practice, handling mainly bankruptcy cases until his 1989 appointment to the bankruptcy court.[80] Judge Flannagan retired from the bench in October of 2003.[81] He has belonged to the American and Kansas Bar Associations, the National Conference of Bankruptcy Judges, the American Bankruptcy Institute, and the Association of Insolvency Accountants.[82]

Judge Robert E. Nugent

On June 14, 2000, the judges of the Tenth Circuit appointed Robert E. Nugent to the United States Bankruptcy Court for the District of Kansas to succeed retiring Judge John K. Pearson.[83] Nugent attended the University of Kansas, earning a BA in English and Political Science in 1977 and

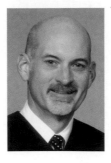

a JD in 1980. He was admitted to the Kansas and Federal Bars in 1980 and then practiced for seven years in Hutchison, Kansas. After also serving as a Chapter 7 panel trustee and a Chapter 11 examiner, he joined the Wichita firm of Morris, Laing, Evans, Brock & Kennedy, where he remained until his appointment to the federal bankruptcy bench in Wichita.[84] Since 2002, Judge Nugent has served as the district's chief bankruptcy judge and as a member of the United States Bankruptcy Appellate Panel for the Tenth Circuit.[85] Chief Judge Nugent also belongs to and has held leadership positions in the National Conference of Bankruptcy Judges and the Committee on Federal and State Jurisdiction of the Judicial Conference of the United States, and is a former president of the Wichita Bar Association.[86] He speaks frequently to bankruptcy organizations and continuing legal education groups, coedits and is a chapter author of the *Kansas Bankruptcy Handbook, Third Edition*, Kansas Bar Association, and is a member of the Board of Editors of the *Journal of the Kansas Bar Association.*[87]

Judge Janice Miller Karlin

Janice Miller Karlin became the eighth bankruptcy judge for the District of Kansas when she was appointed on October

16, 2002, to fill the vacancy created when Judge Robinson was appointed to a seat on the Federal District Court bench.[88] Karlin was born on August 24, 1953, in Pittsburg, Kansas.[89] She enrolled at the University of Kansas, earning a BA in 1977 and a JD in 1980. After being admitted to the bar, she joined the United States Attorney's Office, where she served as an assistant United States attorney and later as the assistant U.S. attorney in charge of the Kansas City office until her appointment to the bench in 2002.[90] Judge Karlin has served on the Board of Governors of the University of Kansas School of Law, where she has served as an adjunct professor of Trial Practice. She received the Federal Bar Association 2010 Section Chair Award,

which recognized her work chairing the Bankruptcy Section of the Federal Bar Association.

Judge Dale L. Somers

Dale L. Somers became the District's ninth bankruptcy judge on September 19, 2003, when he was sworn in to succeed Judge Pusateri.[91] Somers was born on March 7, 1946, in Norton, Kansas.[92] He attended Kansas State University, earning a bachelor's degree in 1968 before enrolling at the University of Kansas School of Law.[93] After graduating from law school in 1971, he entered private practice in Topeka, Kansas, with the firm Eidson, Lewis, Porter and Haynes. In 1989 he joined Wright, Henson, Somers, Sebelius, Clark and Baker, where he remained until his appointment to the bench. Judge Somers has belonged to and held leadership positions in the Topeka and Kansas Bar Associations, serving as president of the KBA in 1996–97.

Judge Robert D. Berger

In 2003, the judges of the Tenth Circuit selected Robert D. Berger to fill the vacancy created by Judge Flannagan's retirement.[94] Berger was born in Topeka, Kansas, in 1961.[95] He earned a BA in history from the University of Kansas in 1983 and a JD from the Washburn University School of Law in

1986. After graduation, he entered private practice with Lentz and Clark.[96] Prior to his appointment in 2003, he practiced law as a bankruptcy and insolvency specialist representing bankruptcy debtors and creditors.[97] He was among the first group of attorneys in Kansas and Missouri certified by the American Board of Certifications in both consumer and business bankruptcy law. Judge Berger has written numerous articles on bankruptcy issues, including Chapter 13 tax matters, and is a contributing author for the Kansas Bar Association's *Bankruptcy Handbook*. Judge Berger has also served as a frequent lecturer on bankruptcy, insolvency, and related tax issues. He counts among his affiliations membership in the American Bankruptcy Institute and the National Conference of Bankruptcy Judges.

The Fred Phelps Family

Fred Phelps Sr. and his family have had an interesting relationship and history with the District of Kansas federal court and the federal courts in general. As an attorney, Fred Phelps Sr. filed and tried many federal suits, most of which involved civil rights claims. By most accounts, he was a gifted trial lawyer who rankled a lot of important people and business leaders. But he was also subject to disciplinary and ethics actions in state and federal courts. Phelps received his first suspension in 1969, when the Kansas Supreme Court suspended him from practicing law in Kansas for two years for ethics violations. Ten years later, the Kansas Supreme Court permanently disbarred him after finding he had again committed ethics violations. The same ethics violations caused the District of Kansas judges to suspend him shortly thereafter from practicing in that court for two years.

In 1985, nine federal judges filed a disciplinary complaint against Phelps and members of his family for falsely accusing some of the judges of racial and religious prejudice. To resolve the complaint, Fred Phelps Sr. eventually agreed to give up his license to practice in federal court if the other family members would be allowed to continue.

The Phelps family continues to be legally and politically active. The family has picketed multiple court proceedings as

Fred Phelps Sr.

well as the funerals of some of the court's judges. They also picket the funerals of soldiers killed in line of duty to communicate their belief that God hates the United States for its tolerance of homosexuality. In fact, the family recently argued a case involving their First Amendment right to picket a soldier's funeral before the Supreme Court of the United States, and won.

Notes to Chapter 8

1. Federal Judicial Center, *History of the Federal Judiciary/Magistrate Judgeships*, http://www.fjc.gov/history/home.nsf/page/judges_magistrate.html (last visited Mar. 17, 2011).

2. *See* 28 U.S.C. §§ 631-650.

3. Judicial Improvements Act of 1990, Pub. L. No. 101-650, 104 Stat. 5089.

4. Act of October 21, 1976, Pub. L. No. 94-577, 90 Stat. 2729.

5. Federal Magistrate Act of 1979, Pub. L. No. 96-82, 93 Stat. 643.

6. Federal Judicial Center, *History of the Federal Judiciary/Magistrate Judgeships*, http://www.fjc.gov/history/home.nsf/page/judges_magistrate.html (last visited Mar. 17, 2011).

7. 28 U.S.C. § 631(e).

8. *Id.* at § 631(f).

9. *Id.* at § 631 (b).

10. *Id.* at § 631.

11. *Id.* at § 633 (b).

12. Federal Judicial Center, *History of the Federal Judiciary/Magistrate Judgeships*, http://www.fjc.gov/history/home.nsf/page/judges_magistrate.html (last visited Mar. 17, 2011).

13. 28 U.S.C. §633(a).

14. THE FEDERAL MAGISTRATE JUDGES ASSOCIATION, http://www.fedjudge.org (last visited Jan. 23, 2011).

15. Edward B. Soule, *The Federal Magistrate Act in Kansas*, 10 WASHBURN L. J. 45 (1970-71).

16. *See* Soule at 45.

17. Tim Carpenter, *Former Chief Justice Dies*, TOPEKA CAPITAL-JOURNAL, Sept. 10, 2009, *available at* http://cjonline.com/news/state/2009-09-10/former_chief_justice_dies (last visited Mar. 22, 2011).

18. *Obituaries*, 78 J. Kan. B. Ass'n Nov.-Dec. 2009, at 17.

19. 152 F.R.D LXXVII.

20. Id at LXXVIII.

21. *Id.* at LXXIX.

22. *Id.* at LXXVII.

23. *Id.* at LXXX.

24. J. Milton Sullivant, http://signal.baldwincity.com/news/2000/mar/29/j_milton_sullivant (last visited Jan. 23, 2011).

25. *The American Bench: Judges of the Nation*, 1016 (Mary Lee Bliss et al. eds., 19th ed., Forster-Long, Inc. 2009).

26. John Thomas 'Tom' Reid, http://www.thekansan.com/obituaries/x1772950994/John-Thomas-Tom-Reid (last visited March 30, 2011).

27. 1 *Almanac of the Federal Judiciary* 30 (Megan Rose ed., Aspen Pub. 2011).

28. 3 Martindale-Hubbell Law Directory: Iowa-Mississippi, 1980 at 373B.

29. *Magistrate remembered for service, mediation*, 68 J. Kans. B. Ass'n . Nov.-Dec. 1999, at 5.

30. Hon. Karen M. Humphreys, THOMSON REUTERS, http://pview.findlaw.com/view/ 1818178_1?channel=LP (last accessed Jan. 23, 2011).

31. Interview by Ryan Schwarzenberger and Jessica McCloskey with Hon. Karen M. Humphreys, Chief Magistrate Judge, Federal District Court of Kansas, in Wichita, Kan. (June 23, 2010) [hereinafter Humphreys Interview].

32. Humphreys Interview.

33. *The American Bench: Judges of the Nation*, 1021 (Mary T. Finn et al. eds., 21st ed., Forster-Long, Inc. 2011).

34. *Id.* at 1047.

35. 1 *Almanac of the Federal Judiciary* 30 (Megan Rose ed., Aspen Pub. 2011).

36. *The American Bench: Judges of the Nation*, 1037 (Marie T. Finn et al. eds., 21st ed., Forster-Long, Inc. 2011).

37. Press Release, Shughart Thomson & Kilroy, Attorney James P. O'Hara Named U.S. Magistrate Judge (2003) (on file with author)[hereinafter O'Hara Press Release].

38. *The American Bench: Judges of the Nation*, 1042 (Marie T. Finn et al. eds., 21st ed., Forster-Long, Inc. 2011).

39. Hon. K. Gary Sebelius, THOMSON REUTERS, http://pview.findlaw.com/view/16958 17_1?channel=LP (last visited Jan. 24, 2011).

40. 6 Martindale-Hubbell 1991 at 99B.

41. 62 J. Kan. B. Ass'n, April 1993 at 24.

42. Hon. K. Gary Sebelius, THOMSON REUTERS, http://pview.findlaw.com/view/16958 17_1?channel=LP (last visited Jan. 24, 2011).

43. 4 Martindale-Hubbell KS-670 (2010).

44. Hon. Kenneth G. Gale, THOMSON REUTERS, http://pview.findlaw.com/view/1040736_1?channel=LP (last visited April 21, 2011)

45. 1 *Almanac of the Federal Judiciary* 30 (Megan Rose ed., Aspen Pub. 2011).

46. *See, e.g.*, Burton v. R.J. Reynolds Tobacco Co., 170 F.R.D. 481 (D. Kan. 1997).

47. *See In re Hague Child Abduction Application*, No. 08-2030-CM, 2008 WL 913325 (D. Kan. May 17, 2008).

48. *See Williams v. Sprint/United Management Co.*, 230 F.R.D. 640 (D. Kan. 2005).

49. *See* Humphreys Interview.

50. *See Williams v. Sprint/United Management Co.*, 230 F.R.D. 640 (D. Kan. 2005).

51 2 Stat. 19, repealed in 1803.

52. 14 Stat. 517.

53. Nelson Act, ch. 541, 30 Stat. 544 (1898).

54. Chandler Act, ch. 575, 52 Stat. 883 (1938).

55. Bankruptcy Referees, http://www.fjc.gov/history/home.nsf/page/admin_03_03.html (last visited April 29, 2011).

56. Bankruptcy Reform Act, Pub. L. No. 95-598, 92 Stat. 2549 (1978).

57. *Northern Pipeline Constr. Co. v. Marathon Pipe Line Co.*, 458 U.S. 50 (1982).

58. *Id.* at 87-89.

59 The Bankruptcy Amendments and Federal Judgeship Act of 1984 (98 Stat. 333).

60. KANSAS CITY STAR, June 29, 2005, 2005 WLNR 22784538

61. 62 J. Kan. B. Ass'n, May 1993 at 18-19.

62. Bankruptcy Judge Retires, TOPEKA CAPITAL-JOURNAL, May 29, 2003, http://cjonline.com/stories/052903/loc_bankjudge.shtml (last visited Jan. 25, 2011).

63. 2 Who's Who in America (52nd ed 1998) at 3493.

64. Bankruptcy Judge Retires, TOPEKA CAPITAL-JOURNAL, May 29, 2003, http://cjonline.com/stories/052903/loc_bankjudge.shtml (last visited Jan. 25, 2011).

65. Who's Who.

66. 59 J. Kan. B. Ass'n, June 1990 at 6.

67. Who's Who.

68. Bankruptcy Judge Retires, TOPEKA CAPITAL-JOURNAL, May 29, 2003, http://cjonline.com/stories/052903/loc_bankjudge.shtml (last visited Jan. 25, 2011).

69. Kathryn A. Plonsky, *Anchors Aweigh: The Creation of the U.S. Bankruptcy Appellate Panel of the Tenth Circuit*, 46 http://catalog.lib.campbell.edu/web2/tramp2.exe/do_ccl_search/guest?setting_key=english&servers=1home&index=ckey&query=546509, 2010).

70. 2 Who's Who at 3341.

71. John K. Pearson, *Resume*, http://www.deb.uscourts.gov/mediation/BIOs/peajo_11-2010.pdf (last visited April 22, 2011).

72. 2 Who's Who at 3341.

73. John K. Pearson, *Resume*, http://www.deb.uscourts.gov/mediation/BIOs/peajo_11-2010.pdf (last visited April 22, 2011).

74. John K. Pearson, *Kansas Bankruptcy Handbook*, About the Authors (John K. Pearson et al. eds., 2nd ed. 1986).

75. John K. Pearson and J. Scott Pohl, *A Brief Overview of the Revised Article 9 in Kansas*, 72 J. Kan. B. Ass'n. No. 8 at p. 22 (September 2003).

76. Adorno & Yoss, Retired U.S. Bankruptcy Judge John Pearson Joins Adorno & Yoss Law Firm, http://www.yoss.com/uplds/docs/PressRelease-JudgeJohnPearsonM1881652.PDF (last visited Mar. 21, 2011).

77. John K. Pearson, *Resume*, http://www.deb.uscourts.gov/mediation/BIOs/peajo_11-2010.pdf (last visited April 22, 2011).

78. 59 J Kan.B. Ass'n, June 1990 at 5

79. *Id.* at 6.

80. *Id.* at 5.

81. Topekan Named Bankruptcy Judge, Topeka Capital Journal, August 2, 2009, http://cjonline.com/stories/08023/loc_topekajudge.shtml (last visited May 20, 2011)

82. *About the Authors*, Kansas Annual Survey of Law, 2000, at vii, viii.

83. *The American Bench: Judges of the Nation*, 1014 (Mary Lee Bliss et al. eds., 20th ed., Forster-Long, Inc. 2009).

84. 77 J. Kan. B. Ass'n, January 2008 at 6.

85. *The American Bench: Judges of the Nation*, 1014 (Mary Lee Bliss et al. eds., 20th ed., Forster-Long, Inc. 2009).

86. 77 J. Kan. B. Ass'n, January 2008 at 6.

87. Interview by Timothy M. O'Brien with Hon. Robert E. Nugent, Chief Bankruptcy Judge, Kansas Bankruptcy Court, in Wichita, KS (April 22, 2011)

88. *The American Bench: Judges of the Nation*, 1010 (Mary Lee Bliss et al. eds., 20th ed., Forster-Long, Inc. 2009)

89. Interview by Timothy M. O'Brien with Hon. Janice Miller Karlin, Bankruptcy Judge, Kansas Bankruptcy Court, in Topeka, KS (April 22, 2011).

90. Kathryn A. Plonsky, *Anchors Aweigh: The Creation of the United States Bankruptcy Appellate Panel of the Tenth Circuit*, 53-54 (2010)

91. Topekan Named Bankruptcy Judge, Topeka Capital-Journal, August 2, 2003, http://cjonline.com/stories/080203/loc_topekajudge.shtml (last visited May 10, 2011).

92. Interview by Timothy M. O'Brien with Hon. Dale L. Somers, Bankruptcy Judge, Kansas Bankruptcy Court, in Topeka, Kan. (April 22, 2011).

93. Topekan Named Bankruptcy Judge, Topeka Capital-Journal, August 2, 2003, http://cjonline.com/stories/080203/loc_topekajudge.shtml (last visited May 10, 2011).

94. Topekan Named Bankruptcy Judge, Topeka Capital-Journal, August 2, 2003, http://cjonline.com/stories/080203/loc_topekajudge.shtml (last visited May 10, 2011).

95. Interview by Timothy M. O'Brien with Hon. Robert D. Berger, Bankruptcy Judge, Kansas Bankruptcy Court, in Kansas City, Kan. (April 22, 2011) [hereinafter Berger Interview].

96. Dan Margolies, New Bankruptcy Judge, Kansas City Star, March 2, 2004, at D19.

97. Berger Interview.

9

PALACES OF JUSTICE *

In the earliest days of the American republic, judges, both state and federal, were often required to hear cases in whatever buildings they could find space. But the majesty of the law and those who administer it has long been the inspiration for buildings built specifically for the purpose of housing the judiciary and those who assist judges in doing justice. The Federal District Court for the District of Kansas has occupied a number of courthouses in the past one hundred and fifty years.

During the territorial period, territorial judges appointed by the president held court wherever it was convenient, but primarily in Leavenworth—then the home of federal troops and a fort—and at Lecompton, the territorial capital, where the territorial governor made his home.[1] But once Kansas became a state, federal courts were generally held in multipurpose federal buildings. Beginning in the1880s, federal court buildings, often combined with post offices, were constructed to serve the growing needs and caseloads of federal district judges in Kansas. Six cities in Kansas have had federal courts constructed within their precincts since 1884: Fort Scott, Salina, Topeka, Leavenworth, Wichita, and Kansas City, Kansas.

Fort Scott

The combined Fort Scott federal courthouse and post office was approved by Congress on March 4, 1885.[2] Building was contingent upon the state legislature ceding jurisdiction to the United States, which it did the next day.[3] Construction began in 1888 and was completed in 1890. It was designed by the noted architect Mifflin E. Bell. Bell served as the supervising architect for the U.S. Treasury from 1883 until 1886.[4] He designed courthouses and post offices across the United States in a variety of styles. The federal courthouse and post office he designed for Fort Scott was an imposing building at First Street and Scott Avenue in the style known as Richardsonian Romanesque, a style also seen in Trinity Church in Boston, Massachusetts.[5] According to newspaper records, the total cost of the building alone was $100,000.[6] The building was used by the Federal District Court until 1936.[7] Demolition of the structure was finished in January 1946.[8]

The second Fort Scott post office and federal courthouse building was designed by then supervising architect of the Treasury, Louis A. Simon. Work began on the structure at Second and National Avenue in 1935 and completed in April 1936.[9] U.S. District Judge Richard Hopkins was to "preside in the splendidly equipped federal courtroom when the May term" of court opened.[10] This new building is very much a product of its age. It is a four-story blockish structure with little ornamentation built of stone. The first-story windows are larger than those of other stories and all of the windows are uniformly interspaced throughout the façade in the modernist or moderne style, i.e., plain and utilitarian, as one would expect from a building built during the Depression. It is not an inviting building but does convey the power of the federal government, very much in keeping with the politics of the time. This building continues to be used by the post office today and the courtroom is now a storage facility.

* This chapter relies heavily on the text and photographs identified through research for courthouse exhibits developed by Jean Svadlenak & Associates in 1994 and 1999.

Top: The original Fort Scott U.S. Courthouse and Post Office. c. 1890. The Kansas Federal District Court met here until 1936 and the U.S. Circuit Court for the District of Kansas met here until that court was abolished in 1912. Bottom: Fort Scott U.S. Courthouse and Post Office, 1936. Facing page: Exterior stone carvings on the Wichita U.S. Courthouse.

Leavenworth

The federal post office and courthouse was built in Leavenworth in 1890.[11] It, like the Fort Scott federal building, was designed by Mifflin E. Bell in the Richardson Romanesque style. It was a three-story corner building with a monumental arched entrance and a corner tower.[12] It was used by the Federal District Court of Kansas from its opening until 1959. The U.S. Circuit Court also met in the building until that court was abolished in 1912.[13]

By 1948, the Leavenworth Courthouse had deteriorated and the courtroom was gloomy. According to a newspaper account, Judge Mellott said it was a disgrace to hold court in such surroundings and that very little court business had been held in Leavenworth for that reason.[14] The Leavenworth County Bar appointed a committee to draft a resolution to be sent to Judge Mellott recommending improvements to the courtrooms and related facilities.

By 1959, the need for a new building was clear. The old courthouse was razed and construction began on a new facility on April 4, 1959.[15] The new Federal Building at the corner of Fourth and Shawnee was designed by George Tewksbury and built by the W. W. Bennett Construction Company. It was formally dedicated on July 16, 1960. District Judges Delmas Hill and Arthur J. Stanley, along with Circuit Judge Walter Huxman, were in attendance. The building continues to be used by the post office. The former courtroom on the second floor is now used as a meeting room.

Above right: The original Leavenworth U.S. Courthouse and Post Office, c. 1901. The U.S. District Court for the District of Kansas met here until 1959, when the building was razed. The U.S. Circuit Court for the District of Kansas also met here until 1912. Right: The current Leavenworth U.S. Courthouse and Post Office.

Art in the Courthouses

Fort Scott

On the north wall of the former courtroom in the Fort Scott courthouse is an impressive mural entitled "Border Gateways" commemorating the passage of the Enabling Act of the Kansas Territories. The oil-on-canvas mural shows settlers in covered wagons and stagecoaches, on horseback and walking west on the first day of the land rush. Three Native Americans are in the foreground sitting on horses and watching the procession. A legend printed across the bottom of the mural states: "The Passage of the 'Enabling Act of Kansas Territory' brought many Settlers through the Border Gateways—1854."

The artist who painted the mural, Oscar E. Berninghaus, was born in St. Louis in 1874, studied at the St. Louis School of Fine Arts, taught at Washington University, and eventually settled in Taos, New Mexico. His paintings are in the collections of many museums.

"Border Gateways," a mural in the Fort Scott United States Courthouse.

He also did commission work for several major clients including Anheuser-Busch Brewing Company and the Denver and Rio Grande Railroad.

Salina

Salina's first federal courthouse and post office was completed in 1896 and was the work of Will A. Freret, supervising architect of the Treasury from 1887 to 1889.[16] It was in the Richardson Romanesque style and was built of brick with stone trim. A large tower with a round turret graced one side. The top story had several attic windows and a large chimney. It was typical of its style and evoked a sense of tradition and age, characteristics that supported the authority of the courts and federal agencies it housed. Its entrance was at the corner and introduced by pillared arches and was fronted by an elaborate three-globed street light. The building straddled Seventh and Iron Streets and was used by the Federal District Court from 1896 until 1938. Unfortunately, like so many structures of its era whose architectural beauty was outweighed by their lack of modern amenities, the federal building was razed in 1962 and replaced by one far less attractive. A scale model of the courthouse is presently located in the lobby of the Smoky Hill Museum.

The second federal courthouse and post office in Salina is located at 211 West Iron Street and was designed by Louis A. Simon, supervising architect, and Lorimer Rich.[17] The building is a two-story, flat-roofed, limestone building with a northern façade orientation. The building is adorned with two sculptures by Carl C. Mose. The first, "Land," is a man with an ax. The second, "Communication," is a mother with a young boy. The building was placed on the National Register in 1989 and currently serves as the home of the Smoky Hill Museum.[18]

Above: Original Salina U.S. Post Office and Courthouse, c. 1914. Below: Second Salina U.S. Post Office and Federal Building, c. 1989.

The cornerstone of the second Salina U.S. Post Office and Federal Building (now Smoky Hill Museum).

Salina

Carl C. Mose designed the sculptures "Land" and "Communication" that flank the entrance to the former Salina Post Office and Federal Building. According to the registration form for National Register of Historic Places, the pieces were designed to be considered as architectural abstractions when put into place in 1940. "Land" is a workingman dressed in boots, overalls, and a long-sleeved shirt holding an ax. "Communication" is a woman standing with a young boy at her side. The figures are stoic individuals with blank faces and heroic proportions. The simple, yet powerful depictions represent the individuals who inhabit central Kansas.

"Land," left, and "Communication," right, two sculptures by Carl C. Mose which adorn the second Salina U.S. Courthouse and Post Office, which is now the Smoky Hill Museum.

Topeka

The first federal courthouse constructed by the U.S. government in Topeka was the United States Post Office and Customs Building completed in 1884 at the corner of Fifth and Kansas Avenues.[19] James Hill was the supervising architect of the Treasury responsible for the design of the building, but the Treasury also brought in the popular Kansas architect John G. Haskell to modify the Treasury design.[20] Haskell was popular at the time and known for the Richardson Romanesque style he favored. Among the changes made by Haskell were dormer windows to improve light in the interior.[21] The building's tower incorporated a large clock manufactured by Seth Thomas Clock Company, which was installed in February 1884. When completed, the new building incorporated the postal service, the Federal District Court, and the Circuit Court.

By 1925 the courthouse façade was in serious need of restoration, so the U.S. government authorized the repair and cleaning of the outside of the building at the substantial cost of $40,000.[22] Although this work improved the visage of the building, it did nothing for the increasing inadequacy of the interior space and the growing needs of the tenants. The U.S. Congress agreed to fund the cost of constructing a replacement building in 1932.[23] The old building was demolished in 1933.[24]

The second federal building in Topeka was completed in 1933, designed by James A. Wetmore, and located at the corner of Fifth and Quincy.[25] Its opening ceremonies featured the postmaster general of the United States, James A. Farley.[26] The new building abandoned the Romanesque style of its predecessor and was built of steel faced with limestone and marble trim.[27] But within twenty years it was becoming apparent that the building was too small. A 1953 General Services Administration study concluded that at least 170,000 additional square feet were needed.[28] In 1977 construction on the new Frank Carlson Federal Building at 444 S.E. Quincy St. was completed.[29] The new building houses the Federal District Court, as well as a number of different federal agencies. It is adjacent to the old post office, which remains in use.

Detailed woodwork on a bench from the original Topeka U.S. Courthouse.

Original Topeka U.S. Courthouse and Post Office, c. 1915. Construction began in 1879 and was completed in 1884, at a cost just over $286,000.

Second Topeka U.S. Post Office and Federal Building, c. 1934.

Frank Carlson Federal Building and U.S. Courthouse, 2010. On January 31, 1981, the building was redesignated to honor former U.S. Senator Frank Carlson, who served eighteen years in the Senate, two terms as governor of Kansas, and six terms as congressman.

Exterior façade of the second Topeka U.S. Post Office and Federal Building.

"White Tornado," a sculpture inside the Frank Carlson Federal Building and U.S. Courthouse.

Wichita

The first federal building that housed both the post office and the Federal District Court was completed in 1890 and located on the corner of Market and William Streets.[30] Like its contemporary in Salina, it was designed by Will A. Freret in the Richardson Romanesque style, complete with clock tower. It was built of smooth-dressed stone with interior walls and floors of iron and tile, making it practically fireproof.[31] In 1908 the original structure was expanded to cope with increased demand for more post office space.[32] It was used continuously by the Federal District Court until 1932, when a new building was constructed.[33] From 1934 to 1936 it housed offices of several federal agencies created as part of the New Deal.[34] The old federal building was demolished in 1936.[35]

The new courthouse was designed by James A. Simon and its construction was supervised by James Wetmore.[36] Like others constructed during this period, the new building was in the modernist style and constructed of steel and limestone facade.[37] Under pressure from the Wichita Chamber of Commerce, the building was graced by two "front" entrances, one on Market Street and the other on Main. By 1986 the post office had moved out of the building and its former space was converted into additional courtrooms.[38] In 1989 the building was placed on the National Register of Historic Places.

Right: Original Wichita U.S. Courthouse and Post Office, c. 1900.
Below: Current Wichita U.S. Courthouse, c. 1932.

Wichita Architectural Craftsmanship

The U.S. Courthouse in Wichita at 401 North Market Street is a magnificent structure with outstanding craftsmanship throughout. The building, which originally also housed the U.S. Post Office, was constructed from Bedford limestone and was completed in 1932. Sixteen varieties of marble from Arkansas, Colorado, Georgia, Minnesota, Missouri, Montana, Tennessee, and Vermont were used in the interior construction. Significant stone carvings appear throughout. The exterior carvings feature such regional subjects as eagles, buffalo, Native Americans, wheat, and ears of corn. Inside, there are fine examples of stone carving, such as a large bust of a Native American chief. The interior of the courthouse also features a number of bronze works including a cast-bronze cornice with four bronze eagles across the framework of the interior doors. Wood carvings adorn the courtrooms and surrounding areas.

Stone Indian carving from first-floor lobby of the current Wichita U.S. Courthouse.

Top: Restored courtroom currently used by Judge Thomas Marten, Wichita U.S. Courthouse. Left: One of four bronze eagles which sit across framework of the interior doors. Above: Filigree vent. Below: Plaster ceiling detail.

As part of visual arts program supported through the New Deal's Works Progress Administration program, 1 percent of construction costs of new federal buildings was set aside for art in 1934, meeting the objective of making art a part of America's everyday life. Artists were selected who were born in the state or in nearby states. Two oil-on-canvas murals were painted in the courthouse in 1935 and 1936 by J. Ward Lockwood (1894-1963), born in Atchison, Kansas, and Richard Haines (1906-1984), born in Marion, Iowa. Lockwood's mural is a collage of images associated with the evolution of the Postal Service during the settlement of the western United States. The mural by Haines depicts various aspects of rural life and farm production, focusing on the importance of urbanization, industrialization and technology to the economic growth of the region.

In 1986 and 1998, projects were completed to restore the building to its original grandeur– especially the fine detail work of skilled artisans in stone, plaster, and bronze–from light fixtures and paneling to the intricate and colorful plaster ceilings and moldings.

Artist rendering of the original U.S. Courthouse and Post Office, Kansas City, Kansas, c. 1900. John C. Pollock was the first federal judge to preside at this location. Below: Post Office sign featuring a mail carrier on a horse from the original Kansas City Courthouse.

Kansas City, Kansas

In 1900 the federal government constructed a new post office and federal courthouse at the corner of Seventh and Minnesota in Kansas City, Kansas.[39] It was designed by James Knox Taylor in the classical style. Its exterior was graced by two-story columns and the main façade incorporated classical arches framing both the entranceway and the windows. It was home to the Federal District Court from its completion until 1959. It also was used by the U.S. Circuit Court from 1948 until 1959. The building was demolished in 1962.[40]

The second federal courthouse in Kansas City was completed in 1959 at 812 North Seventh Street.[41] It was designed by the architectural firm of Radotinsky, Meyn, and Deardorff of Kansas City. The building was approximately fifty-three thousand square feet, and cost $2.5 million to construct.[42] The new courthouse also housed federal agencies including the Civil Service Commission, Housing and Home Finance Agency, Internal Revenue Service, and departments of Agriculture, Defense, Treasury, and Health, Education, and Welfare.[43] One office was used by the Kansas Second

District's congressional representative in Congress.[44] It was dedicated in 1960, and used by the Federal District Court of Kansas from its opening until 1994, when the present federal courthouse was completed.

Construction for the present federal courthouse at 500 State Avenue in Kansas City, Kansas, was begun in July 1991.[45] It was designed by the Wichita architectural firm of Gossen, Livingston Associates.[46] Three years later it was dedicated on June 10, 1994.[47] Then Chief Federal District Judge Earl O'Connor played an important role not only in securing the new courthouse building but also in its design.[48] Traditionally, each judge was assigned his or her own courtroom, chambers, and law library. The new courthouse at 500 State Avenue departed from tradition and features some shared courtrooms and a shared law library.[49] Separate facilities for staff and holding cells were also incorporated into the building as well as secured parking.[50] The new design not only fosters interaction among the judges but provides for significantly enhanced security, necessary in today's more violent times. The courthouse is named for Senator Bob Dole, who was instrumental in its creation.

Left: Program from dedication of second Kansas City, Kansas, Federal Building on February 12, 1960. Above: Second Kansas City, Kansas, U.S. Post Office and Courthouse, 1959. The onset of World War II and subsequent postwar inflation had delayed construction of this new building until the mid 1950s, though by the late 1930s the original courthouse at 7th & Minnesota was considered inadequate for the volume of postal and court business there.

Robert J. Dole U.S. Courthouse, 2010.

Notes to Chapter 9

1. *See generally* George Templar et al, *Kansas: The Territorial and District Courts, in* THE FEDERAL COURTS OF THE TENTH CIRCUIT: A HISTORY 17 (James K. Logan ed., U.S. Court of Appeals for the Tenth Circuit, 1992).

2. *$50,000! Appropriated by Congress for the Erection of the Federal Building in Fort Scott.* FORT SCOTT DAILY MONITOR, March 5, 1885, at 4.

3. *The Way Clear for the Public Building.* FORT SCOTT DAILY MONITOR, March 6, 1885, p. 1.

4. Historic Federal Courthouses, Fort Scott, Kansas, U.S. Court House and Post Office (n.d., ca. 1890), FEDERAL JUDICIAL CENTER, http://www.fjc.gov/history/courthouses.nsf/getcourtho use?OpenAgent&chid=951837C7306201018525718B005DB639.

5. http://en.wikipedia.org/wiki/Richardsonian_ Romanesque.

6. The U.S. Courthouse Post Office, FORT SCOTT DAILY MONITOR, January 1, 1890, at 1.

7. Fort Scott Courthouse (1890), *supra* note 3.

8. *Old Post Office Lot Bought by H. Hicks.* FORT SCOTT TRIBUNE, January 26, 1946, at 1.

9. Historic Federal Courthouses, Fort Scott, Kansas, United States Post Office and Court House (1936), FEDERAL JUDICIAL CENTER, http://www.fjc.gov/history/courthouses.nsf/ getcourthouse?OpenAgent &chid=959D17930ED31F508525718B005DC34E (last visited Jan. 24, 2011).

10. *In New Federal Building.* FORT SCOTT TRIBUNE AND MONITOR, April 26, 1936, at 1.

11. Historic Federal Courthouses, Leavenworth, Kansas, U.S. Court House, Post Office (1890), FEDERAL JUDICIAL CENTER, http://www.fjc.gov/history/courthouses.nsf/ getcourthouse?OpenAgent& chid=E226868577D1A1338525718B005DD7DC (last visited Jan. 24, 2011).

12. U.S. Treasury Department, *A History of Public Buildings* (Washington D.C.: GPO 1901) p. 182-83.

13. Leavenworth Courthouse, *supra* note 11.

14. *A General Opinion on the Federal Courtroom-- Something Must Be Done.* LEAVENWORTH TIMES, December 12, 1948, http://skyways.lib.ks.us/genweb/leavenwo/library/ FEDCOURT.htm.

15. Dedication Program, Federal Building–Post Office, July 16, 1960 (on file with author). Also available at the Leavenworth Public Library.

16. Historic Federal Courthouses, Salina, Kansas, U.S. Post Office and Courthouse (1896), FEDERAL JUDICIAL CENTER, http://www.fjc.gov/history/courthouses.nsf/getcourthouse?Op enAgent&chid=006141A1F0393D438525718B005DDF40 (last visited July 28, 2011).

17. Historic Federal Courthouses, Salina, Kansas,

U.S. Post Office and Federal Building (1938), FEDERAL JUDICIAL CENTER, http://www.fjc.gov/history/courthouses.nsf/ getcourthouse?OpenAgent& chid=BDF5FEECB85407278525718B005DE321 (last visited Jan. 24, 2011).

18. Salina Courthouse (1938), *supra* note 16.

19. F. W. Giles, *Thirty Years in Topeka.* Orig. publ. 1886, reprint. 1960; John M. Peterson, *John G. Haskell: Pioneer Kansas Architect.* HM Ives and Sons, 1984, p. 116-18.

20. F. W. Giles, supra note 19.

21. John M. Peterson, *supra* note 19 at 118.

22. *Its End Is Near: Old Post Office Building Soon to Be Thing of Past.* TOPEKA DAILY JOURNAL, February 25, 1933.

23. *Topeka New $1,000,000 Post Office and Federal Building.* TOPEKA STATE JOURNAL, December 11, 1931.

24. *Its End Is Near: Old Post Office Building Soon to Be Thing of Past.* TOPEKA DAILY JOURNAL, February 25, 1933.

25. Dwight Thacher Harris, *Topeka Begins Use of Its New Post Office Building.* TOPEKA JOURNAL, December 9, 1933.

26. Ketchum M'Gill, *Great Crowd at Dedication of New Post Office.* TOPEKA CAPITAL, August 21, 1934.

27. Dwight Thacher Harris, *Topeka Begins Use of Its New Post Office Building.* TOPEKA JOURNAL, December 9, 1933.

28. *3-Story Federal Building Here Planned; May Seek New Site.* TOPEKA STATE JOURNAL, October 9, 1953, at 1.

29. Frank Carlson Federal Building, U.S. General Services Administration, http://www.gsa.gov/portal/ content/101470 (last visited July 28, 2011).

30. Historic Federal Courthouses, Wichita, Kansas, U.S. Post Office and Court House (1890), FEDERAL JUDICIAL CENTER http://www.fjc.gov/history/courthouses.nsf/getcourthouse?Ope nAgent&chid=C75784C870374ADB8525718B005DF457.

31. *Federal Edition—Stone: Public Building Committee Reports New Bill.* WICHITA EAGLE, March 12, 1908.

32. *Arrange for Post Office Addition: Needed Room for Mailing Department Assured.* WICHITA EAGLE, February 19, 1908.

33. *Evolution of Wichita's Post Office from Log Cabin to $1,200,000 Structure Opening for Business Today.* WICHITA EAGLE, April 1, 1932, at 1.

34. *Reopen Old Federal Building this Week: Basement and First 2 Floors to Be Used by CWA, CWS and U.S. Transient Service,* WICHITA EAGLE, February 10, 1934.

35. *Old Federal Site Cleared.* WICHITA BEACON, February 19, 1937.

36. Historic Federal Courthouses, Wichita, Kansas, U.S. Post Office and Court House (1932), FEDERAL JUDICIAL CENTER, http://www.fjc.gov/history/courthouses.nsf/ getcourthouse?OpenAgent& chid=426DD5B8AB2DBF928525718B005DF8FE (last visited Jan. 24, 2011).

37. *U.S. Courthouse, Wichita, KS,* U.S. GENERAL SERVICES ADMINISTRATION, http://www.gsa.gov/portal/ext/html/site/

hb/category/25431/actionParameter/exploreByBuilding/buildingId/017 (last visited Jan. 25, 2011) [hereinafter Wichita Courthouse].

38. Wichita Courthouse (1932) *supra* note 36.

39. Historic Federal Courthouses, Kansas City, Kansas, U.S. Post Office (1902), FEDERAL JUDICIAL CENTER, http://www.fjc.gov/history/courthouses.nsf/getcourthouse?OpenAgent&chid=07CF5A9A8245C90D8525718B005DCB8A (last visited Jan. 25, 2011).

40. *Old Post Building is Sold Piece by Piece.* KANSAS CITY STAR, September 16, 1962.

41. Historic Federal Courthouses, Kansas City, Kansas, Federal Building (1959), FEDERAL JUDICIAL CENTER, http://www.fjc.gov/history/courthouses.nsf/getcourthouse?OpenAgent&chid=574E754434805E2C8525718B005DD2CA.

42. *Federal Building Ahoy!* KANSAS CITY STAR, December 21, 1957.

43. *The United States Courthouse and Federal Office Building to Be Built in Kansas City, Kansas.* KANSAS CITY STAR, May 25, 1956.

44. *Debut Near for Federal Building.* KANSAS CITY STAR, September 27, 1959.

45. Exhibit Script for Federal Courthouse-Kansas City, KS, Jean Svadlenak & Associates (June 23, 2010) (on file with author).

46. Bob Cox. *KC Courthouse Breaks Design Rules.* WICHITA EAGLE, February 21, 1994.

47. *COURTHOUSE DEDICATION PROGRAM*, June, 1994.

48. *See generally* Robert W. Richmond, EARL E. O'CONNOR: SENIOR UNITED STATES DISTRICT JUDGE 28 (1997).

49. Bob Cox. "KC Courthouse Breaks Design Rules." WICHITA EAGLE, February 21, 1994.

50. *See generally* John T. Dauner, *KCK's New U.S. Courthouse Sets a National Standard*, KAN. CITY STAR, Dec. 26, 1993, at B1.

Appendix A: Court Support Officers and Personnel

CLERKS OF THE UNITED STATES DISTRICT COURT FOR THE DISTRICT OF KANSAS

John T. Morton..1861–1863, Topeka
Franklin G. Adams ....1863, Topeka
Clark J. Hanks ....1863–1865, Topeka
Adolphus S. Thomas..............................1865–1874, Topeka
Joseph C. Wilson....................................1874 – 1895, Topeka
George F. Sharritt...................................1895 –1899, Topeka
Frank L. Brown..1899 –1904, Topeka
Morton Albaugh.......................................1904 –1918, Topeka
Frank L. Campbell....................................1918–1933, Topeka
W.G. West...1933–1936, Topeka
Howard F. McCue.....................................1936–1944, Topeka
Harry M. Washington ....1944 –1959, Topeka
Charles W. Cahill.....................................1959–1972, Wichita
Arthur G. Johnson...................................1972–1986, Wichita
Ralph L. DeLoach.....................................1986–1997, Wichita
1997–2007, Kansas City
Timothy M. O'Brien ....2008–present, Kansas City

Marlin Miller, the retired Wichita division director of the Clerk's office, researched and assembled this list. See also, Daniel W. Wilder, *The Annals of Kansas*, (1875) (found at http://skyways.lib.ks.us/genweb/civilwar/October.htm); William G. Cutler, *History of the State of Kansas* (1883) (found at: http://www.kancoll.org/books/cutler/sthist/annals-p18.html).

UNITED STATES CHIEF PROBATION OFFICERS FOR THE DISTRICT OF KANSAS

William C. Robinson .... 1959–1977, Wichita
Thomas Warders.................................... 1977–1983, Wichita
Perry D. Mathis .... 1983–1991, Kansas City
Leonard J. Bronec.................................. 1991–1996, Kansas City
Arlo D. Lindsey...................................... 1996–1998, Kansas City
Gary Howard .... 1998–2004, Kansas City
.... 2004–2009, Wichita
Ronald G. Schweer................................ 2009–present, Kansas City

LIBRARIANS FOR THE DISTRICT OF KANSAS

Sue Ann Berard........................ Oct 24, 1988–Aug 14, 1992, Wichita
Sharon L. Hom .... Dec 12, 1992–April 16, 2010, Wichita
.... and Kansas City
Meg K. Martin .... Oct 11, 2010–present, Kansas City

BANKRUPCTY CLERKS OF THE UNITED STATES BANKRUPTCY COURT FOR THE DISTRICT OF KANSAS

G. Clarice Farmer[1] .... July 1, 1962–Feb 28, 1972
Arthur Johnso..Feb 28, 1972–July 20, 1984
G. Clarice Farmer..................................July 21, 1984–June 1, 1985
Russell L. Brenner................................Sept 16, 1985–July 31, 1998
Fred W. Jamison....................................Aug 3, 1998–present

1. For her initial term, Ms. Farmer was officially a clerk to the bankruptcy referees. On February 28, 1972, the District Court for the District of Kansas consolidated the U.S. District clerk and clerk to the referees under the direction of Arthur Johnson, the incumbent clerk of the District Court. Ms. Farmer later became the clerk of the Bankruptcy Court.

Appendix B: Other Court Officers and Personnel

FEDERAL PUBLIC DEFENDERS FOR THE DISTRICT OF KANSAS

Leonard Munker....................................1973–1982
Charles Anderson 1982–1994
David Phillips..1994–2008
Cyd Gilman..2008–present

UNITED STATES MARSHALS SERVICE FOR THE DISTRICT OF KANSAS

James L. McDowell .... March 23, 1861 (S)
Thomas A. Osborne .... April 20, 1864 (S)
Charles C. Whiting .... March 7, 1867 (S)
David W. Houston................................... January 24, 1870 (S)
William S. Tough.................................... March 22, 1873 (S)
Charles H. Miller.................................... March 27, 1876 (S)
Benjamin F. Simpson............................. March 18, 1878 (S)
April 28, 1882 (S)
William C. Jones..................................... August 5, 1885 (R)
March 12, 1886 (S)
Richard L. Walker .... May 17, 1889 (R)
January 20, 1890 (S)
Shaw F. Neely .... January 12, 1894 (S)
William Edgar Sterne............................. January 10, 1898 (S)
Littleton S. Crum................................... January 28, 1902 (S)
William H. Mackey, Jr. .... August 4, 1902 (R)
December 9, 1902 (S)
January 8, 1907 (C)
John R. Harrison .... July 24, 1911 (C)
Otho T. Wood.. June 9, 1914 (C.A)
June 25, 1914 (C)
July 6, 1918 (C)
Fred R. Fitzpatrick .... September 27, 1921 (C)
December 21, 1925 (C)
Donald H. MacIvor................................. February 19, 1930 (C)
Lon Warner... May 4, 1934 (C)
May 31, 1938 (C)
William M. Lindsay................................. March 18, 1940 (C.A.)
April 12, 1940 (C)
May 9, 1944 (C)
Joseph P. Regan .... July 27, 1949 (C)
Eugene L. Kemper................................... September 3, 1953 (R)
March 11, 1954 (C)
May 8, 1958 (C)
Vance W. Collins..................................... November 20, 1961 (R)
March 12, 1962 (C)
July 22, 1966 (C)
Jack V. Richardson.................................. October 3, 1969 (C)
November 20, 1973 (C)
Bernal D. Cantwell................................. September 15, 1977 (C)
Kenneth L. Pekarek .... December 9, 1981 (C)
Richard Rand II Rock............................. February 11, 1994 (C)
Walter R. Bradley.................................... May 10, 2002 (C)

The abbreviations:
"R"– Recess Appointment Date
"S"– Senate Confirmation Date (used from 1789 to 1903)
"C"– Commission Date (used from 1903 to present)
"C.A."– Court Appointment Date

Illustration Credits

To the many archivists, librarians, photographers, and court family members contacted for illustrations for this book, we extend our gratitude. We'd particularly like to thank Nancy Sherbert, curator of photographs, and her staff at the Kansas State Historical Society, who were always helpful and patient throughout our search.

Photographs and other illustrations are from the files of the U.S. District Court, District of Kansas except as noted here.

The following sources have been abbreviated:

EPLM: Eisenhower Presidential Library and Museum

KSHS: Kansas State Historical Society

LOC: Library of Congress

NARA: National Archives & Records Administration

SC/KCPL: Special Collections, Kansas City Public Library

SHSMo: State Historical Society of Missouri

SRL/KU: Spencer Research Library, University of Kansas

UMKC/SL: University of Missouri Kansas City School of Law

USTD: U.S.: Treasury Department

WUSL: Washburn University School of Law

WyCoHSM: Wyandotte County Historical Society & Museum

Page ii. KSHS.

iii. KSHS.

vi. Row 1, left: U.S. Treasury Department; row 1, center & right: NARA; row 2, left: NARA; row 2, center: NARA; row 2 ,right: U.S. Treasury Department; row 3, left & right: NARA; row 4, left: NARA.

x. SC/KCPL, Albert D. Richardson's *Beyond the Mississippi.*

Page 2. Map: KSHS.

3. Top: KSHS; bottom: NARA.

4. KSHS.

5. KSHS.

6. SHSMo.

7. KSHS.

8. LOC.

9. KSHS.

10. KSHS.

11. Top left: Collection of the Supreme Court of the United States; right: (three documents) NARA.

14. Top left: tombstone: Jean Dodd; bottom: KSHS.

16. KSHS.

17. KSHS.

18. KSHS.

20. Leavenworth: KSHS; Justice David J. Brewer, Collection of the Supreme Court of the United States.

23. KSHS.

25. KSHS.

30. KSHS.

32. KSHS.

33. Winfield: Cowley County Historical Museum.

35. KSHS.

36. Top: KSHS; Prisoner identification photograph: Robert Franklin Stroud, 594-AZ, U.S. Penitentiary, Alcatraz, CA, Warden's Notebook; Records of the Bureau of Prisons, The National Archives at San Francisco.

38. KSHS.

39. Garden City, Kansas: KSHS.

40. KSHS.

41. Top and bottom: KSHS; center: *Pittsburg Daily Headlight,* Dec. 19, 1921. Photograph courtesy of Linda O'Nelio Knoll *"Army of Amazons – An Oral History of Southeast Kansas,"* © White Buffalo Press, 2000.

42. Top left: KSHS.

43. Badge: U.S. Bureau of Alcohol, Tobacco and Firearms.

46. United States Court of Appeals for the Tenth Circuit.

47. UMKC/SL.

48. Rex Ingram: LOC.

49. Wamego Historical Society & Museum.

50. Top left: Wamego Historical Society & Museum.

51. United States Probation Office for the District of Kansas.

52. Hon. J. Thomas Marten.

54. Time & Life Pictures/Getty Images.

55. KSHS.

56. Top right: National Park Service; classrooms: KSHS.

57. Time & Life Pictures/Getty Images.

58. Time & Life Pictures/Getty Images.

59. KSHS.

60. KSHS.

61. Left: Time & Life Pictures/Getty Images; right: NAACP Legal Defense Fund.

63. LOC.

64. Time & Life Pictures/Getty Images.

68. Carolyn Stanley Lane.

69. Carolyn Stanley Lane.

70. Top left: *Kansas City Star.*

71. KSHS.

72. Top: WUSL; center: SRL/KU; bottom: EPLM.

74. Kansas Department of Wildlife and Parks.

75. Left, top & bottom: *Wichita Eagle*; right: The Oklahoma Publishing Co.

76. The Oklahoma Publishing Co.

77. Barn: Alson Martin.

79. Washburn University School of Law.

81. Top & bottom left: *Wichita Eagle*; bottom right: Deborah Godowns.

82. Elaine Saffels and Deborah Godowns.

83. Top left: WUSL; center: Elaine Saffels and Deborah Godowns.

84. Bottom left: Alleen VanBebber.

85. Michael Fortier: Associated Press.

86. Farrar, Straus and Giroux, LLC.

92. Top right: *Wichita Eagle.*

99. Left and bottom right: Judge J. Thomas Marten.

100. Top right: *Kansas City Star.*

101: Top left: Administrative Offices, U.S. Courts.

117. Fred Phelps: AP Photo/David Zalubowski.

121. NARA.

122. Top right: U.S. Treasury Department; center: Leavenworth Public Library; mural: Tim O'Brien.

123. Top right & center: NARA; sculptures and cornerstone: Tim O'Brien.

124. Top right & center: NARA.

126. NARA.

128. Top: U.S. Treasury Department; Post Office sign: Monte Gross/WyCoHSM.

129. Top right: NARA.

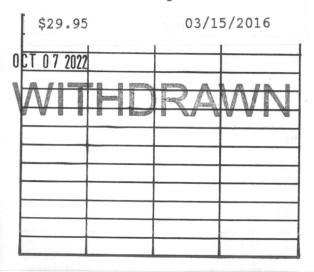